DEMOCRACY AND EQUALITY

DEMOCRACY AND EQUALITY

Theories and Programs
for the
Modern World

RONALD M. GLASSMAN

PRAEGER

New York
Westport, Connecticut
London

Library of Congress Cataloging-in-Publication Data

Glassman, Ronald M.
  Democracy and equality : theories and programs for the modern
world / Ronald M. Glassman.
    p. cm.
  Bibliography: p.
  Includes index.
  ISBN 0–275–93100–5 (lib. bdg. : alk. paper)
  1. Equality. I. Title.
JC575.G63 1989
320′.01′1—dc19   88–27574

Library of Congress Catalog Card Number: 88–27574
ISBN: 0-275-93100-5

First published in 1989

Praeger Publishers, One Madison Avenue, New York, NY   10010
A division of Greenwood Press, Inc.

Printed in the United States of America

The paper used in this book complies with the
Permanent Paper Standard issued by the National
Information Standards Organization (Z39.48–1984).

10 9 8 7 6 5 4 3 2 1

Copyright Acknowledgments

Acknowledgment is made for extracts from the following sources: Aristotle, *The Politics*, edited and translated by Ernest Barker, 1958, by permission of Oxford University Press; scattered excerpts from *The General Theory of Employment, Interest, and Money* by John Maynard Keynes, reprinted by permission of Harcourt, Brace & Jovanovich, Inc.; from *Losing Ground: American Social Policy 1950–1980*, by Charles Murray, copyright © 1984 by Charles Murray, reprinted by permission of Basic Books, Inc., Publishers; John Rawls, *A Theory of Justice*, © 1971 by the President and Fellows of Harvard College, reprinted by permission; excerpts from *The Old Regime and the French Revolution* by Alexis de Tocqueville, translated by Stuart Gilbert, copyright © 1955 by Doubleday, a division of Bantam, Doubleday, Dell Publishing Group, Inc., reprinted by permission of the publisher.

Contents

PART I

NONSOCIALIST THEORIES OF EQUALITY

Introduction: The Death of Socialism and Its Ramifications

SOCIALISM IS DEAD. WE ARE ALONE IN SOCIETY

In recent years we have witnessed the decline of socialism as a motivating ideology and as an immanent utopian model. Socialism no longer engenders a romantic image of a classless, stateless society or a workers' democracy. No stage of pure communism is envisioned in the impending future. The realities of government power, bureaucratic inefficiency and authoritarianism, and class divisions linked to the new technocratic economy overshadow the once bright vision of a socialist-utopian future.

Romantic socialism is dead, killed by the power of the State, killed by the authoritarian tendencies of bureaucracy, killed by the inefficiency of centralized, bureaucratized economy, and killed by its abandonment of the enlightened political principles of law, the limitation and separation of powers, and open electoral participation.

The decline of romantic socialism has saved us from the now apparent political and economic dangers of despotic statism and inefficient bureaucratic economy. However, the decline of socialism has also left us with an ideological vacuum and a moral dilemma. What becomes of the quest for equality and the ethic of social justice? Are we simply to accept, in the name of freedom and democracy, as wide a range of inequality as laissez-faire corporate capitalism engenders? Are we morally bound to ignore the Dickensesque wretches who accumulate at the bottom of the economic ladder and the overbearing and often selfish individuals who emerge at the top?

There were, and are, theorists who have been so fearful of the despotic results of socialism that they have asked us to eschew all theories of equality. de Tocqueville has been revived because of his warnings about creating a society in which the individual becomes entrapped in a web of governmental control, and therefore loses his or her civic independence.[1] Weber argued with Lukacs[2] against romanticized socialism, and precisely predicted the despotic potentialities within the Bolshevik program.[3] Hayek warned that socialist planning, even within a democratic society, would lead us down the "road to serfdom."[4] Popper effectively labeled Marxist socialism as one of the major enemies of an "open society."[5]

Today, theorists such as Nozick,[6] Murray,[7] and the contemporary neo-conservatives[8] argue for a minimalist state, so worried and skeptical are they about the results of state intervention of any kind in the economic or social spheres.

Is it historically correct, however, that laissez-faire policies produce the best of all possible worlds? Is the proper counter-theory to socialism the enshrinement of corporate capitalism? In order to avoid the despotism of socialism, do we wish to revive the lifestyle of Oliver Twist[9] for a large segment of our population?

Keeping the warnings about socialism presented by the theorists mentioned above always in mind, there are still critical reasons for not dropping the idea of equality altogether. The reasons for continuing to search for a regrounding of the theory of equality are fourfold:

First, it has been known since the days of Aristotle that extreme inequality of wealth undermines the stability of democracy and drives the polity toward oligarchy or tyranny.

Second, it has been known since the days of Charles Dickens that unbridled inequality of wealth undermines our Judeo-Christian ethical tradition of humanism and social justice, which must be maintained in order to modify the excesses of our parallel ethic of rugged puritanic individualism.

Third, it has been known since the Great Depression that laissez-faire capitalism becomes unstable without certain forms of government intervention.

Finally, it is now apparent—and it is a frightening specter—that the growth of the power of the bureaucratic state[10] and the corporate leviathan[11] have continued apace, even where the welfare state has been severely reduced and the industrial economy deregulated.

Thus, even with the death of socialism, democracy and government by law must continue to be safeguarded from the growing power of the modern state and economy. Taking this safeguarding as pre-eminent, the objectionable aspects of unbridled corporate capitalism must still be modified for the political, economic, and ethical reasons mentioned above.

THE THEORY OF EQUALITY GROUNDED ON A NONSOCIALIST BASE

Given the death of romantic socialism, the question becomes, what theories and programs exist, or should exist, so that the quest for equality within legal-democratic societies is not totally lost?

As it turns out, there are nonsocialist theories and programs for equality already in existence. And there are also democratic–socialist programs tailored to the legal-democratic system that are also being experimented with.

In this volume we will focus on three theoretical systems that take legal democracy as a given, necessary, uncompromisable first principle, but that then attempt to moderate the extremes of wealth and power that emerge as a result of the independence of the capitalist economic sphere from governmental control.

The three theoretical systems are, respectively, those of Aristotle, Rawls, and Keynes. Why pick these three theorists? Each represents a watershed in theorizing critical for the conception of democracy and equality. Aristotle has given us, from the world of the Greek Polis, the best practical solution to the problem of democracy and equality. Rawls has revised the Enlightenment social contract theories, presenting us with an updated conception focusing on the dilemma of balancing claims for democracy and equality. And Keynes has created a post-Depression revision of capitalist theory that attempts to modify the theory's worst excesses without destroying its undergirding system of law and democracy.

Aristotle's theory of *proportionate equality with a middle class majority* arose, of course, in the classic world of the Greek city-state. His argument, however, remains the basis for modern day nonsocialist theories. Aristotle's compromise between pure communism and uncontrolled capitalism may yet be the most sophisticated and practical solution to the problem of "equality" ever created, and it is applicable even within the context of modern society.

Contemporary neoconservatives may chafe at the use of Aristotelian theory to support any theory of greater equality, since his theory of "distributive justice" suggests an unequal distribution of wealth based on merit, superior achievement, or superlative contribution to the polity. I hope to show, however, that Aristotle's theory of proportionate equality—though the greatest single argument against pure equality ever produced—was intended to be institutionalized alongside his theory of the ethical "golden mean," which in social structural terms meant, for Aristotle, the principle of a middle class majority.

As we will show, Aristotle presents us with specific theoretical and policy formulations, the goals of which are to expand the size and prosperity of the middle class, upgrade the poor to middle class status, and encourage the rich to give of their wealth for the common good. Within this context, his critique of pure communism and his theory of proportionate equality take on a different meaning.

Rawls' theory is derived from the philosophical foundations of the Enlightenment. It embodies the intent of the Enlightenment thinkers as to the primacy of law, the limitation of power, and the free reign of economic processes. However, his principle of *justice as fairness*, through an extension of Enlightenment logic itself, creates a modification of laissez-faire theory designed to ameliorate its worst effects.

Rawls goes back to the "state of nature" and attempts to re-establish, not only the theory of equality, but also the theory of democracy. Discarding the

Enlightenment's first premise, that certain "inalienable rights" are granted by "natural law," as unacceptable to modern rationalist thinkers, Rawls creates a new basis for political rights and economic justice logically consistent with his first premise, namely, the "veil of ignorance." Behind a "veil of ignorance," would anyone establish a society in which they would likely be politically oppressed or economically impoverished? Rawls thinks not, and goes on to establish principles by which a society could be maintained so as to minimize the latter phenomena.

Rawls's theory was chosen because it at once reaffirms the Enlightenment principles of the limitations of power and government by law, while modifying the Enlightenment tendencies to legitimate oligarchy over democracy[12] and to enshrine individualist-competitive market economics as the magical provider of a prosperous and just world.[13]

Keynes' theory arose from the depths of the Great Depression. It was an attempt to resurrect and reformulate the theory of capitalist economics. We have chosen to concentrate on the work of Keynes because his theory seeks to ameliorate the worst features of capitalist industrialism: the business cycle, unemployment, and excesses of wealth accumulation among the rich. Although Keynes's theory of economic stabilization and social fairness is an economic theory, its consistency with the political theories of Aristotle and Rawls is remarkable.

Accepting the legal-democratic polity as a given, worth preserving at all costs, as with Aristotle and Rawls, Keynes presents us with an economic program designed to produce greater equality while at the same time *increasing the efficiency* of the capitalist-industrial system.

We will establish that the modern day institutionalization of "Keynesianism" embodies very little of the actual theory and program that Keynes presented. Monetary "fine tuning" and military spending were hardly the heart of Keynes's program, which was calculated to achieve full employment, progressive taxation, low interest rates, and the partial "socialization of investment." His theory is a complex and comprehensive one, the goal of which is to preserve the strengths of capitalism while compensating for its weaknesses. The end results of Keynes' program were to be the creation of increased equality and economic stability within a framework of law and democracy.

TOWARD A COMPREHENSIVE THEORY OF EQUALITY WITHIN CAPITALIST DEMOCRATIC SOCIETIES

The goal of this work is to establish the theoretical principles and practical programs through which a greater degree of equality may emerge in capitalist democratic societies. The safeguarding of democracy remains primary and becomes the limit beyond which the theories and the programs must not stray. Within the limits set by the preservation (and extension) of legal-democracy, however, theories and programs for the expansion of economic equality should be undertaken.

We shall attempt to show that the reduction of extreme inequalities of wealth and the expansion of the middle class helps to stabilize and strengthen legal democracy; that in fact such processes tend to reduce oligarchic and tyrannical tendencies in the polity, and help to safeguard democracy from bureaucratic authoritarianism and meritocratic elitism as well.

Furthermore, as we will illustrate in our section on Keynes, the theories and programs established to engender a greater degree of equality can improve the functioning of the technocratic, capitalist, industrial economy. For, though Soviet-style centralized-bureaucratized socialist economies are on their way out, modern corporate capitalism is hardly functioning as a laissez-faire model. Thus some of the programs intended to produce greater equality also create a greater degree of economic stability and industrial growth.

These latter processes, if even partially successful, help to ameliorate the social ills engendered by capitalism, and in so doing, reduce the moral dilemma accompanying competitive individualism. The spirit of humanism must be nurtured within an individualistic, democratic society, or a nihilistic narcissism takes its place.

We shall, in this treatise, attempt to show that politically, economically, and morally, the quest for equality within the framework of legal-democratic polity is socially beneficial.

1

Aristotle: Democracy, Equality, and the Majority Middle Class

INTRODUCTION

Ancient Greece was the birthplace of democracy as we know it. Assemblies of citizens gathered (in some Greek city-states) to debate and decide upon public policy. Such debate and decision making was often constrained within the parameters of constitutional law. Office holding was limited in tenure, open to all citizens, and regulated by constitutional-legal restraints.

Not all the Greek city-states exhibited legal-democratic political processes, but those that did brought to the world a process of politics dramatically different than that of the divine-right despotic monarchies surrounding them.

Democracy had existed in a pre-polis form among many "uncivilized" tribes, including the early Greeks themselves. The earlier form of democracy consisted of tribal councils with campfire debates, and often included electoral representative procedures linked to the clans.[1] Clan leaders deliberated on policies, influenced by the general assembly of adults who debated these decisions in their presence. Custom, rather than written rational law, acted as the constraint on political decisions and political process.[2] Nonetheless, the system of tribal democracy was "government of the people, by the people, and for the people."[3]

Greek city-state democracy, however, represented a quantum leap beyond tribal democracy. The Greek citizen was a citizen of the city-state at large, and not the representative of a predominantly-familial clan. Secular law[4]— rational, debatable and changeable—replaced custom, which was immutable and sacred, as the basis for political process and political decision making. These latter produced a higher order of political freedom and democratic participation.

Thus, although preceded by tribal societies in which genuine democracy may be said to have existed, the Greek city-states became the model from which a modern form of democracy would, centuries later, emerge. The rebirth of democracy during the British, French, and American Enlightenment (which we will discuss in our next chapter) was motivated by the rediscovery of the theories and practices of ancient Greece. Once rekindled, these ideas and programs shone like a beacon, obliterating the long night of the Dark Ages.

And if democracy was established on a new and rational base, beyond that of the tribal case, so too was equality.

In pre-polis tribes, cooperation was necessary for survival. The coordinated efforts of men in hunting were absolutely essential, while the combined efforts of women were critical for gathering (and/or gardening). The sharing of meat and vegetable food between the men and the women then ensured the survival of the individuals within the group.[5]

Private property existed in the form of crafted weapons, clothing, shelter, ornaments, religious articles, and so on. However, although private property existed, it was communal in use.[6] That is, an arrow produced by the best craftsman would be shared with the best hunter—a choice share of the kill returning to the craftsman. Or a pair of moccasins would be given to another in need, with honor accruing to the maker and giver.

Private property with communal use was the norm for most tribal societies. Families could leave a tribal group for another encampment with most of their possesions in hand; however, the selfish use of private property and the hoarding of goods were strictly forbidden and violently punished.[7]

Finally, tribal societies produced no surplus of goods—no storehouses of luxury, no excesses of food. Therefore, the accumulation of personal private property and the allocation of surplus and luxury goods never became an issue. The ethic of sharing was linked to the harsh realities of survival in nature. Private possessions were niceties, the sharing of which could bring honor and the hoarding of which could bring no gain. The conflict between the ethic of sharing and the ethic of private property development would not occur until a huge surplus of goods occurred and the distribution of that surplus could result in an unequal arrangement of power, status, and living standards.

In the divine kingly empires, this dilemma was resolved by way of an ideological sleight of hand: Through the religious machinations of the pagan priesthood, the aristocracy and the king were declared divine. Once the royal aura had been cast over the aristocracy, the showering of surplus goods upon them became logical.[8] The godly gained the surplus and were adorned with the luxuries. So adorned, they appeared god-like, and so the circle of exclusion was complete.[9]

Below the deified aristocracy, a communal ethics—modified, yet similar to tribal ethics—continued to prevail.[10]

Enter the trade-merchants. At the behest of the godly-aristocracy, a new class of trading merchants were encouraged in their task. The merchants invented, as their "tools of the trade," money and contract law.[11] Armed with their new tools, and forced by necessity to learn the arts of calculation, writing, and foreign language, the merchants became a rational, intellectual, and wealthy stratum of ancient civilized society.

However, within the context of the divine kingly empires, the merchants' wealth and status could never become legitimated. They were not gods, therefore their accumulation of wealth and luxury was unacceptable—to both the aristocracy and the profane classes. The merchants were hated by the lower classes and demeaned whenever possible by the aristocracy.

Thus, although their accumulation of private wealth continued (because their craft was essential to the functioning of the empires), an ethic of private property and private wealth accumulation was never accepted as a general principle of economic distribution or a moral ideal.[12] The money economy and contract law were limited to trade transactions, while the communal storehouses, the internal distribution of goods, and the corvee labor projects continued to be controlled by the pagan priesthood and kingly officials. The aristocracy, of course, continued to accrue its godly share.

In the Greek city-states—founded as military associations and not as divine kingly empire centers,[13] and also in the Phonecian trading cities—merchant activity engendered a far more profound effect. Private wealth accumulation and private property became commonplace. But the unequal accumulation of wealth among a citizenry that was equal in political power and status would create an ethical dilemma that would have to be resolved. For the accumulation of great private wealth would generate hatred and jealousy unmitigated by any divine aura. Within a rationally oriented military society in which the individual citizen was educated to political equality and trained in military prowess, jealousy in the economic sphere was bound to spillover into violence in the political sphere. And so it did.

As the landed military elite (which was never "divine" in Greece) was replaced by a new merchant elite, a cycle of revolution and counter-revolution was set off that threatened to destroy Greek society.[14]

Within the dual context of emerging constitutional democracy and growing class violence, Greek thinkers, more as practical policymakers than as ivory-tower philosophers, attempted to establish schemas that would balance the claims of a democratic citizenry possessed of legal equality, with the parallel but conflicting claims of a free-trading institution generating enormous differentials in the accumulation of personal wealth (and the property, power, and status that this wealth could buy).

Amid the turmoil generated by the rise of political democracy and the concommitant rise of economic inequality, thinkers such as Plato, Aristotle, Phalleus, Thucidides—and later Polybius and Plutarch—wrote, offering their analyses and solutions to this problem enveloping Greek society.

Reacting to the turbulence of both political democracy and excessive economic inequality, Plato put forth a schema demanding a return to the military-ascetic and regimented society of the Greek past. Such a society, in part, still existed in Sparta. But, unlike the Spartan model, Plato exalted the virtue of intellectual development above that of the military. He rejected Sparta's "timocracy," or system of government based on military honor alone, and would have replaced it with true aristocracy, or government by the "best" (*aristoi*)—the "best" meaning, in Plato's terms, the intellectually most superior.

These "aristoi" would rule for the rest of the people, as the "guardians," the government in Plato's ideal republic thus taking the form of an oligarchy of the intellectually superior few.[15] Plato rejected democracy, or rule by all the people (*demos*), for he relegated the populace below the intellectually superior aristocracy to a second class political status, divested of the right to participation in the political process and socialized to accept their own inferiority.[16] For Plato, the masses had no wisdom, and therefore democracy was an unwise political system.

In the economic sphere, Plato demanded pure communism for his intellectual guardians. He believed that the pursuit of the accumulation of wealth, and the life of luxury that its success resulted in, would corrupt the aristoi. Therefore, they were to hold no private possessions, no wealth but the bare necessities. Even wives and children were to be held in common, children being cared for and socialized by the state—raised up or cast down according to their intellectual capacities—and meals would be taken in common at a public mess.

Some of these institutional arrangements existed in Sparta, where the public mess was part of the military routine and property was left in the hands of the women (and developed by the serfs). The term "spartan" has come to denote a lack of luxuries, and so Plato's schema was not considered far-fetched or utopian within his own time.

As for the economy of those below the aristoi–guardians, Plato says little. In Sparta, they were serfs with no political rights. For Plato, they were artisans and farmers and slaves, with essential economic functions but no political rights.

Plato's schema does not attempt to establish or preserve in any way political democracy or legal freedom. Plato does not mention that the Spartans were murderously cruel to their serfs,[17] a situation of course that he would never have recommended for his guardians. But we in the modern world have so recently witnessed the monstrous horrors of Nazism, Fascism, and Stalinist-communism[18]—which Plato would have abhorred, but from which his schema offers us no protection[19]—that we must reject Plato's model for the modern world.

Other theorists, such as Phaleus, attempted to create schemas in which a system of equal property would undergird a process of political democracy. But in Phaleus' program, constant state intervention would have become necessary to ensure the continuation of equality in property. For success in economic activity would produce an increase in wealth and property for a successful entrepreneur, and inheritance could also increase one's wealth and property. Therefore, a process of continual "levelling and divestiture" conducted by the state would become a necessity in his system. Although poorer property owners might appreciate this, wealthier ones would certainly revolt against it. Further, Phaleus' program would actively discourage dynamic economic motivation, the results of which would bring civic shame and negation, rather than private power and wealth.

Enter Aristotle. After years of reflection, Aristotle produced a theory and program that sought to balance the contradictory claims of legal-democratic political equality and accumulation of private wealth. The bases of the theory were: proportionate equality, private property with public use, and a majority middle class. In the following section we will attempt to show that the theory of the majority middle class is the architectonic theory upon which all other theories of equality must be built.

A caveat: Aristotle, as with most of the Greek thinkers, accepted militarily-derived slavery as a fact of social existence; nor did he support freeing the slaves or making them citizens. On women's participation in politics, Aristotle was also regressive, considering women as inferior to men, whereas Plato was progressive and would have included intellectually superior women in his guardian class.

On legal protection of the people against the state, however, Aristotle's position is above reproach: "He who commands that law should rule may thus be regarded as commanding that God and Reason alone should rule; he who commands that a man should rule adds the character of the beast" (Aristotle: *Politics*, p. 146).

For this reason, let us begin with Aristotle.

DEMOCRACY AND EQUALITY IN ARISTOTELIAN BALANCE

Aristotle begins with a sociological formulation that could have come from a modern textbook. Unlike the Enlightenment thinkers of a later age (whom we will discuss in the next chapter), he does not begin with individuals in a "hypothetical state of nature," but rather with the reality of society: human beings in an association without which they could not survive.

The Polis exists by nature and that it is prior to the individual . . . not being self-sufficient when they are isolated, all individuals are so many parts all equally depending on the whole (which alone can bring about self-sufficiency). The man who is isolated—who is unable to share in the benefits of political association, or has no need to share because he is already self-sufficient—is no part of the polis, and must therefore be either a beast or a god. (A:6)

Aristotle then establishes the ethical uniqueness of humans as opposed to other group animals.

It is the peculiarity of man, in comparison with the rest of the animal world, that he alone possesses a perception of good and evil, of the just and the unjust, and of other similar qualities; and it is association in (a common perception of) these things which makes a family and a polis. (A:6)

Man, when perfected, is the best of animals; but if he be isolated from law and justice he is the worst of all. (A:7)

In his quest to determine the just ordering of society, Aristotle analyzes political institutions, property relations, and class relations. In so doing he reviews, first, schemes for ideal or utopian societies put forth in his day (A:BkII, pp. 39–72), and then actual states existing in his day (A:BkII, pp. 73–91).

For our purposes—that is, for our exposition of a new basis for a theory of equality within a framework of uncompromisable democracy—let us begin with Aristotle's critique of Plato's idea of "pure communism" and his counter-scheme of "proportional equality."

Aristotle's Critique of Plato's Ideal of Pure Communism

In Aristotle's day there were many schemes offered for establishing the community of property. Private property—as commercially developed, money-making property—had only recently emerged in Greece with the expansion of Ionian naval-military power and the increased trade and imperialism that had emerged with it.[20]

The Greeks had existed with traditional, quasi-tribal, communal property arrangements in an earlier epoch, and the Dorian Greeks (most notably those of Sparta and Crete) had refashioned and reinforced these earlier communal property arrangements on a new ultra-military basis (utilizing slave agricultural labor).

Given the existence of these communally oriented Greek city-states, and given the remembrance of the Greek tribal-communal tradition, it is no wonder that there was a reaction against the commercial private property arrangements that were emerging. The reaction was not only from among the poorer classes, who found themselves in a disadvantaged situation with regard to property, but from the landed military aristocrats who rejected the commercial and democratic orientations of the newly emerging Ionian city-states.[21]

Aristotle plunges directly into the debate that was raging in his day: "The next subject for consideration is property. What is the proper system of property for citizens who are to live under an ideal constitution? Is it a system of communism, or one of private property?" (A:48).

Aristotle then states unequivocally: "Communism cannot remedy evils which spring from the defects of human nature: it is also based on a false conception of unity, and neglects the true unity which comes from education; finally, it is contradicted by experience . . . and the system of government which he [Plato] connects with his scheme is too absolute and is likely to cause discontent" (A:48).

Aristotle then criticizes Plato's idea of communism further, and the critique reads as if it were written yesterday:

Legislation such as Plato proposes may appear to wear an attractive face and to argue benevolence. The hearer reviews it gladly, thinking that everybody will feel towards everybody else some marvelous sense of fraternity—all the more as the evils now existing under ordinary forms of government (lawsuits about contracts, convictions for perjury and obsequious flatteries of the rich) are devoured as due to the absence of a system of common property. None of these evils, however, is due to the absence of communism. They all arise from the wickedness of human nature. (A:50–51)

Aristotle is warning the utopian thinker that the establishment of communism will not suddenly remove all of the ills of society. He points out from observations of his day that: "Indeed, it is a fact of observation that those who own common property, and share in its management, are far more often at variance with one another than those who have property in severality . . . " (A:51).

Whether the one or the other group has more conflict is irrelevant, but that common ownership of property would not remove all human ills and all human conflict is the message Aristotle wishes to impart. However, he goes much further in his critique of communal property, for he asserts that, not only will the ills of mankind not suddenly disappear, but certain positive results of private ownership would also be lost: "Another consideration must also be pressed. Justice demands that we should take into account not only the evils from which men will be liberated when once they have turned their property into a common stock, *but also the benefits of which they will be deprived*" (A:51; italics added).

Aristotle argues that private property is loved and cared for as if it is part of oneself. Therefore, the efficient development of such property would be more likely than that held in common: " . . . to think of a thing as your own makes an inexpressable difference . . . and it may well be that regard for oneself (and, by extension, for what is one's own) is a feeling implanted by nature, and not a mere random impulse" (A:50).

He then goes on to argue that since love of property is like self-love, giving from private property produces a feeling of "kindness, of goodness," which would be absent in a system of communal property. However, Aristotle was not naive in this sentiment. He did not mean by this that the owners of private property would all be kind and good and give of their own free will to those in need and to the civic good in general. In fact, he goes on to outline his plan for the best form of property holding and property use (in contradistinction to Plato and Phaleus and others who had been suggesting communistic plans).

A System of Private Property With Public Use

Aristotle proposes a system of property in which "ownership is private and use is common" (A:48). He argues brilliantly for a system of private property, which through proper *legal and social pressure* is put to public use. His argument proceeds in this manner, and provides us with a remarkably contemporary set of guidelines and basic principles:

The present system (of private property) would be far preferable, if it were adorned by customs (in the social sphere) and by enactments of proper laws (in the political). It would possess the advantages of both systems, and would *combine the merits of a system of community of property with those of the system of private property.* (It would be the ideal); *for property ought to be generally and in the main private, but common in one respect (i.e., in use). . . . It is clear . . . that the better system is that under which property is privately owned but is put to common use*; and *the function proper to the legislator is to make men so disposed that they will treat property in this way.* (A:49–50; italics added)

In this arrangement, Aristotle is able to utilize the strength of private property (i.e., that it will be developed to its utmost as if it were part of oneself) but to modify its weakness (i.e., that the private owners would use their property for their own selfish ends).

No coercion or confiscation is allowable in Aristotle's schema of "public use," but rather the power of the legislators (as attached to a middle class majority) and a proper system of education and socialization would pressure the rich and middling property owners toward contributing to the common good. We will describe the details of this noncoercive system shortly. The rule of law and a majority middle class are its cornerstones.

Before presenting the details of Aristotle's theory of the private ownership and public use of property, let us present his theory of *proportionate equality*. For, although Aristotle argues in favor of private property, one could still argue for a system of private property in which each individual gained equal shares, and in which adjustments of property differentials toward equal shares were built into the system. Phaleus argued for such a schema (A:62–7); Aristotle, however, did not argue for pure equality.

The Theory of Proportionate Equality: Aristotle's Meritocracy

Aristotle argues against a system of pure equality on the grounds that it would be unfair and unwise: unfair because those who contribute more to the society deserve more in return; unwise because those who contribute more, if unrewarded, would cause trouble and destabilize the political system. He states his views this way, enunciating his famous system of *distributive justice* and *proportionate equality*: "Those who contribute most to an association . . . [i.e., who contribute most to good action] have a greater share in the polis [and should therefore, in justice, receive a larger recognition from it] than those who are equal to them [or even greater] in free birth and descent, but unequal in *civic excellence*, or than those who surpass them in wealth but are surpassed by them in excellence" (A:120).

Aristotle goes on to argue that: "Men of education would be aggrieved by the system, feeling that they deserved something more than mere equality; indeed, as a matter of actual observation, they often rise in revolt and cause civic discord for this very reason. Indeed there would be a general revolt against pure equality" (A:67).

Not only would Aristotle reward those of merit with a greater share of property, but he would also reward them with a greater share of political offices, thus utilizing the talents of those with merit while extending them greater authority as a reward.

It is necessary to deal with office, or political power, as well as with property: civil discord arises not only from inequality of property, but also from inequality of the offices which men hold. But here we must note a difference. The distribution of property works in the opposite way from the distribution of office. The masses become revolutionary when the distribution of property is *unequal.* Men of education become revolutionary when the distribution of office is *equal.* (A:65)

Thus, Aristotle's meritocracy offers greater rewards of office and property for those exhibiting "civic excellence." Notice that wealth alone is not the standard of merit used by Aristotle, but rather excellence and superior education. Nor is free birth, or democratic citizenship, alone the standard for reward, but again, the superior contribution of an individual.

It is this Aristotelian formulation—that of *proportionate* equality, rather than pure equality—that forms the basis for modern day theories of meritocracy, including Rawls' theory of justice. However, in contradistinction to contemporary neoconservative and liberal theorists who rest their case with the theory of pure meritocracy (Daniel Bell), or worse, with the theory of unfettered capitalist distribution (Fredrich Hayek), Aristotle tempered his theory of proportionate equality with his architectonic theory of the majority middle class. (And as we will show, Rawls tempered his theory of distributive justice with the "difference principle.")

In establishing the principle of the majority middle class and its link to the stability and lawfulness of democracy, Aristotle offers a set of proposals directed toward: the expansion of the middle class, the upgrading of the poor, and the legal, noncoercive encouragement of the rich to use their property for the common good. In so doing, he adds a communal dimension to his theory in which the system of proportionate equality (or just reward for greater civic contribution) becomes an advantage to the society, without becoming a destabilizing disadvantage. That is, the elitist tendencies of his meritocracy are reduced, because the advantages gained by individuals of superior merit (or superior wealth) occur within the context of legislative control by the majority middle class.

Let us now present Aristotle's theory of the majority middle class, for contained within it is the best practical proposal for the attainment of a realistic degree of equality in society, within a context of stable, legal-democracy. Again, Aristotle's argument reads as if it were written today.

Aristotle's Theory of the Majority Middle Class: Stable Democracy With Practical Equality

Aristotle believed that extremes of wealth destabilize society and lead to political conflict and violent crime. However, he did not believe that the communist programs for eliminating these wealth differentials were viable or desirable. He sought, therefore, to create a practical program for the containment of the conflict engendered by extreme wealth differentials.

The program centers on: (1) the expansion of the middle class, (2) the absorption of the poor (so that they become part of the middle class in political as well as in economic activity), and (3) the legal, social, and educational persuasion of the rich to share their wealth with the poor and the middle class.

Here is Aristotle's argument for the middle class as the basis for the best political system: "We are here concerned with the best constitution and way of life for the majority of men and states. Goodness itself counts in a mean; and in any state the middle class is a mean between the rich and the poor. The middle class is free from the ambition of the rich and the pettiness of the poor: it is a natural link which helps to ensure political cohesion. We may thus conclude that a constitution based on this class—i.e., a 'polity'—is most likely to be stable" (A:179).

We will explain Aristotle's use of the term "polity" to denote the form of government linked to the majority middle class shortly. First, let us present Aristotle's theory of the majority middle class more completely.

In all states there may be distinguished three parts, or classes, of the citizen body: the very rich, the very poor and the middle class which forms the mean. *Men who are in this (middle) condition are the most ready to listen to reason.* Those who belong to either extreme—the over-handsome, the over-strong, the over-noble, the over-wealthy; or at the opposite end the over-poor, the over-weak, the utterly ignoble—find it hard to follow the lead of reason.

Men in the first class tend more to violence and serious crimes: men in the second tend too much to roguery. It is a further merit of the middle class that its members suffer least from ambition, which both in the military and the civil sphere is dangerous to states.

It must be added that those who enjoy too many advantages—strength, wealth, connections and so forth—are both unwilling to obey and ignorant how to obey.... But there are also defects in those who suffer from the opposite extreme of a lack of advantages: they are far too mean and poor-spirited.... The result is a state, not of freemen, but only of slaves and masters: a state of envy on one side and on the other contempt.

Nothing could be further removed from the spirit of friendship or the temper of a political community. Community depends on friendship; and when there is enmity instead of friendship, men will not even share the same path.

A state aims at being, as far as it can be, a society composed of equals and peers (who as such can be friends and associates); and the middle class, more than any other, has this sort of composition. (A:181; italics added)

Thus, although Aristotle puts forth a theory of proportionate equality that rewards merit, he does not leave the social situation in such a condition as to encourage nothing but competition and elitism. This would be far from Aristotle's ideal of the just society. Instead, he emphasizes social policies that would ameliorate the disparities arising from a meritocracy (whether the merit be natural, or gained through advantageous class position). By insisting on policies that would upgrade the poor and cajole the rich into contributing their wealth to the common good, Aristotle directs society toward becoming, "as far as it can be, a society composed of equals and peers," so that such equals will act as "friends and associates" who care about one another. Within this society of caring associates, wherein the middle class makes up the vast majority, meritocratic reward for those showing some form of civic excellence is encouraged.

It must also be emphasized that Aristotle, by inserting the phrase, "as far as it can be," turns us away from utopian or coercive schemes of pure levelling, such as those of Phaleus or Plato. Let us go further with Aristotle's reasoning on this. Why does he prefer a society wherein the middle class forms the majority?

It is clear from our argument, first, that the best form of political society is one where *power is vested in the middle class*, and, secondly, that good government is attainable in those states where there is a *large middle class*—large enough, if possible, to be stronger than both of the other classes. . . .

It is therefore of the greatest blessings for a state that its members should possess a *moderate and adequate property*. Where some have great possessions, and others have nothing at all, the result is either an extreme democracy or an unmixed oligarchy; or it may even be—directly, and as a reaction against both these extremes—a tyranny. Tyranny is a form of government which may grow out of the headiest type of democracy, or out of oligarchy; but is is much less likely to grow out of constitutions of the middle order. (A:182)

For Aristotle, a society dominated by the rich or the poor would become undemocratic, tending toward oligarchy, democracy-of-the-poor, or tyranny. A large middle class, however, serves to stabilize the democracy, creating an arena of economic compromise between the rich and the poor, and an assembly of political compromise in which reason and law supersede the passions (that are inflamed by differences in wealth and status).

Aristotle states it this way: "The reason why democracies are generally more secure and more permanent than oligarchies is the character of their middle class, which is more numerous and *is allowed a larger share in the government, than it is in oligarchies*. *Where democracies have no middle class, and the poor are greatly superior in number, trouble ensues, and they are speedily ruined*" (A:182; italics added).

Aristotle continues his warning about the instability of democracies wherein the middle class is too small: " . . . the middle class is in most states generally small; and the result is that as soon as one or the other of the two main classes— the owners of property and the masses—gains the advantage it oversteps the mean, and *drawing the constitution in its own direction* it institutes, as the case may be, either a democracy (of the poor) or an oligarchy" (A:183). In other words, where the middle class is small, the rich and the poor will draw the constitution away from democracy, and it may degenerate into tyranny.

Aristotle distinguishes democracy-of-the-poor from democracy-of-the-middle-class. He uses the term "polity" to denote democracy of the middle class. He uses this term because in a democracy of the middle class, *both the rich and the poor are encouraged to participate in governance* (in an atmosphere of reason and compromise, reinforced through the establishment of constitutional law), whereas democracy of the poor tends to degenerate into either mob rule, demagogic domination, or dictatorship (tyranny).

By mob rule, or what Polybius later called ochlochracy,[22] Aristotle meant that the majority, by assembly vote, might attack a minority, or change its laws from month to month so that individuals would be punished one month for what they had been encouraged to do the month before, or vote the whim of the moment, swayed by the passion of debate (and crowd psychology) with no legal-constitutional guidelines to stabilize the democratic process.

Demagogic domination also emanated from "extreme democracies," for the crowd psychology at large assemblies would bring forth charismatic orators who could sway the citizen body. Sometimes such charismatic demagogues ruled the democracies nobly, sometimes villainously, but in either case these "heady democracies" drifted dangerously toward tyranny under the sway of the demagogues. Again, this was too unstable for Aristotle, who demanded that the rule of law—carried by the more rationally oriented middle class—was necessary for the proper functioning of democracy.

He who commands that law should rule may thus be regarded as commanding that God and Reason alone should rule; he who commands that a man should rule adds the character of the beast. (A:146)

Law should be sovereign on every issue, and the magistrates and the citizen body should only decide about details. (A:169)

We have always to remember that rightly constituted laws should be the final sovereign, and that personal authority of any sort should only act in the particular cases which cannot be covered by general law. (A:123).

Demagogues arise in states where the laws are not sovereign. The people then become an autocrat made up of many members. (A:168).

Democracy . . . under which everything is managed by decrees, is not even a democracy, in any real sense of the word. Decrees can never be general rules and any real constitution must be based on general rules. (A:169)

It is critical for us here that Aristotle links the middle class to "law"—the middle class becomes the carrying class for constitutional law and political rationality: "It also must be considered a proof of its value that the best legislators have come from the middle class" (A:183).

Let us return to our discussion of Aristotle's distinction between democracy-of-the-middle-class—"polity"—and democracy-of-the-poor—which degenerates into extreme (non-legal) democracy, or worse, tyranny. Let us discuss this latter possibility.

Democracy-of-the-poor, or extreme democracy, often degenerated into tyranny, wherein a dictatorial leader would begin by ruling in the name of the poor, but end by ruling for himself and his supporting clique. Such a tyranny could emerge from oligarchy of the rich as well, especially during periods of counter-revolution against the poor.

Thus Aristotle rejects both ''unmixed oligarchy'' and ''extreme democracy'' for their instability, unlawfulness, and selfish, self-interested rule. He carefully distinguishes democracy-of-the-middle-class from these forms of government. And, because democracy-of-the-middle-class majority would not exclude the rich or the poor, but rather include them, he terms democracy based on the middle class majority, ''polity.'' This is a generic term, an inclusive term, and Aristotle's best form of government would include elements of oligarchy of the rich and democracy of the poor, within a system of constitutional law. The keys for us here are *the paramountcy of law and the middle class majority.* The best government and the best society can only be approached when law is established as inviolable and the middle class is nurtured and expanded ''as far as it can be. . . . ''

Before presenting Aristotle's policy proposals concerning the expansion of the middle class, one more point needs to be highlighted. Aristotle links the problem of violent crime to the destabilization of classes (as part of the problem of political instability). His analysis, though in no way meant as a total theory of crime (as, say, that presented in the modern world by Durkheim and his followers[23]), sheds a good deal of light on the causality of certain kinds of crimes. Here is the way Aristotle analyzes the situation:

There is also a further point which has to be taken into account. We have to consider, not only the cause of civil discord, but also the cause of ordinary crime. There are some crimes which are due to the lack of necessities; and here, Phaleus thinks, equality of property will be a remedy, and will serve to prevent men from stealing simply through cold and hunger. . . . What is the remedy for this kind of crime?. . . . Some modicum of property and some sort of work. (A:65–66)

Aristotle does not stop with an analysis only of the crimes of the poor. He is just as worried about the rich: ''The greatest crimes are committed not for the sake of necessities, but for the sake of superfluities. Men do not become tyrants in order to avoid exposure to cold. . . . We thus see that the general scheme proposed by Phaleus avails only against lesser crimes'' (A:65–66).

Aristotle put forth proposals for the containment of the excesses of the rich as well as the poor. Let us now present Aristotle's practical policy proposals for the expansion of the middle class, the upgrading of the poor, and the persuasion of the rich to contribute to the common good of all.

Policies for Maintaining Democratic Stability Through Increased Equality

Besides constructing democracies on a sound basis, it is also necessary to ensure their permanence. The true policy is not one which guarantees the greatest possible amount of democracy, but one which guarantees its largest possible duration. Moderation is therefore advisable. On the one hand, *the rich should not be alienated by a policy of confiscating their riches . . .* on the other hand, *measures should also be taken to improve the lot of common people by a system of social services, both public and private.* (A:267; italics added)

Economic and Political Policies Concerning the Poor

Aristotle presents us with a set of policies concerning the economic improvement, and the political participation, of the poor. He makes it clear that he does not recommend simply handing over redistributed money-wealth to the poor. Rather, *career and property* must be provided to the poor such that they may be absorbed into the middle class. This latter would make them more reasonable and rational in their political orientation.

Further, the political participation of the poor in the assembly and the courts was to be mandatory:

. . . measures should . . . be taken to improve the lot of the common people by *a system of social services, both public and private.* (A:267)

It is the habit of demagogues to distribute any surplus among the people; and the people in the act of taking ask for the same again. To help the poor in this way is to fill a leaky jar . . . yet it is the duty of a genuine democrat to see to it that the masses are not excessively poor. (A:268)

Poverty is the cause of the defects of democracy. That is the reason why measures should be taken to ensure a permanent level of prosperity. This is in the interest of all classes, including the prosperous themselves; and therefore, the proper policy is to accumulate any surplus revenue in a fund, and then to distribute this fund in block grants to the poor. The ideal method of distribution, if a sufficient fund can be accumulated, is to make such grants sufficient for the purchase of a plot of land: failing that they should be large enough *to start men in commerce or agriculture.*

If such grants cannot be made to all the poor simultaneously, they should be distributed successively, by tribes or other divisions: and meanwhile the rich should contribute a sum sufficient to provide the poor with *payment for their attendance at the obligatory meeting of the assembly . . .* [and the law courts]. (A:267)

Notables who are men of feeling and good sense may also undertake the duty of *helping the poor to find occupations*—each taking charge of a group, and each giving a grant to enable the members of his group to make a start. (A:269)

Aristotle is clear on his policies for the poor. The proper policy would be that which provided the poor with careers and property, rather than money per se. This would enable the poor to rise to near middle class status. The poor would also be incorporated as citizens, since they would be paid a small sum so that they could attend the assembly and the law courts.

Policies Concerning the Rich

Aristotle wished to create policies that would encourage the rich to give of their wealth, but that would be noncoercive. "The demagogues of our day, jealous to please the peoples of their states, cause a large amount of property to be confiscated to public use by means of the law courts. . . . Such prosecutions are usually brought against notables only, and not against those who belong to the popular party; but the proper policy, whenever it can be pursued, is to keep all citizens alike attached to the constitution and the government under it, or at any rate, failing that, to prevent any citizen from regarding the government as his enemy . . . '' (A:268).

Aristotle believed that through a proper policy of education, socialization, and legislation, the rich could be encouraged to give of their private wealth for the common good. Aristotle was not naive in this. He knew that the rich would have to be pressured by the middle class-controlled legislature, and that the education of the rich would have to include a heavy dose of socialization emphasizing communal good will.

It is worth repeating Aristotle's conception of ''private property with common use'' to illustrate his policy toward the rich:

The present system (of private property) would be far preferable, if it were adorned by customs (in the social sphere) and by enactment of proper laws (in the political). It would possess the advantage of both systems, and *would combine the merits of a system of community of property with those of the system of private property.* (It would be the ideal); for *property ought to be generally and in the main private, but common in one respect (i.e. in use).* . . . It is clear . . . that *the better system is that under which property is privately owned but is put to common use;* and *the function proper to the legislator is to make men so disposed that they will treat property in this way.* (A:49–50; italics added)

Thus the legislators are entrusted with the task of pressuring the rich to use their wealth for the common good. Aristotle hoped especially that the rich would use their wealth to upgrade the condition of the poor, for this would enhance the stability of the democracy. It is worth repeating this statement of Aristotle's: ''Notables who are men of feeling and good sense may also undertake the duty of helping the poor to find occupations—each taking charge of a group, and each giving a grant to enable the members of his group to make a start'' (A:269).

The middle class-dominated legislature would also guide the rich away from using their money for frivolous or self-aggrandizing projects: ''It is a policy, too, to prevent the rich, even if they are willing, from undertaking expensive, and yet useless, public services'' (A:229).

Policies for the Expansion of the Middle Class

Aristotle is clear when he suggests that policies should be established that ensure: (1) the numbers of the middle class increase (this includes the upgrading of the poor to middle class economic, political, and educational standards); (2) the wealth and property of the middle class be adequate and secure; and (3) that the middle class play a majority role in the legislature and law courts.

It is clear from our argument, first, that the best form of political society is one where power is vested in the middle class, and secondly, that good government is attainable in those states where there is a large middle class. . . . It is therefore of the greatest of blessings for a state that its members should possess a moderate and adequate property. (A:182)

Aristotle goes on to affirm:

The reason why democracies are generally secure and more permanent than oligarchies is the character of their middle class, which is more numerous, and is allowed a larger share in government than it is in oligarchies. Where democracies have no middle class, and the poor are greatly superior in number, trouble ensues, and they are speedily ruined. (A:182)

Thus, policies for the expansion, prosperity and political empowerment of the middle class would, for Aristotle, become the architectonic policies for the creation of a stable, lawful democracy with the greatest practical amount of equality.

A state arrives at being, as far as it can be, a society composed of equals and peers (who as such can be friends and associates); and the middle class more than any other, has this sort of composition. (A:181)

POLICY FORMULATIONS DERIVED FROM ARISTOTLE

Aristotelian Policies for the Poor

Careers for the Poor

Aristotle favored policies that would upgrade the poor to middle class status. Careers, property, and political participation were the goals of his policies: "[M]easures should be taken to improve the lot of the common people by a system of social services, both public and private" (A:267).

Aristotle makes it clear that he does not favor simply giving money to the poor: "It is the habit of demagogues to distribute any surplus among the poor; and the people in the act of taking ask for the same again. To help the poor in this way is to fill a leaky jar . . . yet it is the duty of a genuine democrat to see to it that the masses are not excessively poor" (A:268).

From the Aristotelian system, we can see that the welfare system, the poor laws, or the dole are the wrong approach to upgrading the condition of the poor. The welfare system is the "leaky jar" approach, the dependency approach.

Everyone knows that the welfare cycle of perpetuated dependency must be broken. From the Aristotelian system, the solution becomes apparent. Long-term careers must be created for the poor, even if this process takes two generations, or even three, to establish. And property and political participation must also be part of the social goals of this process.

In the modern context there are numerous sub-classes of the poor. There are: (1) the unemployed working class displaced by automation; (2) the working poor, who have jobs, but whose income is too far below middle class standards; (3) the urban poor who have never had a stable job and whose educational level and socialization level leave them nearly unemployable; and (4) the rural poor— indigenous and immigrant—who collect in urban centers or remain in rural areas, and who are also educationally unready for the modern economy.

We will discuss the displaced workers in the section on Keynes, and the working poor in the section on Rawls. Here we focus on the urban and rural poor whose educational and social level make them the least likely to find employment in a competitive market economy.

Workfare vs. Welfare

From the Aristotelian system, workfare programs would replace welfare programs. For with the welfare programs, "in the act of taking, the people will simply ask for more again," and thus the poor cannot gain upward mobility.

Workfare programs would provide jobs for the poor in *underserviced* areas of society. Such jobs would help to inculcate stable habits of work and socialize children into a culture of work and upward mobility (instead of a culture of poverty, vice, drugs, and crime). The targeted populations for workfare job programs are: welfare mothers and their children, and unemployed men who have never worked.

Welfare Mothers and Their Children

To the surprise of the majority of the middle class—liberal and conservative— most welfare mothers want to work. When offered job opportunities, they are grateful. However, we must not be naive. Welfare mothers are willing to work, but their skills are minimal, their attitude is sometimes hostile and negative, they may be on drugs, they may engage in occasional prostitution, and they may spend their money on numbers/gambling. Furthermore, they will have children, and therefore excellent day-care centers with educational enrichment programs will be necessary.

In Massachusetts, and now in New Jersey, workfare programs are being initiated. Both these programs are nonpunitive. The key, of course, is that jobs must be found for, or created for, welfare mothers. Here is the way Governor Tom Kean of New Jersey presents his program. He states the case for careers for the poor as well as it can be stated.

Nothing is higher on my agenda in 1987 than an ambitious effort to reduce the welfare rolls by giving our recipients a real opportunity to gain economic independence. Our existing system has failed to do this while wasting our taxpayers' dollars; we must fix it.

Liberals and conservatives have been arguing for a generation now about why welfare has failed. The time has come to stop arguing and start acting. . . .

It is time to re-cast public assistance. We must move from a system that encourages dependence to one that emphasizes work, self-sufficiency, and opportunity. It is time to build a system that gives our poor a real chance to better themselves.

[The new program] will *require* education, job training, or work of *all* able-bodied recipients as a condition for obtaining welfare. The state will guarantee the job training, child care, medical coverage, and other support necessary for a woman to take a job, enter job training or finish school. "REACH" (our program) will be the first state program to make prevention its major theme by concentrating on young mothers, the group most vulnerable to becoming longterm recipients.

. . . although REACH initially will require a significant investment of state money, *REACH will pay for itself, even if we reduce the welfare rolls by only 15 percent.*

If we want recipients to have a genuine shot at getting off welfare, they must be trained to hold and be able to maintain real, private sector jobs. . . . To encourage this, we also hope to offer tax breaks to employers. . . . The alternative to workfare is to "continue to pour billions of our taxpayers' dollars into a system that has miserably failed us [the "leaky jar"].[24]

Along with tax breaks, the government may have to supply subsidies to private corporations, hospitals, nursing homes, and so on, in order to ensure that jobs would be made available for workfare mothers.

Government-created jobs will also be necessary in order to absorb those work-fare mothers who simply cannot be absorbed by the private sector. The government could subsidize jobs in some needed underserviced areas of our society. For instance, job sectors that could absorb poor women include: maids and housekeepers, babysitters for dual career couples, hospital work, nursing-home work, day-care centers, waitresses in luncheonettes and restaurants, department store and shopping center positions, garment district labor, and factor assembly line work (where this is not automated or sent to the Third World).

Once the jobs are found or created, two sets of *support systems* become necessary: educational enrichment programs for the children and social work support systems for the adults (and children).

With the workfare mother working, the children must be cared for at good day-care facilities. The ratio of childcare workers and teachers to children must be kept such that the children get a high level of nurturance and supervision. The children represent the generation that could be most effectively helped. Middle class dual-career couples never leave their children in a situation where more than four or five children are supervised by a babysitter, and middle class nursery schools are very attentive to the children's emotional and educational needs.

Along with nurturant childcare, educational enhancement programs are needed at the day-care facilities. These already exist at many day-care centers, but should be upgraded in terms of program and numbers of personnel. Again, no naivete or romanticism should be tolerated. The children of the poor are deficient in language, vocabulary, reading skills, abstraction ability, math skills, and so on. They may be street-wise or farm-wise, but this knowledge will not get them anywhere in modern society.

Another warning: the educational enhancement programs must run from the cradle to college in order to be really effective. This latter is not problematical if the society in question is willing to service the poor properly. Further, such educational programs will pay for themselves if welfare payments are substantially reduced through their partial success.

More reality: social work support systems are necessary for working mothers, since they may have bad work habits, bad attitudes, are often hostile mothers, and have drug, alcohol, or other problems. Well-trained social workers are needed to help workfare mothers get to their jobs on time, cope with the stress of their job, nurture their children, manage their budgets, deal with government bureaucracies, and so on. Many workfare mothers will need very little support; others a great deal. But such social work support must be available or workfare programs may not succeed.

From an Aristotelian perspective, the creation of careers for poor women and their children must replace the practice of giving welfare payments to them and allowing them to remain dependent.

Unemployed Poor Men

The condition of unemployed poor men is usually worse than that of their welfare women. The big differences are the hostility and criminal factors. Reality again: lower class boys may be members of gangs. They grow up in a street culture of violence and crime where the heroes are the gangsters, killers, numbers runners, drug dealers, pimps, and so on.[25] The literature is well known, the results, of course, highly problematical. One is dealing with an unskilled, uneducated (school dropouts at an early age), hostile, sometimes violent, sometimes addicted stratum of young men whom one is attempting to place in stable, career-line jobs.

Can poor men be placed in jobs and can they succeed? Can they eventually be re-attached to the family?

The kind of jobs preferred by poor men are similar to those preferred by working class men. Police, guards, transit jobs, truck drivers, auto mechanics, taxi drivers, heavy factory work—macho type career lines. However, these jobs are not available precisely because the working class and the working poor compete for and gain these jobs.

What kind of jobs are available? Short-order cooks and counterwork in small restaurants, stock jobs in department stores, and little else. We must face it: jobs must be created for this population of men. Park and sanitation work should be doubled in most American cities—America's parks are the least manicured, our cities the dirtiest in the industrial world.

For the majority of the workfare men (who have not received the educational and job training support the next generation will receive), Jobs Corps- and C. C. C.-type structures will probably have to be re-created.

The Job Corps has great advantages as a job program for urban and rural poor men. It is organized like the military. It is a civilan army corps. That is, tough masculine supervisors act like army sergeants, commanding a work brigade. Such supervisors can and should be drawn from union personnel, so that co-operation, instead of conflict, is fostered between the unions and the unemployed.

Lower class men respond well to such a situation. However, along with the tough army-style discipline, social work and educational support systems are necessitated and must be included. Just as with the women, attitude problems, work habit problems, hostility, and addiction problems must be dealt with. Social workers are needed for those who cannot respond to army-style discipline. Support groups and individual counseling will be needed. Non-authoritarian work situations will be needed for a certain percentage of poor men.

Educational and job training programs should, of course, be made available, as they would be for the women.

Will all this be expensive? Less so than the cost of prison incarceration, which presently runs at about $25,000–$50,000 per inmate per year!

We will discuss job training and retraining programs along with job placement programs in our section on Keynes. Here we wish to focus on one other Aristotelian principle: the idea of *property* for the poor.

Property for the Poor

The long-range goal is to make the poor less dependent. Careers, education—these are the critical factors. However, once careers are established for the poor, housing, property, and perhaps business property might be a next step for independence. In terms of housing, the situation for the urban poor is so catastrophic that no alternative exists except to build large-scale housing projects. But we know from the experience of the 1960s that the rehabilitation of smaller houses with the option of private ownership—the usual American dream—produces better results. Ownership creates an attitude of independence and encourages maintenance and improvements. If loans are made to the poor, they do fix up old houses and they do care for them. Such programs do exist; they should be dramatically expanded. Housing property does help create independence and stability. In this case, however, subsidies and low cost long term loans, with the least bureaucratic harassment, are necessitated. Again, this may be the cheaper long-term policy than the current one, based on payments to welfare hotels and welfare landlords.

As to small business, certain ethnic immigrants excel at this, such as Arabs, Koreans, and Indians (and in the past Italians and Jews). Latins are moderately successful with small business; American Blacks not very successful. Where immigrant competition is not overwhelming, poor Blacks and Latins should be encouraged and helped to open small businesses. Such programs exist, but need expansion.

Political Integration of the Poor

Aristotle advised that every effort be made to encourage the poor to attend the assembly and the law courts. He even suggested cash payments to the poor to facilitate such participation.

In the modern context, voter registration, such as that now being done, is a proper policy. Whether such voter registration focuses on the Blacks and Latins[26] or on the white rural poor (as in the South in reaction to the attempt to register Blacks[27]), it is a good policy. If the poor become politically integrated, they are more likely to make a commitment to work in, and for, the society at large. They are also more likely to channel their anger and their activity into political organization and rhetoric, rather than into petty crime.

Again reality: such political activity by the poor may be radical in nature. But, as Aristotle so wisely understood, radical politics within a democratic system is much less dangerous than that which develops outside the system. Radical politics within the system gets channelled into party organization, electoral processes, and eventually toward charismatic or demagogic figures contained within the electoral process and the law. The awakening of the poor outside of the system leads to the rise of tyrannical charismatic leaders, revolutionary violence, and despotic styles of control.

Some of this tyrannical violence emanates from the poor, even when they are organized within the system. But, with the slightest improvement in the career condition of the poor, this quickly gives way to democratic styles of leadership and organization. Where the condition of the poor is utterly wretched and hopeless, and where they are a vast majority, tyranny will prevail. Where the poor are a minority, and where their integration into economic society is improving, their political integration will be more successful, and will be part of the process of upgrading their social status.

Crime and the Poor

One last Aristotelian dimension of the program must be mentioned. That is the problem of crime and violence emanating from the poor.

We have to consider, not only the cause of civil discord, but also the cause of ordinary crime. There are some crimes which are due to the lack of necessities; and here Phaleus thinks equality of property will serve to prevent men from stealing simply through cold and hunger . . . What is the remedy for this kind of crime? . . . . Some modicum of property and some sort of work. (A:65–66).

Aristotle in no way meant this as a total theory of crime and its remedy. He discusses the crimes of the rich shortly thereafter. And we in the modern world are aware of Durkheim's comprehensive theory of crime and the vast literature it has spawned.[28] Sutherland's analysis of "white collar crime" and the epidemic of drug use among the middle class alert us against any theory linking crime to the poor alone.

It is important, nonetheless, to add this Aristotelian dimension to the problem of the poor and the crimes emanating from the poor. For Aristotle believed that crime among the poor could be substantially reduced if the poor were upgraded to middle class life styles. Of course, there would still be crime, but the "pathological"[29] crime rate, to borrow Durkheim's term, emanating from the poor might be substantially reduced.

For instance, in the United States certain petty crimes arising from the poor are routinely accepted as "normal." The theft of radios from cars is so ordinary that removable radios had to be invented, and signs saying "no radio" have been mass produced. The same is true of battery theft from cars and car theft itself. The police accept car theft as part of the system, only occasionally attempting to reduce it. Bicycle theft is almost automatic in our cities. Even "kryptonite" locks don't prevent wheels and seats from being stolen.

Muggings are considered part of urban life in the United States. If you live in a city, you will be mugged. Except for the elevation of an occasional vigilante to hero status, no action is demanded against what is perceived as inevitable. Rates of murder and rape—emanating from the poor and the unemployed working class and linked especially to young men in these two groups—are astronomical in the United States. The majority of these murders and rapes are directed at the poor themselves, the poor being the victims more often than the middle class. Gang killings in poor neighborhoods are routine, and barely investigated by the police—who often know the perpetrators, but cannot cope with the scale of the problem. Drug related crime and violence is also, of course, more concentrated in lower class areas.

A number of years ago a movie was made, spoofing Italian divorce laws (or the lack of them). It was called "Divorce Italian Style" (i.e., murdering your mate). Today we could make a movie called "*Re-distribution of Income American Style*," in which the cars, bikes, radios, televisions, clothing, and jewelry of the middle classes would be stolen by the poor, and then the middle class reimbursed by the insurance companies and their insurance rates subsequently raised. The result is the distribution of consumer goods to the poor, payed for by the middle class. All this stimulates the economy, because the middle class re-purchases new products, while paying higher insurance rates at the same time. The rich, thus, get more, the poor get a share, and the middle class pays for it all. This is bad policy by Aristotelian standards—and it is about as funny as murdering your mate because divorce is against the law.

We mention the problem of crime and the poor because, if Aristotelian theory is correct, the upgrading of the poor through careers, education, property, and political participation would yield a corresponding decline in the crime rate. Such a decline would bring with it a reduction in insurance rates (car and household), thus increasing the security and stability of the middle class, and also a reduction in prison costs. This would go far toward the financing of career programs and housing for the poor. This, of course, would be a long term gain on an initial investment, but it would be a remarkable gain indeed, both financially and socially.

Aristotelian Policies for the Rich

From Aristotle's theory we can derive a program of taxation and education produced by legislators to encourage the rich to give of their wealth. The system of private charities within capitalist societies is so extensive that we might think that this would be sufficient to generate revenue for the poor. This is not the case, however, in part because of the protestant ethic, in part because of the capitalist economic system itself.

In terms of protestantism, the individual is supposed to make it on his or her own, and hard work puts one on the road to salvation and heavenly grace. Those who do not work, those who fail—in other words, those who are poor—deserve their lot. Little sympathy for the poor exists; they are considered slothful, corrupt, of the devil—it is their own fault. Therefore, charities in capitalist countries tend to be directed toward the infirm and the handicapped, rather than the poor.

Secondly, the capitalist economic system flourishes with a "reserve army" of unemployed workers, which keeps wages down. Both these factors, the religious and economic ethic, combine to prevent the rich, even where they are charitably generous, from helping the poor to gain careers or property.

Given this modern situation, taxation of the rich becomes the key way in which poor and middle class legislators—the majority—can persuade the rich to give of their wealth. One could envision, in the modern context, a special added five percent surcharge tax on the rich, the revenue from which could be legally earmarked for a career fund for the poor. Such a fund could be directed toward education, job training, job placement, and job creation. Second, a minimum tax on the rich, barring all loopholes, may be the best devise for obtaining a portion of the wealth of the rich in the modern context. We will discuss the minimum tax, and the much more complex process of corporate taxation, in the sections on Rawls and Keynes that follow.

In any case, Aristotle is clear about the role of the legislature in relation to the rich. They should intervene, noncoercively, in order to persuade the rich to direct their "goodwill" toward upgrading the poor.

Aristotle also speaks of educating the rich and socializing them to the benefits of maintaining political stability. This is important in the modern context. Because, as inadequate as the protestant ethic was in terms of the rehabilitation of the poor, it at least spurred the conscience of the rich to give lavishly to charities for the infirm and the disabled. Today, with the decline of world religion, an ever more selfish attitude could come to prevail.

We have already seen a growing "me-first," sensual, selfish, narcissistic attitude[30] in the new generation. A humanistic helping attitude may have to be re-inculcated in the modern population in order to avoid the emergence of a morally vacuous, sociopathic society. Is ours to become a society of "sensualists without heart run by technicians without soul" as Max Weber warned it might?[31] There is evidence to suggest that modern society will not become anti-humanistic. In fact, there are signs that we are becoming more humanistic than our predecessors. There is, for instance, a worldwide revulsion against torture, unlawful imprisonment, inhumane warfare, and despotism in any form.

How does all of this apply to a policy for the rich? From Aristotle's system, the rich should be taught, through the educational process itself, to give for the common good, taught that this is one of their roles—that in giving a portion of their wealth and developing an attitude of goodwill, they will benefit from it by adding to the stability and prosperity of the society. As Aristotle stated it: "Notables who are men of feeling and good sense may also undertake the duty of helping the poor to find occupations—each taking charge of a group, and each giving a grant to enable the members of his group to make a start" (A:269).

Aristotle in no way suggested that an attitude of condescension, or noblese oblige, be inculcated. The educational process was to ingrain a *rational attitude* of *civic consciousness* in the rich. An attitude through which (having gained wealth or possessing access to high office) they could cooperate with the legislature in upgrading the poor and enhancing the general civic good.

Operationalizing this, one could envision a new program of civic responsibility becoming required at the elite private and public schools and colleges. Civics could be revived as it once was meant to be taught—as a course inculcating citizenship and legal-democratic procedures.

Can this be done without offending sectarian believers? Yes, civics—the old course in good citizenship (which Hannah Arendt warned could disappear[32])— in no way conflicts with religious beliefs nor does it have anything to do with blind patriotism. Rational political and economic participation within a legal-constitutional context is what civics encourages.

The kind of education that Aristotle suggested may be needed more than ever now. For, as the rich become corporate managers rather than business owners, the responsibility for economic actions becomes de-personalized. The managerial rich operate behind the facade of corporate entities possessing legal status separate from the managers who operate them. Corporations have no moral conscience and corporate managers usually have no public persona. (Lee Iacocca is the exception that proves the rule.) Therefore, the inculcation of an ethic of responsibility and sharing among the emerging managerial elite[33] is absolutely essential to modern society in that the managers may act more selfishly and sociopathologically than their capitalist predecessors.

Policies for the Expansion and Prosperity of the Middle Class

Since pure equality may be neither possible nor advisable, especially within the context of modern society, Aristotle's theory of the middle class majority becomes the architectonic theory of equality.

The basis for Aristotle's theory of equality is that the larger and more prosperous the middle class is, the more stable the polity will be. To foster this, Aristotle favored policies that would lead to the expansion of the middle class, the assurance of its economic prosperity, and its political control of the legislature.

It is clear from our argument, first, that the best form of political society is one where power is vested in the middle class, and secondly, that good government is attainable in those states where there is a large middle class. . . . It is therefore of the greatest of blessings for a state that its members should possess a moderate and adequate property. (A:181–82)

How does one ensure the prosperity of the middle class and provide them with adequate property?

Taxation

The middle classes provide society with the bulk of its tax revenues. Therefore, it is urgent that the middle class pay its fair share of taxes. However, taxes on the middle class should always be set at a moderate rate. For, at the same time that taxation of the middle class is absolutely essential to modern societies, a high consumption rate[34] among the middle class is also necessary for the proper functioning of our modern over-productive, technologically advanced[35] market economy. Further, as Aristotle has insisted, the prosperity of the middle class is necessary for political stability. Therefore, taxation of the middle class must be set at a moderate rate.

The taxation programs of most modern societies were originally set as "progressive"—that is, heavy on the rich, moderate on the middle class, and light on the poor. This system of taxation was correct in its inception and is still correct.[36] From the Aristotelian system, a moderate taxation of the middle class becomes a central principle.

The taxation system that emerged in the United States after WWII allowed the rich and the upper-middle classes to avoid their tax burden. It placed the brunt of that burden on the middle class. And it allowed the poor to remain unemployed and therefore untaxed. This was a disastrous system from the Aristotelian point of view.

The recent revision of the tax laws still does not tax the rich enough, nor does it reduce the taxes of the middle class enough. The correct ratio for the taxation system should emerge from the desired direction of class balance. And, of course, it should serve to improve the market economy, not impair it. As we shall see in our section on Keynes, taxing the rich and investing such capital, while allowing the middle class to increase their "propensity to consume" is good capitalist economics.[37] From the Aristotelian system, it is also good politics.

Further, from the Aristotelian system, career creation for the poor expands the tax base of the society in the long run, and thus bolsters the possibility of maintaining a moderate taxation of the middle class.

One more factor should be mentioned within this perspective. The progressive taxation should not be set so as to harm the upward mobility of the upper middle class. The income differential between the upper middle class and the rich is very great. It is not difficult to set the tax rates such that the rich pay a large minimum tax (a tax containing no loopholes), while the upper middle class is taxed moderately.

Conversely, from the Aristotelian system, the upper middle class would not be encouraged to utilize the bulk of their income on superficial luxury items, but rather to focus it on education, property, and stability. Therefore, a luxury tax, such as will be discussed in the section on Rawls, levied on "conspicuous consumption" items, would be consistent with Aristotelian theory. For, the upper middle class would be protected and nurtured by the income tax system, whereas income spent on superfluities would be more heavily taxed.

To conclude, then, moderate taxation of the middle class is essential to their economic prosperity, and this latter is essential for political stability. This, however, brings up the question of the rising cost of the "welfare state," with its medical and social security "safety net" programs. In the modern context, this must be analyzed in terms of taxation of the middle class. How can the middle class remain moderately taxed if the costs of the welfare state escalate? Do we jettison the welfare state or overtax the middle class? From an Aristotelian point of view, one must not overtax the middle class, whose moderate prosperity is absolutely essential for legal-democratic political stability. Therefore, we must look for alternative ways in which the welfare state can be funded, its bureaucracy limited, and its costs held down. Unless this last problem is solved, moderate taxation of the middle class cannot be maintained. The solution put forth by the neoconservatives—that the welfare state be dismantled—will be analyzed in a later chapter. We will show, however, that this is not likely, given the technological success of modern medicine, the popular desire to maintain social security retirement benefits, the expanding need for unemployment insurance due to automation, and so forth.

The Aristotelian principle, however, of moderate taxation of the middle class, is a critical principle, and one that should not be compromised if at all possible.

Housing Property

Property in the modern world means: housing, cars, televisions and other technological products, plus stock property (rather than direct business ownership in all but small businesses).

From the Aristotelian system what one derives is the need to maintain a moderate but adequate property for the middle class. This has profound modern implications. For instance, in terms of home ownership, every effort should be made to make available middle class homes. This means that suburban houses and apartments should be priced within the buying range of the middle class. It also means that urban apartments and condominiums should also be kept within this price range.

The trend toward building luxury homes, apartments, and condominiums is disastrous for the middle class—especially for the children of the middle class.

Those children left out of the inheritance of a residence may not be able to maintain their middle class status at all. Such a situation is anathema to the long term expansion and prosperity of the middle class.

What would an Aristotelian policy be? The major thrust of housing should be the production of middle class homes, apartments, and condominiums. This means that there must be: (1) a major effort to keep inflation in housing prices down; this can be done. At present in the United States (1988), the rise in housing prices has far outstripped the cost of materials or labor. The market can be moderated by increasing the supply of housing and subsidizing builders, land-lords, and mortgage institutions. (2) A program of mortgage assistance to the middle class may be absolutely essential, given market conditions; G. I. Bill-type low interest, long-term mortgages should be made available. Even down payments should be lowered. (3) Government subsidies to builders of middle income housing should be generously extended. (4) Rents should be fairly sta-bilized so as to avoid both tenant gouging and landlord bankruptcy. This latter can be accomplished. Rents have risen far beyond the fair profit level for land-lords, while rent-controlled apartments are maintained at rents far below the landlords' ability to care for the buildings. Fair rentals are necessary for young people just starting out in life, for the divorced, and for the elderly. I repeat, fair rental prices should be set such that the inflationary tendencies of the market are moderated to support the needs of the middle class. (We have already dis-cussed housing for the poor in this same vein.)

One more point on housing for the middle class: ownership may be better than renting. For ownership of property, as Aristotle pointed out, makes one care for the property as one cares for oneself. It also creates a greater degree of independence than renting. Furthermore, it attaches the owner to the realities of maintenance costs and market conditions. All of this is good for the stability of the middle class. However, the market tends to drift toward luxury housing where profits are far higher, and usually needs some modification or incentive program geared to the needs and means of the middle class (and the poor).

Stock Property

The days of direct ownership of big business are fading rapidly in this era of mergers, remergers, conglomeration, takeovers, break-ups, and so on. Further-more, the split between ownership and managerial control has been understood since the days of Berle and Means.[38] Business ownership, in today's corporate-capitalist world, means stock ownership. This does not mean that a concentration of stock ownership does not exist. The major industrial and financial assets are held by a small percentage of rich families, financial organizations, giant insti-tutional investors, and top managers.

However, even with this concentration of stock ownership, the actual control of stock property is remarkably complex. There are competing groups vying for control within the upper financial circles. Managers are in a struggle with financial cliques for both ownership and control of corporate property, and managers are also in a struggle with wealthy families, who own the majority shares of the corporations they founded.

Two examples should suffice here. Uniroyal was going to be bought out by a financial clique. Its managers, however, sold off huge chunks of its assets, and then bought the stock itself. The managers of Uniroyal now own controlling stock shares. In another case, the managers of Getty Oil attempted to block the succession bid by J. Paul Getty's son, after J. Paul Getty died. The managers were able to stack the Board and take over control of the CEO position, even though the Getty family still controlled the stocks. In other cases, financial cliques and family ownership have won out. However, the struggle has been fierce.

Some Marxists, such as Maurice Zeitlin,[39] believe that stock ownership is still basically in the hands of capitalist families—and they certainly do continue to hold enormous assets. Other Marxists, such as G. William Domhoff,[40] document the increasing control by corporate managers, along with the capitalist families.

Assuming that there is currently a mix of ownership and control, our job here is to establish the relationship of the middle class to stock ownership and an Aristotelian policy for such ownership.

As things now stand, stock ownership is in the hands of six different groups: (1) rich capitalist families, who established the industrial revolution and own vast empires of corporate stock; (2) corporate managers, who have steadily increased their stock ownership in both diversified portfolios for general investment purposes, and controlling shares of their own companies; (3) financial cliques, who have been "raiding" corporations, buying them out, selling them off, merging them, splitting them, and reconstituting them in a maze of conglomerate and oligopolistic identities; (4) giant institutional investors, such as mutual funds and insurance companies, who own fortunes of diversified stocks, but also own large blocks of certain corporate stocks; (5) speculators and arbitragers, who own stocks only transitionally and only for financial gain, rather than direct managerial control; and (6) the middle class—largely the upper middle class—acting as small investors who own dispersed shares of stocks and bonds with neither any controlling interest nor the financial impact to reap great windfalls, but with the ability to gain higher financial gains than through savings banks, and with a hedge against inflation.

What would an Aristotelian policy be concerning stock property?

First, property should remain private, for this ensures a high motivation level for its development. Second, the fortunes of the rich would be left intact, their ownership of stock property being determined by their own efforts (or efforts on their behalf) to develop their private property. Third, the managers, of course, are a new class unforeseen by Aristotle. Their ownership of their own company stock could increase their efficiency and emotional investment in the success of the company, but it would also increase their power. As an uppper class power group, they would have to be checked in their ambitions by the middle class, just as the commercial-rich or landed-rich had to be checked, or they might draw the constitution toward oligarchy—or worse, tyranny.

The middle class, in Aristotelian terms, should develop two strengths in regard to stock property: (1) they must gain a moderate share of stock property, so as to maintain their own economic prosperity, and (2) they must maintain the political ability to check the power excesses of the newly emergent managerial class.

First, general stock ownership of diverse investment stocks should be extended to a broader spectrum of the middle class. This latter is more like advanced banking, however, than "ownership" of property.[41] Second, ownership of company stock should be extended to the middle class employees. It may take white collar unions[42] to gain such stock ownership, or it may not, depending on the company in question.[43]

This second category of stock ownership does imply real property ownership. Employee stock ownership plans (ESOPs),[44] where they exist, grant large ownership shares to the employees below the elite managerial level, and in many cases gains the new middle class the right to elect representatives to the corporate boards, along with the managerial representatives and those of the wealthy families.[45]

The implications of the ESOPs are profound, because the greater economic share in the corporate stock ownership gives the middle class a greater political check on the managers and the capitalist rich.

The system of property remains private, and equality proportionate. However the prosperity and power of the middle class is actively maintained to ensure the continuation of the rule of law and to check the potential drift toward oligarchy or tyranny.

Private Property With Public Use

The whole question of stock ownership and managerial control of giant corporations brings us to Aristotle's idea of private property with public use.

The contemporary Communist experiment wherein property is held in common through government ownership has exhibited the flaws that Aristotle theorized such a system would, plus a greater flaw. Aristotle theorized that without private ownership there would be a loss in initiative; a loss in property development. This has occurred in the Soviet Union and in China. Government ownership, of course, added the element of despotic control, anathema in its totality to anything Aristotelian.

Having accepted private property as superior to communistically shared property, however, Aristotle had then to come to grips with the problem of selfishness. For if property is held privately, why should personally earned profits be shared? Aristotle, therefore, further theorized that a system of legislation and education encouraging the public use of private property should accompany its institutionalization.

The present system (of private property) would be far preferable, if it were adorned by customs (in the social sphere) and by enactments of proper laws (in the political). It would possess the advantages of both systems, and would combine the merits of a system of community of property with those of a system of private property. (It would be the ideal); for property ought to be generally and in the main private, but common in one respect (i.e., in use). . . . It is clear . . . that the better system is that under which property is privately owned but is put to common use; and the function proper to the legislator is to make men so disposed that they will treat property in this way. (A:49–50)

How would the principle of private property with public use be operationalized in the modern world?

First, of course, there is taxation. We have already described this in terms of taxation of the rich.

Second, through the legislature, public works programs should be undertaken for the benefit of all. The financing of such programs will be analyzed in the section on Keynes. However, the principle is Aristotelian. Property remains private, but the wealth derived therefrom is put to public use. More on this later.

Lastly, there is the question of the giant corporation. Corporations are private property in that they are not government-owned. However, since ownership is stock ownership, and this is usually separated from day-to-day managerial control, enactments should be undertaken by legislators to ensure a greater degree of public use of corporate property.

Berle and Means[46] wrote years ago of "quasi-public" corporations and suggested the "public utility" model of use. That is, private property with government regulation, or at least some government input to ensure that communities served by corporations were fairly served.

Others, like Ralph Nader[47] and Robert Dahl,[48] have suggested plans for middle class representation on corporate boards to ensure the public use of such property. Keynes[49] theorized on the necessity for a partially government-directed/partially corporate-directed investment program in order to achieve more public utilization of private wealth (and in order to avoid the business cycle and high unemployment).

This whole issue must be discussed in a more modern context of social structure, and this we will do later. However, we wished to establish the Aristotelian principle of private property with public use as the best practical solution to the problem.

Political Empowerment of the Middle Class and the Threat of the Mass Media

Within Aristotle's system, the rich, given their access to education and their economic contribution to the polity, should be rewarded with high offices. However, Aristotle makes it clear that the best legislators come from the middle class.

In the modern context, the rewarding of the rich with high appointive offices in the cabinet and foreign service occurs routinely. This would be consistent with Aristotelian theorizing. Most legislators, on the other hand, come from the middle class, and this too would be consistent with Aristotelian ideas.

However, since the introduction of the mass media, especially television, into political campaigns, a disturbing new factor has emerged. The cost of campaigning has risen so high that millionaires have been drawn more directly than ever into the electoral process, even at the congressional level. Either they have been running for office themselves, or become visibly involved as chief funder of a middle class candidate.

The Senate has already become a "millionaire's club," and the House has drawn more and more wealthy candidates to its midst.[50] Again, even when the candidates are middle class, they have become far more dependent on the rich for funding than they had been prior to the advent of television campaigning.

As Max Weber pointed out in *Politics as a Vocation*,[51] the rich are less likely to be corrupted by taking graft and make for good leaders in a democracy. Weber's point has some truth to it. However, if taken beyond the appointment to high offices and extended to congress or parliament, such a trend could be disastrous. If Aristotelian logic is correct, and the rich come to control the legislature, they draw the constitution toward oligarchy. This may be a subtle process in the modern context. But subtle as it may be, if it weakens middle class political power, it weakens the legal-democratic polity. The disempowering of the middle class not only affects the middle class themselves, who become withdrawn and alienated, but also the entire body politic. If the rich are over-represented they naturally tend to support policies that work to their advantage.

This is not to assert that many wealthy legislators are not good legislators or that many of them may not be liberal legislators—even champions of the cause of the poor and the middle class. But the quality of democracy is diminished if the middle class believes it cannot run for office on its own. It does not matter if the rich surrogates are the best representatives in the world, it only matters that they are surrogates. The situation would become more like the Rome of Caesar than the Athens of Pericles.

What should be done to ensure that the middle class remains empowered in the legislature?

Stringent new election laws are necessary, which either provide finances for those running for office, or ensure free media time.[52] Fairly determined free media time for rightfully endorsed candidates may be the best way to go.

The point to be emphasized here is that television campaigning should not be so institutionalized as to favor the rich (or their PAC surrogates). Let us repeat the Aristotelian dictum: the middle class must be empowered in order to ensure political stability. Therefore, the drift toward rule by the rich in the legislature should be stopped, and the mass media, after a good deal of trial and error, should be brought more thoughtfully into the electoral process. The French system (newly established) of free time should be carefully analyzed in this regard.

Lobbying and the Middle Class

To continue in the same vein, lobbying by the rich (and organizations representing the rich and the corporations) has also been having the effect of driving the legislature toward oligarchic tendencies. Lobbyists for the rich have always had great influence, but recently the situation has become skewed.[53] How can the lobbying process be modified so that the middle class can make their effect felt in the legislature?

First, new limits should be set on lobbying efforts. Perhaps an ombudsman system should be set up by the legislative branch itself to monitor and contain lobbying efforts, making public disclosures regular and routine. Second, middle class organizations, and those of the poor, should perhaps be modestly funded through a small tax credit, with a check-off list for those organizations favored and those not. Recently there has been an effort by middle class organizations to extend the lobbying efforts of the average citizen. Lobbying training classes and volunteer lobbyists have been giving their time to this effort. This is a good start; more is needed.

Whatever the program for mass media and lobbying modification, the principle of the strengthening of the middle class politically and economically must be kept paramount.

The Split Between the Upper Middle Class and the Lower Middle Class

There has been a growing and dangerous split in the middle class over the last fifteen years in the United States. The upper middle class has been able to float with the inflationary trend through its stock and housing investments. The lower middle class, lacking the funds for the stock or bond markets, has not been able to keep abreast of inflation. The housing owned by the lower middle class has not risen as fast as that of the upper middle class, whose luxury condominiums and houses have risen rapidly in value. Further, the salaries of the upper middle class have risen with the inflation, while those of the lower middle class have lagged slightly behind inflation.

Benefitting from the inflation through stocks, bonds, and real estate investments, the upper middle class has come to identify more closely with the rich, while the lower middle class, declining, struggling, and faced with blocked mobility for its children, has grown angry and frustrated. Unable to identify with the upper middle class, but desirous of its life style, the lower middle class could not turn its anger upward, and therefore has turned that anger outward and downward—downward toward the poor and outward at foreign "villains" such as the Soviets and Iranians.

The weakening of the lower middle class, and the growing attachment of the upper middle class to the rich, leaves the middle class in general greatly dissipated in political impact. In Aristotelian terms this is dangerous, for such a weakening reduces the balancing power of the middle class. The nation then drifts toward policies favoring the rich, while the lower middle class and the poor are increasingly left out.

We know that the poor have been left jobless and homeless, but now the lower middle class is going through a period of increasing unemployment, debt-foreclosures, and difficulty in financing college education for their children. The children of the lower middle class are finding it increasingly difficult to sustain college loans and almost impossible to find post-college housing. At the same time, the children of the upper middle class are going to expensive private high schools and colleges, and having condominiums bought for them—as good investments—upon graduation.

Increasing violence has emanated from the lower middle class: murder, rape, child abuse, spouse abuse, drug-use, drinking, and teen suicide. Economic decline and political disempowerment can be cited as partial causes of this increased violence.[54]

At the same time, the upper middle class has become more selfish, less humanistic, more acquisitive, and less charitable.[55] Such attitudes and actions by the upper middle class then push the rich toward the same uncharitable worldview (the effect being the opposite of the moderating and civic-oriented effect the middle class should assert over/against the rich). In order for the legal-democratic polity (with a capitalist economy) to work for the good of all, the rich must be pressured toward philanthropic activities and toward generosity for the poorer classes. Therefore, the split between the upper middle and lower middle classes is disastrous in its long-term social impact.

Policies must be formulated that will encourage the upper middle class to scale down its conspicuous consumption and upscale its humanistic concern for the society at large. Educational programs for the upper middle class, and humanistic career lines as well, will be discussed in the section on Rawls. Also in that section we will discuss fair taxation for the upper middle class—not over-taxation, but fair taxation, especially a tax on luxury items.

Programs for the economic security of the lower middle class and for the educational upward mobility of this class will be discussed in the sections on Rawls and Keynes.

The class balance of a polity is best when the middle class is unified and in a large majority. Any tilt in the balance disrupts the stability of the polity. The split-off of the upper middle class and the decline of the lower middle class represents just such a tilt.

If the "American Dream" is closed off from an increasing number of the lower middle class, while the "lifestyle of the rich and famous" is dangled in front of them and extended to an increasing few, instability and violence are even more likely to escalate.

Who can deny that a polity in which the numbers of the homeless poor accumulate on the streets while luxury apartments shoot up everywhere is out of balance? Who can be so foolish as to believe that trouble will not ensue from such policies?

Can the New Middle Class Function as an Aristotelian Middle Class?

C. Wright Mills in *White Collar*[56] and *The Power Elite*[57] has described the dramatic change in the structure of the middle class that has occurred since

WWII. The "old middle class" was an economically independent class engaged in small business, small farming, and shopkeeping. The old middle class lived modestly, but answered to no one directly. On the other hand, the "new middle class" is a dependent middle class, working as a salaried stratum employed by giant corporations, government bureaus, and service agencies.

The new middle class must answer to elite managers and top bureaucrats—they are entrapped within the authority structure of bureaucratic hierarchies. The new middle class may live more affluently than the old middle class, but the structural conditions in which they must function inhibit their independence.

Locked into such bureaucratic hierarchies, can the new middle class act as an Aristotelian middle class? I have written an entire volume on this problem, entitled *The New Middle Class and Democracy*.[58] In that volume, I present both a positive and a negative scenario, and then describe the conditions under which the new middle class could retain its empowerment.

Though the future may produce an "Iron Cage of Bureaucracy,"[59] as Max Weber worried, the world of democracy and law has not yet been overwhelmed by bureaucratic authoritarianism. We will have more to say about this in our section on "Objections to Equality."

At this juncture, in order to develop our theory of equality, let us assume that the new middle class can fulfill its Aristotelian functions, continuing to engender moderation, reason, and law to the polity. For, as long as electoral democracy and constitutional legal protections continue to exist, the new middle class can act independently of bureaucratic hierarchies within the political sphere. Voluntary associations such as Amnesty International and the American Civil Liberties Union, along with liberal and conservative organizations and political party clubs, continue to function in the private after-work world of the new middle class.

If these latter organizations and processes are retained and protected by law, and if they are combined with some new democratic institutions—such as the ombudsman[60] or the democratized corporate board,[61] created to limit the power of the new upper managerial class[62]—then the new middle class may continue to function in its Aristotelian role.

Proportionate Equality

Within the context of a politically empowered economically prosperous majority middle class, Aristotle encourages the reward of merit in the system. In fact, he emphasizes at the outset that the meritorious must be encouraged, not inhibited, both for the healthy stability of the polity and for its vibrancy.

Those who contribute most to an association . . . (i.e., who contribute most to good actions) have a greater share in the polis (and should therefore, in justice, receive a larger recognition from it). (A:120)

Both a greater share of property and civic offices should go to those of merit. If it did not, according to Aristotle, "there would be a general revolt against pure equality" (A:67).

Aristotle makes it clear that it is merit, rather than inherited wealth, that he would reward. However, he would reward the wealthy also, as I shall shortly explain. "Those who contribute most . . . should receive a larger recognition [than] those who surpass them in wealth but are surpassed by them in civic excellence" (A:120).

In Aristotle's day, the rich had access to the best education. Therefore, as "men of education," possessing cultural refinements, oratorical skills, and political connections beyond the mean, they would likely excel in merit. In this way, the ambitious among the rich would be rewarded with high offices and greater property.

On the other hand, as Aristotle also tells us, if the meritorious (*aristoi*) and wealthy are rewarded with property and offices, but conditions for the empowerment and prosperity of the middle and lower classes are not firmly established, then the people become jealous and rebellious, stirring up revolutionary and criminal violence.

A full discussion of the operationalizing of the system of proportionate equality follows in the chapter on Rawls. Since Rawls' system is consistent with Aristotle's on this issue, I will not repeat the discussion in both places.

2

Rawls: The State of Nature and Social Justice

Along with that of ancient Greece, the philosophical foundation of the Enlightenment forms the next great basis for democratic theory. One could stop along the historical way with Cicero and Titus Livius of Rome, and Polybius and Plutarch of Roman-dominated Greece, and, of course, at the Italian Renaissance with the insightful work of Machiavelli. However, in terms of the theory of democracy, the works of ancient Greece and the works of the British, French, and American Enlightenment represent the two watershed epochs.

The question, then, is, having selected Aristotle's work from the ancient Greeks, why not pick a representative theorist from the Enlightenment greats? The answer is that Enlightenment thought, although advancing the theory of political democracy beyond that of the Greeks and establishing new ground in the study of economics, is flawed when it comes to considerations of social justice.

Enlightenment political theory is monumental. The works of Hobbes, Locke, Montesquieu, Voltaire, Jefferson, Madison, Hamilton, Paine, and many others set the foundation upon which the structure of modern democracy is built. The Enlightenment theorists developed the system of government by law and constitutional constraints, the principles of the limitation of the power of the state and the protection of the citizen from the arbitrary might of government. They created the system of checks and balances and separations of power within the state. They established the structure of representative democracy and electoral procedures that allowed for the expansion of the democratic principles beyond the bounds of the tiny Greek city-states and to the vast nation-states of the modern world. Modern democracy could hardly exist on the basis established by the ancient Greeks alone.

Furthermore, economic theory likewise burgeoned out of the rational-mind-edness of the Scottish, English, French, Jewish, and American thinkers reacting to the tumultuous events of the just-erupting industrial transformation of national economies. The works of Smith, Ricardo, Malthus, Say, Mill, and others were seminal.

However, when we come to the problem of equality—a problem inevitably arising out of the framework of law and democracy itself, and engendered by the market-industrial economic system that has parallelled political democracy—we find an empty space, or worse, a justification for the denial of economic well-being and a retreat from democracy itself.

The work of Locke is illustrative of this latter problem. Locke worried so much about the power of the monarchical state and the inefficient utilization of property controlled by that state, that he devoted his entire theory to the explicit limitation of the power of the state and to the efficient use and development of property.[1] In Locke's system, those who developed their property to the utmost would gain not only wealth, but political position as well,[2] for a property qual-ification was allowable in Locke's otherwise democratic system. In fact, from Locke's treatise, legal-oligarchy, rather than legal-democracy, emerges.[3] The paradox arises in that, on the one hand, the citizen is provided with the most wonderful set of legal protections from the power of the state ever propounded,[4] while, on the other hand, the majority of such citizens, lacking property qual-ifications, could neither vote nor hold office via the legal-parliamentary structure.

Likewise Montesquieu's work, although establishing the primacy of the rule of law over the rule of men and providing the blueprint for the system of separations of power and checks and balances that later were enshrined in the American Constitution,[5] relates hardly at all to the wealth differentials that emerged with the burgeoning money economy and that would rip France to shreds as that nation attempted to establish his political principles.

This flaw in enlightenment political principles and the parallel defect in the enlightenment economic theories led to a justified socialist reaction to them. The socialist critique, asserting that market economics allowed for poverty and deg-radation and that Enlightenment political theory propounded oligarchy over de-mocracy, was not off the mark.[6]

However, the subsequent socialist rejection (and denigration) of the Enlight-enment political principles of *power limitation, primacy of constitutional law,* and *centrality of the electoral process,* led to a perversion of their very goals. For utopian dreams of classlessness brought about by a temporary dictatorship of the proletariat (guided by the communist party) during the period of transition, evaporated in the face of the reality of the rise of the unlimited, unlawful, all-powerful communist state.[7]

The socialists were obviously wrong in their abandonment of the principles of the Enlightenment, and, since they were wrong, we must go back to those principles and reaffirm them. At the same time, however, we must heed the warning of Aristotle (embodied in the socialist critique) that marked class inequality leads to instability in democracy.

Rawls goes back to the Enlightenment for precisely this reason. And, this is why we have chosen his work rather than that of, say Locke or Montesquieu, as representative of a balanced theory of democracy and equality.

Rawls takes us back to the Enlightenment—to the hypothetical "state of nature," to the "social contract" theory of human rights. He takes us back for two reasons. One, because he feels that it has become necessary to reground enlightenment political theory logically. And two, because he wishes to show that a theory of relative equality emerges from "state of nature" theory even if the conceptions of "private property" and "free market economic action" are accepted as axiomatic, and even if the Enlightenment conceptions of political freedom and democratic political action are held as first principles, uncompromisable.

Of course, we will focus on Rawls' theory of relative equality. However the question must first be answered, why did Rawls believe it necessary to reground Enlightenment political theory?

Rawls saw that the rational-minded citizens of modern society find it difficult to accept the assumptions of the Enlightenment, which undergird the theory of democracy and legal rights. That is, such basic notions as "natural law" and "inalienable rights," though they gain our instant emotional allegiance, demand a rational justification that is lacking in their 18th century formulation. To put it simply, the modern citizen does not believe that political rights are grounded in the "natural order of the universe," or that they are "god-given rights."

The world of nature, though scientifically comprehensible, is no longer seen as regular and lawful. The Newtonian view of the universe as analogous to a giant clock supported the natural-law theory of political rights (by being coextensive with it); it has been replaced by an equally rational, but more complex and chaotic, view of the universe that is totally divorced from any correlation with the political realm.

Furthermore political rights, although cherished in Western tradition, have lost their theistic halo. The Deism of the Enlightenment has become diffused into a vague mysticism, or replaced by a harsh existentialism. "God is dead," or at least so distantly and vaguely conceived that the modern God guarantees nothing, sanctifies nothing.

If, however, nature is not lawfully absolute and God is not immanent, then law is not natural and rights are not inalienable. The very foundation of legal-democracy disintegrates under the impact of modern rationality (ironically, since Enlightenment theory made reason and rationality central). Thus, if we do not want to give up the firm foundation for democracy established by the Enlightenment theorists, we must reground their logic on a contemporary rational base. This is precisely what Rawls has done.

Here is Rawls' presentation of his logical regrounding of the theory of law and rights. He calls it "justice as fairness," and he takes us back to the state of nature in order to begin the "social contract" over again.

In *justice as fairness* the original position of equality corresponds to the state of nature in the traditional theory of the social contract. This original position is not, of course, thought of as an actual historical state of affairs, much less as a primitive condition of culture. It is understood as a purely hypothetical situation characterized so as to lead to a certain conception of justice. Among the essential features of this situation is that *no one knows his place in society, his class position or social status*, nor does anyone know his fortune in the distribution of natural assets and abilities, his intelligence, strength and the like. I shall even assume that the parties do not know their conceptions of the good or their special psychological propensities. *The principles of justice are chosen behind a veil of ignorance.* . . . Since all are similarly situated and no one is able to design principles to favor his particular condition, the principles of justice are the result of a fair agreement or bargain. (Rawls, 1971: 12)

Rawls' logic reminds one of the logic in the folk tale in which two individuals must divide a pie. In order to ensure fairness in the result, they decide that one of them will divide it, but the other will choose which half to take.

In Rawls' scheme, since the participants would be acting behind a "veil of ignorance," not knowing their positions in the society that will emerge, they would have to set up a fair system both politically and economically to avoid the risk of disadvantaging themselves.

For example, if a man knew that he was wealthy, he might find it rational to advance the principle that various taxes for welfare measures be counted unjust; if he knew that he was poor, he would most likely propose the contrary principle. To represent the desired restrictions we imagine a situation in which everyone is deprived of this sort of information. One excludes the knowledge of those contingencies which set men at odds and allows them to be guided by their prejudices. In this manner the veil of ignorance is arrived at in a natural way . . . these conditions define the principles of justice as those which rational persons concerned to advance their interests would consent to as equals when none are known to be advantaged or disadvantaged by social and natural contingencies. (Rawls, 1971: 18–19)

The logic is straightforward and convincing. And as a logical basis for civil and political rights, it is impeccable. The assumption of human rationality (reason) is the only one retained by Rawls from his Enlightenment predecessors, while the notions of "natural rights" or "god-given rights" become unnecessary for sustaining the logic of lawful rights.

Rawls develops two basic principles of justice, which emerge from the social contract entered into behind the "veil of ignorance" in the hypothetical state of nature.

First: each person is to have an equal right to the most extensive basic liberty compatible with a similar liberty for others. Second: social and economic inequalities are to be arranged so that they are both (a) reasonably expected to be to everyone's advantage, and (b) attached to positions and offices open to all. (Rawls, 1971: 60)

The first principle, that of political freedom, is easy to establish through Rawls' logic, and it is consistent with the Enlightenment tradition (as that tradition came to its zenith with the contributions of the British Whigs and the American and French intellectuals).

The basic liberties of citizens are, roughly speaking, political liberty (the right to vote and to be eligible for public office) together with freedom of speech and assembly; liberty of conscience and freedom of thought; freedom of the person along with the right to hold (personal) property; and freedom from arbitrary arrest and seizure as defined by the concept of the law. These liberties are all required to be equal by the first principle, since citizens of a just society are to have the same basic rights. (Rawls, 1971: 61)

Rawls' first principle is consistent with 18th century theory. It logically regrounds that theory in a form acceptable to the 20th century secular-rationalist. However, notice that along with freedom of speech and thought, Rawls includes the right to hold *personal property*. Having established this right as part of his *first principle*, he is allowing for the free development of that property as well. And, as with Locke's original formulation,[8] the development of personal property necessarily leads to the emergence of inequality in economic wealth (and social status).

Locke was content to allow for this, but Rawls cannot be so content. For, behind the "veil of ignorance" in Rawls' state of nature, individuals would never agree to a social contract in which some could become economically disadvantaged in the society that would emerge.

Therefore Rawls, in order to keep his system logically consistent, had to establish his *second principle* of justice.

The second principle, however, is more difficult for Rawls to establish. For, once he accepts, in the first principle, the free utilization of personal property and the *differential abilities* of individuals in the development of that property, he is accepting, as inevitable, the emergence of *economic inequality* within a context of guaranteed *political freedom*.

Rawls fully realizes that behind the "veil of ignorance" a relatively egalitarian system of wealth and authority would be logically arrived at—a system as egalitarian as that arrived at for the establishment of political rights. By his own logic, the hoarding of property would be as unacceptable as the hoarding of power to those entering into the social contract not knowing where their place might be in the eventual scheme of things.

However, having established the first principle—the principle of political rights and freedom—as primary and uncompromisable, he must then establish the second principle—that concerned with economic justice—as limited by the conditions of the first principle. This is the way in which he handles this monumental problem:

The second principle applies, in the first approximation, to the distribution of income and wealth and to the design of organizations that make use of differences in authority and responsibility, or chains of command. While *the distribution of wealth and income need not be equal*, it must be *to everyone's advantage*, and at the same time, *positions* of authority and *offices* of command must be *accessible to all*. One applies the second principle by holding positions open, and then, subject to this constraint, *arranges social and economic inequalities so that everyone benefits*. (Rawls, 1971: 61)

Socialist theorists will be infuriated by Rawls' logic on this, as will liberal theorists (American conservatives and neoconservatives). The socialists will demand to know why it does not logically follow that in ''the initial situation'' the choice for complete equality is not arrived at—for no one knows their position, just as in the case of political rights, and therefore, no one would want to end up among the disadvantaged classes.

Liberals (American conservatives and neoconservatives), for their part, will wonder how equality of opportunity can be fully guaranteed, and how social and economic inequalities can be ''constrained'' so that they work to ''everyone's benefit,'' without massive intervention by the state.

Rawls answers both of these criticisms, and we will treat his answers shortly. For the moment, let us establish Rawls' position more completely.

THE PRIMACY OF DEMOCRACY OVER EQUALITY

One of the key principles of Rawls' system is that *political rights cannot be compromised*. Political liberty cannot be traded off in order to attain improved economic equality. This is the kinship that Rawls' theory shares with Enlightenment theories. Rawls states unequivocally that:

These principles are to be arranged in a serial order with *the first principle prior to the second. This ordering means that a departure from the institutions of equal liberty required by the first principle cannot be justified, or compensated for, by greater social and economic advantages*. The distribution of wealth and income, and the hierarchies of authority, must be consistent with both the liberties of equal citizenship and equality of opportunity. (Rawls, 1971: 61)

   . . . being arranged in serial order they do not permit exchanges between basic liberties and economic and social gains. (Rawls, 1971: 63)

The fact that Rawls makes the principle of civil and political rights primary is critical. The major critique of socialist theories of equality is that they compromise political liberty in order to attain economic equality. Rawls does not do that. Therefore his theory of equality will be fully consistent with—even subordinate to—the theory of legal democracy. In this sense, Rawls provides us with a solid logical grounding for a nonsocialist theory of equality.

Furthermore, the apparent weakness in his theory of equality—that it allows for inequalities in wealth and office if they benefit the good of all (and especially the least advantaged)—is also a strength. It is a strength because it places Rawls' theory in logical synchronicity with liberal political theory in the sense that: (1) no attempt at *coercive* levelling is demanded, and (2) a full recognition and utilization of individual differences in talent and motivation is accounted for.

Further, this acceptance of, and utilization of, highly skilled or motivated individuals is incorporated without the competitive, self-seeking, elitist ethic inherent in theories of "natural aristocracy" or "meritocracy," or the lack of humanitarian conscience inherent in rugged individualist and utilitarian theories.[9] We will discuss this directly under the heading of "meritocracy."

Finally, Rawls' theory, while eschewing the demand for perfect equality, incorporates democratic mechanisms for the facilitation of equality of opportunity, open and equal access to offices, transfers of wealth to those in dire need (and from those who are not), and the use of wealth and talent "for the good of all."

To sum up: (1) Although socialists will reject Rawls' theory as inadequate, we will accept it because of its consistency with the theory of legal democracy. (2) Although neoconservatives will reject Rawls' position as too egalitarian, we will accept it because the classical liberal position allows for too much economic and social misery. In terms of this second point, we will argue, following Aristotle[10] and Acton,[11] that the rich, as well as the poor, become corrupted by extreme differentials of wealth and power.

Thus, we seek a new position on the problem of socioeconomic equality, and Rawls provides us with a new rational grounding for such a position. Let us explicate his theory further.

RAWLS' THEORY OF DEMOCRATIC EQUALITY

At the heart of Rawls' theory of equality is his "difference principle":

Social and economic inequalities are to be arranged so that they are both: (a) to the greatest benefit of the least advantaged and (b) attached to offices and positions open to all under conditions of fair equality of opportunity. (Rawls, 1971: 83)

The principle holds that in order to treat all persons equally, to provide genuine equality of opportunity, society must give more attention to those with fewer native assets and to those born into the less favorable social positions. The idea is to redress the bias of contingencies in directions of equality. In pursuit of this principle, greater resources might be spent on the education of the less rather than the more intelligent, at least over a certain time of life, say the earlier years of school. . . . (Rawls, 1971: 100)

Now the difference principle is not of course the principle of redress. It does not require society to try to even out handicaps as if all were expected to compete on a fair basis in the same race. But the difference principle would allocate resources in education, say, so as to improve the long term expectation of the least favored. If this end is attained by giving more attention to the better endowed, it is permissible; otherwise not. (Rawls, 1971: 100)

Thus, although the difference principle is not the same as that of redress, it does achieve some of the intent of the latter principle . . . the difference principle represents, in effect, an agreement to regard the distribution of natural talents as a *common asset*, and to share in the benefits of this distribution, whatever it turns out to be. Those who have been favored by nature, whoever, they are may gain from their good fortune only on terms that improve the situation of those who have lost out. (Rawls, 1971: 101)

Notice that Rawls accepts the idea of natural differences between individuals. Some will be "better endowed" than others. Rather than attempting to level such differences in a schema that could anger the better endowed or fail to use their talents, Rawls creates a system in which the talents of the better endowed are recognized and rewarded, but only if their superior talents are put to the *use of all* and *to the benefit of the least advantaged*. Rawls states it this way:

The naturally advantaged are not to gain merely because they are more gifted, but only to cover the costs of training and education and for using their endowments in ways that help the less fortunate as well. No one deserves his greater natural capacity nor merits a more favorable starting place in society. *But it does not follow that one should eliminate these distinctions.* The basic structure can be arranged so that these contingencies work for the good of the least fortunate. Thus, we are led to the difference principle if we wish to set up the social system so that no one gains or loses from his arbitrary place in the distribution of natural assets or his initial position in society without giving or receiving compensating advantages in return. (Rawls, 1971: 101)

Rawls then addresses the problem of inherited wealth. In his system, inherited wealth is not "levelled"; however, *the use of inherited wealth for the common good* is all the more logically derivable, since the recipient of inherited wealth cannot claim it by virtue of superior merit. In this sense, it is not a "just dessert," but rather a piece of good fortune (which should not be kept for purely selfish ends). This is quite consistent with Aristotle's position.

The assertion that a man deserves the superior character that enables him to make the effort to cultivate his abilities is equally problematic; for his character depends in large part upon *fortunate family and social circumstances for which he can claim no credit.* The notion of dessert seems not to apply to these cases. Thus the more advantaged representative man cannot say that he deserves and therefore has a right to a scheme of cooperation in which he is permitted to acquire benefits in ways that do not contribute to the welfare of others. (Rawls, 1971: 104)

The Difference Principle Engenders an Ethic of Community Responsibility

Without demanding anything like coerced equalization, Rawls argues against a system of unbridled individual wealth accumulation and inheritance. Whether the accumulation is on the basis of merit or inheritance, Rawls insists that the only justification for such accumulation is that it benefit the good of all (and the least fortunate). For, if it did not, then it could not have been agreed upon behind the "veil of ignorance." In this he is logically correct. In the "initial situation" no rational human would agree to such differential accumulation unless it were to their own eventual benefit.

Thus, although allowing for differentials in wealth based on merit and inheritance (thus making his system consistent with liberalism), Rawls also includes a conception of reciprocity in wealth *use*—thus mitigating the worst excesses of liberalism (as such excesses emerged in actual historical circumstances).[12]

... the difference principle expresses a conception of *reciprocity*. It is a principle of mutual benefit ... the social order can be justified to everyone, and in particular to those who are least favored, and in this sense it is egalitarian. (Rawls, 1971: 102)

Rawls goes even further in this, for not only is his theory egalitarian, at least to some extent, but it encourages a sense of communal participation on a non-socialist basis. That is, no ideology of levelling is made central, and certainly no institutionalization of state ownership of the productive system or coerceive redistribution is demanded. However, within a system of individual assertion, self-actualization, and escalated rewards, the "difference principle" engenders a sense of "fraternity," because differentials of wealth and power can only be justified if they contribute to the good of all and the least advantaged.

A further merit of the difference principle is that it provides an interpretation of the principle of fraternity. . . . The difference principle . . . does seem to correspond to a natural meaning of fraternity: namely, to the idea of not wanting to have greater advantages unless this is to the benefit of others who are less well off. (Rawls, 1971: 105)

Once we accept [the principle of fraternity] we can associate the traditional ideas of liberty, equality and fraternity with the democratic interpretation of the two principles of justice as follows: liberty corresponds to the first principle, equality to the idea of equality in the first principle together with equality of fair opportunity and fraternity to the difference principle. In this way, *we have found a place for the conception of fraternity* in the democratic interpretation of the two principles, and we see that it *imposes a definite requirement on the basic structure of society* . . . (Rawls, 1971: 106)

We will analyze the "requirement" demanded by the difference principle on the structure of society, and the policies engendered by it, later. For now, let us go on with our exposition of Rawls' theory of democratic equality.

The Incorporation of Merit Without Pure Meritocracy

Rawls makes it clear that his system, although allowing for inequalities of wealth and authority emanating from natural talents, motivations, and family and class positions, is not synonymous with *meritocracy*. Pure meritocracy, for Rawls, would be too selfish and too competitive, and offer no mitigating principles for the host of differentiations of wealth and power that would result from it. Such a system could not be agreed upon as just in the "initial" social contract situation.

The democratic interpretation of the two principles will not lead to a meritocratic society. This form of social order follows the principle of careers open to talents and uses equality of opportunity as a way of releasing men's energies in the pursuit of economic prosperity and political dominion. Here exists a marked disparity between the upper and lower classes in both means of life and the rights and privileges of organizational authority. The culture of the poorer strata is impoverished while that of the governing and technocratic elite is securely based on the service of the rational ends of power and wealth. *Equality of opportunity means an equal chance to leave the less fortunate behind in the personal quest for influence and social position.* (Rawls, 1971: 106)

Having rejected unmodified meritocracy, Rawls goes on to insist on the incorporation of the best portion of meritocratic theory, the utilization of the talented for the good of the society, with just rewards for such individuals.

It does not follow that one should eliminate these distinctions (distinctions of talent, natural capacity, family and class advantage). There is another way to deal with them. The basic structure can be arranged so that these contingencies work for the good of the least fortunate. Thus we are led to the difference principle if we wish to set up the social system so that no one gains or loses from his arbitrary place in the distributions of natural assets or his initial position in society without giving or receiving compensating advantages in return . . .

The natural distribution is neither just nor unjust; nor is it unjust that persons are born into society at some particular position . . . what is unjust is the way the institutions deal with these facts . . . there is no necessity for men to resign themselves to these contingencies. In *justice as fairness* men agree to share one another's fate. In designing institutions they undertake to avail themselves of the accidents of nature and social circumstances only when to do so is for the common benefit. The two principles are a fair way of meeting arbitrariness of fortune; and while no doubt imperfect in other ways, the institutions which satisfy these principles are just. (Rawls, 1971: 102)

Rawls thus incorporates the best portion of the meritocracy ideal—that is, that those who succeed through their own efforts and talents (whether naturally or socially endowed) should indeed be rewarded with greater desserts. However, in Rawls' system, the enormous inequities and competitiveness that would result from pure meritocracy would be mitigated by the difference principle (or the institutions based on it). This again is consistent with Aristotle's formulation, which mitigates the inequalities through legislation and education designed to broaden the middle class.

Rawls' modification of the theory of meritocracy is central to a democratic theory of equality. Neoconservatives in America made meritocracy the cornerstone of their program, in contradistinction to 1960s activists, propounding *theories of redress* for the Blacks, the poor, and women.[13] American neoconservatives invoked the ideal of meritocracy against schemas of *mandatory*

compensatory quotas (favoring Blacks, Latins, and women in most cases). However, in reacting against the policies of compensatory quotas and coercive redress,
the neoconservatives demanded a system of meritocracy so unbridled as to result
in a social system that has taken on a "Dickensesque" disregard for the less
fortunate,[14] a narcissistic celebration of self,[15] and a jealous worship of lifestyles
of the rich and powerful[16] (with no demand that the latter contribute to the well-
being of the society at large or to the least fortunate members within it). Rawls'
theory of equality sets us on a logical course between the selfishness of unmodified meritocracy and the coerciveness of unmodified socialism.

Let us now present some further details of Rawls' theory of democratic equality.

The Market Economy and Its Modification

Rawls favors a market economy over a centrally planned economy, sharing
the neoconservative (and Weberian[17]) view that: "It seems improbable that the
control of economic activity by the bureaucracy that would be found to develop
in a socially regulated system would be more just on balance than control exercised by means of prices" (Rawls, 1971: 281). We will have more to say
about this when we present Keynes' views. Rawls does not take a naive attitude
toward the modern economy. He does not assume a Smithian market utopia. In
fact, he will include governmental mechanisms for the regulation of the market
economy in his schema. We wish to make clear, however, that Rawls' theory
of democratic equality is built on a base of corporate capitalism and assumes
some of the logic of market economics. Accepting the existence of the modern
corporate-capitalist economic system, he goes on to explicate his theory of
equality.

I assume also that there is fair (as opposed to formal) equality of opportunity. This means
that in addition to maintaining the usual kinds of overhead capital, *the government tries
to insure equal chances of education and culture for persons similarly endowed and
motivated either by subsidizing private schools or by establishing a public school system.*

It also enforces and underwrites *equality of opportunity in economic activities* and in
the free choice of occupation. This is achieved by policing the conduct of firms and
private associations and by preventing the establishment of monopolistic restrictions and
barriers to the more desirable positions. (Rawls, 1971: 275–6)

Further, Rawls would establish a new branch of government to help create
social equality.

The social minimum is the responsibility of the *transfer branch.* . . . A competitive price
system gives no consideration to needs, and therefore it cannot be the sole device of
distribution. . . . Competitive markets properly regulated secure free choice of occupations
and lead to an efficient use of resources and allocation of commodities to households . . .

whereas the *transfer branch* guarantees a certain level of well-being and *honors the claims of need* . . .

There is with reason strong objection to the competitive determination of total income, since this ignores the claims of need and an appropriate standard of life. . . . But once a suitable minimum is provided by transfers, it may be perfectly fair that the rest of total income be settled by the price system . . . whether the principles of justice are satisfied, then, turns on whether the total income of the least advantaged (wages plus transfers) is such as to maximize their long-run expectations (consistent with the constraints of equal liberty and fair equality of opportunity). (Rawls, 1971: 276–7)

Here again, Rawls is asserting the difference principle. The market economy is accepted, but "corrected" at the point wherein the disadvantaged are left out.

Finally, there is a distribution branch. Its task is to preserve an approximate justice in distributive shares by means of taxation and the necessary adjustments in the rights of property. Two aspects of this branch may be distinguished. First of all, it imposes a number of *inheritance* and *gift taxes*, and sets restrictions on the rights of bequest. *The purpose of these levies is not to raise revenue* (release resources to government) *but gradually and continually to correct the distribution of wealth and to prevent concentrations of power* detrimental to the fair value of political liberty and fair equality of opportunity.

The unequal inheritance of wealth is no more inherently unjust than the unequal inheritance of intelligence . . . the essential thing is that as far as possible inequalities founded on either should satisfy the difference principle.]That is] inheritance is permissible provided that the resulting inequalities are to the advantage of the least fortunate and compatible with liberty and fair equality of opportunity. As earlier defined, fair equality of opportunity means a certain set of institutions that assures similar chances of education and culture for persons similarly motivated and keeps positions and offices open to all on the basis of qualities and efforts reasonably related to the relevant duties and tasks. *It is these institutions that are put in jeopardy when inequalities of wealth reach a certain limit; and political liberty likewise tends to lose its value, and representative government to become such in appearance only.* The taxes and enactments of the distribution branch are to prevent this limit from being exceeded. Naturally, where this limit lies is a matter of political judgement guided by theory, good sense and plain hunch, at least within a wide range. On this sort of question the theory of justice has nothing specific to say. (Rawls, 1971: 277–8)

Rawls, in this statement on wealth inequalities, leads us toward a second level of theoretical grounding. He is suggesting that if wealth inequalities reach "a certain limit," liberty and democracy "lose their value" and "exist in appearances only." Rawls accepts, in principle, that extreme wealth inequalities will dissolve legal-democracy. In this he is absolutely consistent with Aristotle's theory on extremes of poverty and wealth being the "ruin of democracy."[18]

It was Marx, of course, in modern times, who warned that democracy with capitalist wealth inequalities becomes a sham—becomes oligarchy in disguise.[19] But the theory of wealth inequality and its destabilizing effect on democracy is drived originally from Aristotle. Although Rawls' theory of justice has "nothing specific to say" about the "limit" to such wealth inequalities, his theory incorporates Aristotle's warning into his logic in the sense that carefully delineated mechanisms of "taxation and enactments" are established in order "to prevent this limit from being reached."

We must begin again at the point at which Rawls ends. Rawls' theory presents us with a new logical grounding for a theory of democracy and equality replacing the Enlightenment theories—replacing them because "natural law philosophy" will no longer do as a rational justification for legal-democracy, and because the Enlightenment theories were weak on the problem of wealth inequalities and the class structure linked with them. This latter weakness in Enlightenment theory is derived from the immanent struggle with feudal and kingly power occurring at that time and the urgent need to establish private capitalistically exploited property as the base for the new economy and polity that was emerging.[20]

The flaw of Enlightenment theory on the issue of property, wealth, and class engendered the socialist reaction against "bourgeois democracy." The socialist solution, however—that of classlessness—is as much an illusion as the capitalist solution—that of the "invisible hand of the market" ensuring an equitable, if unequal, distribution of wealth.

We must replace both these utopian visions with the realistic possibility derived from theorists such as Aristotle and Rawls. Aristotle's theory of class balance and wealth distribution avoids the socialist demand for pure classlessness and complete levelling, while Rawls' theory allows for the establishment of the primacy of constitutional law, political freedom, and citizens' protection against the power of the state, without the abandonment of the ethic of social justice, economic equity, and personal caring, characteristic of Enlightenment theory.

OPERATIONALIZING RAWLS

The invisible hand of the market and competitive individualism allow, in reality, for disturbing wealth differentials. And Enlightenment political theory, especially that of Locke, legitimated such inequality,[21] offering no palliatives. Enlightenment theorists, though steeped in Aristotle, ignored his warnings about societies split between the rich and the poor and did not include in their theorizing his architectonic principle of the majority middle class.

Rawls, enthralled by Enlightenment principles of freedom, law, and market economics, offers us a system whose strengths remain uncompromised while its weaknesses are overcome. He presents us with a system of corrective processes designed to ensure a fair system of "equality of opportunity" and a just system of "end results." His theory of *education* is geared toward correcting the unfairness of opportunity that usually prevails in legal-democratic societies, while his theory of *transfers* is geared to correcting the extreme inequality of incomes that characterizes market-economy societies. The legal-democratic political system emergent from the works of Hobbes,[22] Locke, Montesquieu, the American intellectuals, and others is preserved at all costs by Rawls, while the market-economy system is taken as basic.

Education

Rawls's system of education is fair to both the advantaged and the disadvantaged. That is, for the disadvantaged, Rawls would have us provide a major effort to upgrade their life chances, while for the advantaged, the best educational programs would be made available, as long as they then used their talent for the benefit of all.

Both these sets of educational principles can be operationalized as follows:

Programs for the Disadvantaged

Before presenting Rawls' proposals, let me discuss the neoconservative objections. These will be discussed in detail in a following chapter, but a word here is necessary. I wish to establish that the neoconservatives' criticisms of the welfare system and of the negative income tax experiment are correct. The welfare system does produce generations of dependency, and the negative income tax can reduce the work incentive. The neoconservative attack on educational programs for the poor, however, has been shown to be wrong. Where such programs have been reduced or removed, school success among the poor has declined—declined in grade school, high school, and college.[23] Furthermore, the neoconservatives have supported "gifted" programs for the middle class and special education programs for the handicapped, while attacking educational programs for the poor. This is mean spirited and smacks of Puritan hostility to the poor—that is, labeling them as slothful and of the devil.[24]

Rawls' program is a balanced program in that it addresses the special necessities of all groups. First, Rawls addresses the very difficult problem of aiding the educationally disadvantaged.

The principle holds that in order to treat all persons equally, to provide genuine equality of opportunity, society must give more attention to those with fewer native assets and to those born into the less favorable social positions. (Rawls, 1971: 100)

If we take Rawls seriously, we have a background of knowledge to draw upon to help the educationally disadvantaged. First of all, we would be dealing with four different categories of disadvantaged individuals: Those disadvantaged because they are (1) poor, (2) working class, (3) learning disabled, and (4) those disadvantaged by their cultural background in an ethnically diverse society.

In terms of the poor, we know that cradle-to-college educational support programs may be necessary in order to ensure equal opportunity. For instance, through day-care centers and nursery schools, toddler and pre-school programs can be initiated. Many such programs have been successfully inaugurated: story-telling, free books, vocabulary-through-conversation, educational television programming, reading tutorials, math games, and so on. Through such programs, every effort can be made to bring poor children up to the level at which middle and upper class children begin school.

Head Start (a pre-school and tutorial program) and Higher Horizons (a cultural enrichment program) should be expanded. And we know now, since the 1960s, that these programs, in order to be effective, must be continued right through to the upper grades in order to maintain their effectiveness.

The Rawlsian program is not meant to be idealistic. The success of the disadvantaged may not be ensured through such programs. However, the effort must be made to give the educationally disadvantaged their best chance. Programs must be found that *do* help, if the present programs do not.

Working class students generally have enough educational background in terms of vocabulary and math skills to get by in school, but not enough to do well. For the working class, pre-school and school programs are important. Programs geared to the working class and their special needs also help alleviate the jealousy and anger they feel toward the poor when they—the working class—are excluded from such programs. The working class, whether they are Protestant, Catholic, or whatever, may say they do not want "help." However, when educational enrichment programs are provided for them, as general school programs, they appreciate them greatly. The working class accepts reading, writing, and arithmetic programs—especially when they are rigorous, "non-coddling" programs consistent with their ethical principles.

Though the working class, generally, may not be receptive to special art, music, and literature programs, these do benefit their children greatly—especially in terms of preparation for college. In most nations, the working class and the poor are not exposed to high culture of any kind. Therefore, cultural enrichment programs can be very beneficial for them in terms of success in higher education.

Again, if such programs are made part and parcel of the general school curriculum, the working class (and the poor) will accept them and benefit from them. If such programs are made available only to the educationally advantaged—or disadvantaged—hostility against the programs and the children who benefit from them will be increased. This atmosphere of jealousy and hostility can be avoided if such programs are made universal. The universality of such programs is important, too, in that the educationally gifted are not ignored in Rawls' scheme.

The Learning Disabled

Special education programs for the learning disabled already exist, and are being expanded. There is little resistance to such programs, because the learning disabled, being physically disabled, are not blamed for their problems, as are the poor.

The Educationally Advantaged

Rawls does not favor "levelling," but rather the utilization of the talents of the advantaged and gifted for the good of all. Rawls favors the development of the educationally advantaged as long as they give back to society what society has given them.

Those who have been favored by nature, whoever they are, may gain from their good fortune only in terms that improve the situation of those who have lost out . . . it does not follow that we should eliminate these distinctions. The basic structure can be arranged so that these contingencies work for the good of the least fortunate. Thus, we are lead to the difference principle if we wish to set up the social system so that no one gains or loses from his arbitrary place in the distribution of natural assets or his initial position in society without giving or receiving compensating advantages in return. (Rawls, 1971: 101)

Using the difference principle in terms of educational programs for the advantaged is really quite simple: (1) provide the best "gifted" programs you can for those with special educational talents and skills, and (2) ask the "gifted," in return, to do service in the tutorial, cultural, and other programs adapted to the disadvantaged. In this way, the meritocratic would receive the best education possible, but would be socialized toward a humanistic, rather than a narcissistic, morality. Such programs of service would not be coercive, but voluntary.

Programs for the educationally talented could include: junior great books, reading groups, mathematics games, logic and concepts, science programs (including theoretical and experimental learning), a variety of foreign language options begun at an early age when children can easily absorb them, music, dance, and art programs.

In return, the advantaged students, later in their development, should become reading tutors, homework helpers, cultural-trip escort helpers, math, science, and language tutors, and so on. These kinds of tutorial programs have been successful in the past. Upward Bound and Higher Horizons worked relatively well, for instance.

However, some warnings from the 1960s' programs should be carefully heeded. Involvement with the poor and working class students by upper middle class students sometimes led to empathy and over-involvement—sometimes led to disappointment by both groups with each other. Disenchantment, hatred, confusion, jealousy, love—all of these emotional involvements occurred.

Naiveté in Rawlsian transfer programs must be avoided. Naiveté can be avoided if: proper *social work supervision* is provided for the advantaged and the disadvantaged educational groups, and if the programs are structured within educational or cultural institutions with *careful administrative supervision*.

Programs such as Upward Bound (a college prep program), Higher Horizons, and Head Start can work wonders if properly structured and supervised. The warning is that we should not allow ourselves to suffer from "social amnesia." That is, we should remember two facts: one, some of the educational programs of the 1960s worked quite well, and two, there were terrible problems and confusions created through naive, romantic, political over-involvement with such programs.

The Rawlsian schema should act as a reminder to conservatives that educational programs for the advantaged and disadvantaged are needed and do work, and, as a reminder to the liberals that it was difficult to establish the programs for the disadvantaged and that they did sometimes engender jealousy, hatred, and over-involvement on both sides of the educational divide.

Having extended this warning against "social amnesia," let us not be afraid to actualize Rawls' ideas.

Higher Education

Rawls accepts the system of elite colleges and private schools. He accepts that individuals of merit and of wealth should get the best education possible, as long as they use this education for the good of all. However, Rawls' difference principle suggests that we do the most for the disadvantaged in order to create a situation of greater social fairness.

In terms of higher education, this means: first, a continuation of educational support and enrichment programs right through college, and second, a system of transfer payments for those qualified applicants from the socially disadvantaged who have shown academic excellence.

Most colleges do have tutoring and counseling services. Some have special support programs for the poor, the Black, and the Latin students. These programs are necessary no matter how good the grade school support programs are. Continuing support—especially in the first two years of college—is often still essential for educationally disadvantaged students. From the 1960s we learned not to isolate disadvantaged students or allow them to isolate themselves. It is better, where possible, to draw disadvantaged students into the academic and social life of the colleges. Black and Latin students are more open to this today than they were twenty years ago. Special support services—especially academic supports—are still very necessary, however, if disadvantaged students are to succeed at the colleges.

In terms of the elite colleges and private schools, the cost of tuition has risen beyond what the middle class can afford. If we are to avoid an elitist system (which Rawls abhors), transfer payments to the middle class and lower class students must occur. Thus a system of scholarships, assistantships, work study, and low-interest loans should be made available to the socially less advantaged. Two different programs should be initiated: first, for those students of merit, who pass examinations for college and high school with high scores, full scholarships and assistantships should be made available; and second, for those students who cannot afford college, but score moderately well, workstudies and assistantships should be made available so that they can attend the good, but less prestigious, universities.

Now comes the most critical point. The "quota" battle that caused so much pain and political reaction in the 1960s and early 1970s can and should be avoided. The way to avoid the quota problem—that of pushing out wealthy or meritorious students with less wealthy or less qualified students—is to institute a 5–10 percent expansion of the student body at the elite colleges, state universities, and private high schools. This expansion would be small, so that the character of any given school in question would not be altered. And this expansion would be subsidized by the transfer branch of government, which is described in the next section and which is central for Rawls' system. Funding for such an expansion would not be expensive. In most cases it would mean the hiring of a handful of professors and the construction or renovation of an additional classroom building.

More money is being spent today on the establishment of unnecessary Deanships and administrative positions. These administrative offices create greater despotic control over university faculties, but they do nothing at all in terms of improving the educational program. It is time to stop punishing the universities for the excesses of the 1960s, which were not of their making anyway! It is time to start directing funding where it belongs—with students and faculty in educational programs.

Let me explain the process again. Within the regular student recruitment progam, a system of "added-on" students would be created. Meritorious and needy students would be included in an expanded enrollment process, so that those with academic merit and those with financial need could still attend prestigious colleges, which would otherwise be beyond their economic means. The regular student body would be selected as usual such that no one could claim that they were displaced by a needy or meritorious student of lesser financial means. No student would be excluded in order to include a disadvantaged student. (This process would hold for medical and law schools as well, though the standards for needy students should be set higher, of course.) There would be no quota system pitting one group against another. Rather, the system would be left intact, but then, through transfer payments (scholarships and assistantships) meritorious and needy students from less advantaged social positions would be added in. This process would help to equalize opportunity, while broadening the talent pool of the nation, without seriously disturbing the equilibrium of the colleges and universities.

What about the high schools?

High Schools

Rawls does not wish to alter the elite private school system as it stands, but again, to create greater equity through ensuring equal opportunity for those in less advantageous positions in the social schema as it exists.

In order to make the situation *fair* in the Rawlsian schema, everyone should have a chance to make it, and the disadvantaged should have a greater share of funding spent on them in order to make up the difference in their chances.

Thus, for the middle class and the poor a system of scholarships to private schools—again on an "add-on" basis, that is through a modest expansion of enrollment—should be created. Scholarship money would be subsidized by government funding, which would be derived from various sources that will be described later on.

Further, the creation of many excellent public high schools should be undertaken. Recently in New York City, for instance, numerous junior high and high schools of high academic excellence were established. The results were heartening indeed, as not only have gifted students received a richer educational background, but many students from disadvantaged social positions have been able to succeed at these schools.

In the Rawlsian schema, one encourages the upper middle class and the rich to continue their educational mobility, then one provides for the mobility of the less advantaged.

The expansion of the program of academic high standards for the high schools and colleges could help take the pressure off the middle class students. It would ensure the moderate-to-excellent student a place in a valued high school and an easier chance to gain a place in an excellent college. As it now stands, the situation is too restrictive, too competitive. The social-psychological burden on our youngsters has become too great. Along with family breakups, divorce, and sexual pressure, school and career pressures have been cited as major causes of teen suicide. If we can do little about the family, let's at least do something to take the pressure off of the teen in terms of educational achievement. Let us expand the opportunities therein.

Taxation: Inheritance and Gift Taxes Levied on the Rich

Rawls is not at all against inherited wealth. However, within his system, the right to inherited wealth must be balanced by the difference principle, otherwise it could never have been agreed to in the initial social contract. Furthermore, since the recipient of inherited wealth cannot claim it by virtue of superior merit, it cannot be considered a "just dessert," but rather it must be considered as a piece of good fortune.

The natural distribution is neither just nor unjust; nor is it unjust that persons are born into society at some particular position . . . what is unjust is the way the institutions deal with these facts . . . there is no necessity for men to resign themselves to these contingencies. (Rawls, 1971: 102).

Rawls' difference principle, when operationalized in this case, calls for "a number of inheritance and gift taxes . . . the purpose of these levies is not to raise revenue . . . but gradually and continually to correct the distribution of wealth and to prevent concentrations of power detrimental to the fair value of political liberty and fair equality of opportunity" (Rawls, 1971: 277–8).

Inheritance taxes need not be detrimental to the ideal of personal property guaranteed in legal-democratic societies. Such taxes have existed in Britain and the United States for years. Nor should such taxes work against the middle class.

An attack on the mobility and prosperity of the middle class was never and should never be intended by a system of inheritance taxes.

The intent in the Rawlsian system is the public use of a percentage portion of the fortunes of the rich, such that such monies be allocated as transfer payments to programs for the less fortunate (and to programs that will benefit all).

The gift tax and taxes on luxury purchases represent another way of reallocating monies from the rich to the poor and middle class. For instance, while the tax on a moderately priced house or car could be kept reasonable, the tax on mansions and luxury cars could be substantially increased. The rich will continue to be able to buy luxury goods, but while doing so will contribute to a fund earmarked for the upgrading of the less advantaged.

One need not wait, in Rawls' system, for the rich to have a fit of good conscience, such as that which struck Andrew Carnegie in the United States or Carlsberg in Denmark.[25] The transfer of such monies would be automatic. Furthermore, as religious ethics have declined, such fits of conscience by the super-rich have also declined.[26] In a sense, contemporary humanism must be institutionalized in the socioeconomic sphere, because it may no longer remain institutionalized within the religious sphere.

Importantly, on the other hand, inheritance, gift, and sales taxes should not be structured so as to inhibit the rich from a high level of consumption. Precisely the opposite. Such luxury consumption should be encouraged, thus ensuring economic demand and motivational emulation for a rising lifestyle—these are both necessary and desirable within modern society. Within the Rawlsian system, these are accepted, but coupled with an automatic humanistic donation for the upgrading of the less advantaged and the improvement of the middle class and society at large.

According to Keynes, as we shall soon see, this can be done, and should be done, for the good of the modern economy, as well as for the moral fibre of society.[27]

That the rich will resist and avoid such taxation transfers is something that Rawls does not deal with. We will discuss this later on.

One other problem needs discussion. What of the effect of inheritance, gift, and luxury goods taxations on the upper middle class? Here a fine balance is necessary. The mobility of the upper middle class should not be closed off, nor should their "propensity to consume"[28] be inhibited. Yet a fair level of taxation to accomplish transfers and establish the difference principle is still necessary.

The kind of taxation suggested by Rawls could be set at a level that would not inhibit the upper middle class, while ensuring that they do pay their fair share. Taxation on housing and education could be reduced, while taxation on nonessential luxury goods, such as jewelry, fur coats, $10,000 watches, and so forth, could be increased.

As for inheritance taxation, it should be set at a high level for the rich and at a moderate level for the upper middle class. In this way great concentrations of wealth would be reduced, as Rawls believes they should be, while the ability of the upper middle class to leave the fruits of its financial success to its children would not be reduced.

The Negative Income Tax and Family Allowance Programs

Rawls does not speak specifically about unemployment. Keynes and Aristotle do, and in their respective chapters we discuss employment programs. However, Rawls is correctly concerned that even where individuals are employed, their incomes may not be high enough to satisfy their minimal needs: "A competitive price system gives no consideration to needs, and therefore it cannot be the sole device of distribution" (Rawls, 1971: 276–7).

As with Keynes, Rawls accepts the market economy as the basic economic institution of society, but wishes to supplement it at its outer fringes.

Competitive markets properly regulated secure free choices of occupation and lead to an efficient use of resources and allocation of commodities to households. . . . [However] a transfer branch [of government is necessary to] guarantee a certain level of well-being and honors the claims of need. (Rawls, 1971: 276–7)

Rawls suggests a *system of wages plus transfers*. Such systems already exist in two forms in modern society. They exist as family assistance programs and as negative income tax programs. Let us look at the family assistance programs first, because they are less controversial and have been generally more successful.

In Northern Europe and Canada, families receive cash payments from the government for each child in the household. They may also receive all sorts of childcare and medical benefits specifically aimed at the maintenance and nurturance of family life. Kammerman and Kahn have written extensively on the different family assistance programs in Denmark, Holland, Germany, and Canada.[29] These programs have been generally well received, and they are important as transfer payments to the middle and working classes in these nations. The middle and working classes have not used the family allowance programs to increase their fertility rate—in fact, there has been a decline in the fertility rate in these nations.

However, in nations with a large underclass of poor people and chronically unemployed individuals, and new immigrants from rural areas of the world, would such family assistance transfers work, or would they encourage the procreation of too many children?

Cash payments for children might be unwise in terms of the poor. If this proved to be the case, family assistance transfer payments to the poor could be made "in kind" instead of in cash. That is, such transfers could be linked specifically to medical, educational, housing, and career needs. Mobility in these areas tends to engender an inhibition of fertility rates. Once such a level of mobility and fertility is reached, then family allowance transfer payments seem to work very well.

Having suggested a modified program for the underclass, I wish to establish that family assistance programs are excellent Rawlsian schemas for the middle and working classes. They encourage family values and reduce the burdens of child rearing, thus providing a humanistic supplement to the income of such families.[30]

The negative income tax has been less successfully applied.[31] The problem with it is that it reduces the motivation to work harder and longer, and in so doing, lessens the chances of the disadvantaged for upward mobility.[32]

Tax cuts to the middle class have not, however, had this kind of effect. The middle classes generally use tax breaks for increased consumption and educational and cultural programs for their children. Why the problem with the poor?

The poor live on the margin, especially the working poor. They work hard, but live badly. They have little chance for rapid upward mobility, even for their children, if their children are and remain educationally disadvantaged. Therefore, if they are given transfer payments directly, as cash payments in the form of a negative income tax, they tend to work less and spend more.[33] They see no future mobility for themselves, so they seek immediate gratification. This is rational behavior on their part.

However, transfer payments could be linked to increased work hours, work performance, promotional possibilites, educational opportunities and job training for job promotions. If transfers are made to the working poor in this latter way, the negative effects of the negative income tax could be avoided. We certainly do not wish to create, through the extension of Rawlsian logic, what Aristotle warned against: a "leaky jar" situation for the poor.[34]

I have asserted, and will assert again, that we do not wish to make the same mistakes we made in the 1960s. Social learning should replace "social amnesia." We have, however, learned not only that the negative income tax reduces work motivation, but also that the working poor cannot make it on their own. Transfer payments, therefore, should be made to the working poor, but made in such a way as to increase their work motivation, while improving their income. Laissez-faire policies do not accomplish the latter, while the negative income tax does not encourage the former.

Nonmonetary Transfer Payments

The Rawlsian ideal of transfers, as supplementary to the wage system of distribution, and corrective of its inequities, can be operationalized beyond the idea of a negative income tax or family allowance program. Other programs could include indirect supplements to wages.

For instance: a mortgage assistance program for the middle class and the working poor could help ensure that members of these classes are able to obtain property. Property, in the form of home ownership in this case, helps ensure the stability and independence of the middle and working classes. Even modest property ownership, according to Aristotle (and Jefferson made this a central principle[35]), is an important element in the stability of democracy. Therefore, mortgage assistance, as a transfer payment to the middle and lower classes, is a wise form in which to supplement the inequitable wage system.

In the same vein, stock-property could be made more readily available to the middle class, through stock dispersion plans that corporations could make available to their employees. Employee stock ownership plans (ESOPs) exist in some corporations. This would be a very good transfer program as it would strengthen employee loyalty and work-motivation, while at the same time increasing the property and the income of the employee.[36]

Of course, with increasing stock market participation by individuals of middling income, a greater degree of government regulation of stock market activities would become necessitated. Market machinations, manipulations, and instability could not be allowed to wipe out the pensions or life savings of individuals, and would have to be insured and regulated as if part of the banking system—which, in point of fact, it would become.[37]

CONCLUSIONS

The Rawlsian program for increased equality helps stabilize democracy by reducing the oligarchic tendencies within the capitalist system.

Fair equality of opportunity means a certain set of institutions that assures similar chances of education and culture for persons similarly motivated and keeps positions and offices open to all on the basis of qualities and efforts reasonably related to the relevant duties and tasks. It is these institutions that are put in jeopardy when inequalities of wealth reach a certain limit; and political liberty likewise tends to lose its value, and representative government to become such only in appearance. (Rawls, 1971: 277–8)

The Rawlsian system also avoids elite-aristocratic-meritocratic domination, while still rewarding merit. The system avoids meritocratic elitism through the difference principle, which demands that the fortunate work for the good of the less fortunate, as well as for their own advancement. "The natural distribution is neither just nor unjust . . . what is unjust is the way the institutions deal with these facts. . . . In *justice as fairness* men agree to share one another's fate" (Rawls, 1971: 102).

Finally, Rawls' system helps create a spirit of "fraternity" in an otherwise individualistic society. Without a concerted attempt to create this spirit of fraternity and humanism, the tendency of the institutional arrangement within capitalist societies is to generate an ethic of selfish individualism and narcissistic nihilism.[38] Rawls would have us modify this.

Within a system of individual assertion, self-actualization and escalated rewards, the "difference principle" engenders a sense of "fraternity," because differentials of wealth and power can only be justified if they contribute to the good of all and the least advantaged. (Rawls, 1971: 105)

3

Keynes: Capitalism with Stability and Equality

Ancient Greek economic theory, unlike ancient Greek political theory, was weak and relatively undeveloped. Neither Plato nor Aristotle gave us much in the way of economic principles. Having raised political theorizing to godly heights, beyond which future generations of theorists could barely rise, they left economics in the murky depths. With slaves to do the dirty work, and military enterprises engaging the basic energies of Greek manhood, little attention was paid to productive forces or trade transactions.

Karl Polanyi has written a brilliant essay entitled, "Aristotle Discovers the Economy."[1] Yet, as wonderful as the essay is, it shows how little there is emanating from Aristotle in terms of economic instruction.[2]

It was not until the British Enlightenment that economic theory would emerge in "classic" form. Of course, this explosion of knowledge was linked to the emergence of the remarkable new mode of production: industrial capitalism. This new mode of production exhibited dynamic characteristics, unknown to the Greeks, which transformed both economic and social life. They include, machine-factory production, market competition, money as capital (beyond its exchange value), and more.

In another illuminating essay, *The Great Transformation*,[3] Polanyi describes the expansion of the market, paralleling the rise of factory-organized machine production. It is this dual institutional change[4] that stimulated the minds of the British economists and set them to building what we now call classical economic theory.

However, as great as classical economic theory is, as with Enlightenment political theory, it emerged with a critical flaw. For the classical economic systems of Smith, Ricardo, Malthus, Say, Bentham, and Mill[5] were supposed to: (1) insure a remarkable productive abundance for the society at large through innovative entrepreneurship; (2) maintain a dynamic use of machinery, labor, and trade; and (3) provide—through market competition—for a relatively equitable distribution of goods and wealth.

The first two factors were fulfilled with world-astounding success, encouraging the adoption of the new economic system by every nation witnessing its miraculous achievement. But market competition, of itself, led to an inequitable distribution of goods and wealth.

Adam Smith believed that through competition the "invisible hand of the market"[6] would ensure relative equity. "It is not from the benevolence of the butcher, the brewer, the baker that we expect our dinner, but from their regard to their own self-interest. . . . The individual is in this, as in many other cases, led by an invisible hand to promote an end which was no part of his intention."[7] Jeremy Bentham was convinced that competitive individualism would work out quite fairly if given full reign.[8] The relative equity, however, did not emerge. And, in fairness to Smith, he warned that *monopoly*-capitalism would prevent such equity.[9] J. S. Mill already saw, in his later years, that Bentham's scheme was not likely to eventuate in anything like an equitable distribution of wealth, and begin speculating about modification of the system.[10]

ENTER MARX

Karl Marx analyzed industrial capitalism as it was in his day, not as it was supposed to be.[11] With monopoly accepted as part of its dynamic, and not as an aberration, and with, therefore, concentrations of wealth in the hands of the few seen as typifying capitalism, rather than deviating from its norms, Marx's conclusions became inevitable. Industrial capitalism—though miraculously productive[12]—must be done away with because of its tendency to engender such disparities in wealth accumulation as to leave society in a violent state of antagonism between the ultra-rich and the wretchedly poor.[13]

In Marx's adult lifetime (approximately from the 1830s to the 1880s), this condition did not improve. His alternative scheme—embodying the abolition of private capitalist ownership of the productive forces, state ownership of these means of production, worker control of factories, and a relatively equal distribution of goods and money—has not, however produced an economic system or an economic theory superior in its productive or distributive capacity.

We must understand, however, that the failure of state-run socialist industrialism and the success of corporate-capitalism were not clearly apparent until well after WWII. Not until industrial capitalism was drastically modified after the Great Depression and during WWII, following the theories and programs of the Swedish economists[14] and Keynes, did it begin to fulfill its promise. And it was not clear until the 1960s that the Soviet and Chinese economies were not functioning up to expectations. Finally, in fairness to Marx, neither the Soviet nor the Chinese despotic-bureaucratic political economies represent anything like the romantic ideal of his worker owned-and-operated factory system. However,

Marx surely deserves blame for his conception of "the temporary dictatorship of the proletariat,"[15] through which the communist parties were able to rule dictatorially during the "transition to true socialism." This latter political phenomenon paved the way for the structuring of a system which, had he lived, Marx would have rejected.

In terms of classical economics and its Marxian critique, we have two social facts that we now cannot avoid dealing with. First, the socialist industrial model, as it has emerged in practice, and not necessarily from Marx's theory, has failed both economically and politically. It provides for no democracy in the here and now, and the equality it achieves is lost in the maze of bureaucratic hierarchies, despotic political accumulations, perennial shortages of goods, and black market machinations.

Second, the capitalist industrial economic model, while successfully undergirding a political system based on law and democracy, remains plagued with an unacceptably unequal distribution of wealth, a continuing high rate of unemployment, and instability in its "business cycle"[16] that continues to drive societies careening between booms and busts. In short, inequity and instability still plague a capitalist industrial system successful in its productive capacity, innovative in its technological development, and supportively enmeshed with a system of government based on law, individual freedom, and democracy.

All of this is written to establish that classical economic theory cannot be utilized in unmodified form to ground a theory of democratic stability and economic equity. Since socialist theory has eventuated in neither, a modified form of classical theory, which minimizes its tendencies toward instability and inequality while retaining its foundational support for legal-democracy, should be looked to.

With Keynes such a modification of classical economic theory was brought forth.

THE KEYNESIAN MODIFICATION OF CAPITALISM

Keynesian economics in the United States has come to mean "monetary fine-tuning" and "pump priming." It has become a mathematical formula through which the corporate capitalist economy is kept running more smoothly—that is, with slightly less violent roller coaster lurches up and down the business cycle.

What we have today is not at all what Keynes envisioned. Keynes was attempting to create a modern capitalist alternative to state-owned centralized socialism. And his program was a rather far-reaching one, embodying the principles of progressive taxation, full employment, low interest rates, and large scale public works projects.

Keynes saw the flaws in capitalist industrialism that had persisted into the modern era: "The outstanding faults of the economic society in which we live are its failures to provide for full employment and its arbitrary and inequitable distribution of wealth and incomes" (Keynes, 1965: 372).[17]

In terms of wealth disparities, Keynes was not a "Leveller"[18] or a socialist. He was not demanding complete equality, nor was he suggesting a radical reorganization of society to accomplish such a goal. Keynes accepted the basic distribution process of capitalism, but wished to modify it so that its results were less extreme: "For my own part, I believe that there is social and psychological justification for significant inequalities of income and wealth, but not for such large disparities as exist today" (Keynes, 1965: 374).

Aristotelian moderation was Keynes' goal, and as with Aristotle, not merely for the sake of a philosophical mean, but for the sake of social, economic, and political stability.

I see no reason to suppose that the existing system seriously misemploys the factors of production which are in use. There are, of course, errors of foresight; but these would not be avoided by centralizing decisions. When 9,000,000 men are employed out of 10,000,000 willing and able to work, there is no evidence that the labor of these 9,000,000 men is misdirected. The complaint against the present system is not that these 9,000,000 men ought to be employed on different tasks, but that tasks should be available for the remaining 1,000,000 men. (Keynes, 1965: 379)

Thus, Keynes would preserve the corporate capitalist economy but would add a government sector of the economy in order to provide employment for those left out of the capitalist economic system. Keynes was well ahead of his time when he observed that: "The authoritarian state systems of today seem to solve the problem of unemployment at the expense of efficiency and freedom" (Keynes, 1965: 381).

Keynes believed that it was possible to retain political freedom and economic individualism, while reducing the socially destructive problem of unemployment: "But it may be possible by a right analysis of the problem to cure the disease whilst preserving efficiency and freedom" (Keynes, 1965: 381).

Keynes was fully aware that laissez-faire theorists and American businessmen might object to his program for an enlarged governmental role in the essentially private capitalist economy, but warned that if the governmental sector of the economy were not established, capitalist economies would not survive. The reader should remember that Keynes was writing at a time when the entire capitalist system was collapsing, and that the incorporation of many of Keynes' proposals helped save the system. Therefore, we should take Keynes' more seriously than ever, when he says:

Whilst, therefore, the enlargement of the function of government . . . would seem to a 19th century publicist or to a contemporary American financier to be a terrific encroachment on individualism, I defend it, on the contrary, both as the only practical means for avoiding the disfunction of existing economic forms in their entirety and as the condition of the successful functioning of individual initiative. (Keynes, 1965: 380)

Furthermore, Keynes makes it clear that "Keynesian economics" does *not* mean a little monetary tinkering by the federal reserve board:

It seems unlikely that the influence of banking policy on the rate of interest will be sufficient by itself to determine an optimum rate of investment. I conceive, therefore, that a somewhat *comprehensive socialization of investment will prove the only means of securing an approximation to full employment*; though this need not exclude all manner of compromises and of devices by which public authority will cooperate with private initiative. (Keynes, 1965: 378)

It is absolutely critical to understand that governments in capitalist societies have been doing exactly what Keynes wanted them to do in terms of "guiding investment," but they have been doing it strictly in terms of military expenditure. The huge military investments of the capitalist governments produce some of the effects Keynes was propounding. However "military-Keynesianism," according to Keynes himself, is wasteful and produces less of a "multiplier effect" than nonmilitary public works. We will describe the multiplier shortly, but first let us look at Keynes' views on "military-Keynesianism."

Keynes was profoundly aware that democratic governments in capitalist societies have been reticent to direct investment into (and create full employment through) socially useful projects (on a large scale), but that such governments were willing indeed—in fact, over-zealous—in their attempts to create massive programs of a military nature. In fact, as long as such programs were military, they would be defended by those who reject the Keynesian schemes, though ironically, as Keynes himself observed, military programs serve the same economic function as the more socially useful projects would. Here are Keynes wry comments on the "military Keynesianism" that has emerged, but which he did not support:

Pyramid-building, earthquakes, even wars serve to increase wealth, if the education of our statesman on the principles of classical economics stands in the way of anything better. It is curious how common sense, wriggling for an escape from absurd conclusions, has been apt to reach a preference for wholly "wasteful" forms of loan expenditure rather than for partly wasteful forms which because they are not wholly wasteful tend to be judged on strict "business" principles. (Keynes, 1965: 128–29)

Continuing his witty, but biting critique, Keynes states:

[I]t would, indeed, be more sensible to build houses and the like; but if there are political and practical difficulties in the way of this, the above would be better than nothing. . . . Just as wars have been the only form of large scale loan expenditure which statesman have thought justifiable, so gold-mining is the only pretext for digging holes in the ground which has recommended itself to bankers as sound finance; and each of these activities has played its part in progress—failing something better. (Keynes, 1965: 129–30)

Obviously, Keynes had "something better" in mind, and we will discuss his program of useful public works. For now, however, let us analyze more closely his reasons for rejecting a centralized government-owned socialist economy, and his reason for rejecting complete wealth equality. There is a consistency in

Keynes position with Aristotle's and Rawl's, and therefore it is important to present Keynes' logic on these matters.

Why Not Full Equality and a Socialist Economy?

It is important to repeat Keynes' position on wealth disparities once again. He states: "For my own part, I believe that there is social and psychological justification for significant inequalities of incomes and wealth, but not for such large disparities as exist today" (Keynes, 1965: 374).

This position of Keynes is similar to that of the ancient Aristotle and the modern Rawls. In the case of all three of these theorists, the system of modified inequality is based on a theory of economic efficiency, political stability, and social fairness, rather than on pure logic or ethical judgments alone.

Keynes goes on to express his views on modified inequality and its advantages, as compared with full equality or laissez-faire inequality: "There are valuable human activities which require the motive of money-making and the environment of private wealth-ownership for their full fruition" (Keynes, 1965: 374).

Here Keynes reminds us of Aristotle's dictum that private property engenders the intensive development of property as if it were part of oneself. Keynes goes on to extoll one of the central virtues of an economy separated from government control. That is, that the separation of economic from political power helps preserve democracy, because so much of the Machiavellian power and domination activity of human leaders is acted out in the economic sphere, rather than in the political:

Dangerous human proclivities can be canalized into comparatively harmless channels by the existence of opportunities for money-making and private wealth, which if they cannot be satisfied in this way, may find their outlet in cruelty, the reckless pursuit of personal power and authority, and other forms of self aggrandizement. It is better that a man should tyrannize over his bank balance than over his fellow-citizens; and whilst the former is sometimes denounced as being but a means to the latter, sometimes at least it is an alternative. (Keynes, 1965: 374)

This is a brilliant statement by Keynes of the theory of the separation of powers. The theory does not imply, as Keynes reminds the reader, that the rich won't use their economic power to tyrannize over the less fortunate citizens; rather, that they will not use the power of "the state" to do so— a seemingly inconsequential differentiation that is actually quite crucial. For the difference between oligarchic over-influence of legal democracy and direct despotic dictatorial domination is all the difference in the world—unless the condition of the majority of the citizens is economically so disadvantageous that political rights and legal protections are irrelevant. This latter condition, of course, is precisely what Keynes' theory was constructed to prevent.

Keynes goes on to make a forceful argument—on both political and economic grounds—that the separation of economic from political power and its concomitant positive effect on the polity in terms of diverting the human "will to power" into financial and entrepreneurial activity, can be successfully maintained without such colossal differentials of wealth as emerge in unbridled capitalist-industrial societies. He states unequivocally that:

It is not necessary for the stimulation of these activities and the satisfaction of these proclivities that the game should be played for such high stakes as at present. Much lower stakes will serve the purpose equally well, as soon as the players are accustomed to them. The task of transmuting human nature must not be confused with the task of managing it. (Keynes, 1965: 374)

If we take Keynes seriously, what is his true program for modified wealth inequality, government-corporate investment, and full employment?

Keynes on Taxation of the Rich

The principle of progressive taxation was considered by Keynes central to a modern capitalist economic system that was to compete with socialist economies.[19] The great differentials of wealth were, for Keynes, a major cause of social unrest and potential political instability. Furthermore, he believed that government investment of the received taxation was central for the maintenance of a more stable economy.

It is worth repeating Keynes' strong feelings on the faults of the economic system under which we live:

The outstanding faults of the economic society in which we live are its failure to provide for full employment and its arbitrary and inequitable distribution of wealth and incomes. (Keynes, 1965: 373)

Keynes embraced a progressive taxation system for the establishment of a more equitable distribution of wealth. What is signficant for us, however, is that he embraced progressive taxation as an economic benefit for capitalism, rather than an impediment to its functioning. Here is his argument:

Since the end of the 19th century significant progress towards the removal of very great disparities of wealth and income has been achieved through the instrument of direct taxation—income tax and surtax and death duties—especially in Great Britain. Many people would wish to see this process carried much further, but they are deterred by two considerations; partly by the fear of skillful evasions too much worthwhile, and also of diminishing unduly the motive towards risk taking, but mainly, I think by the belief that the growth of capital, depends upon the strength of the motive towards individual saving and that for a large proportion of this growth we are dependent on the savings of the rich out of their superfluity. Our argument does not affect the first of these considerations. But it may considerably modify our attitude towards the second. (Keynes, 1965: 372)

We will discuss the first problem mentioned by Keynes, that of "skillful evasions," shortly, for it has become the basic impediment to progressive taxation in the United States. For now, however, let us focus on Keynes' central theory and its support for progressive taxation as a spur to economic development, rather than an impediment to it.

For we may have seen that up to the point where full employment prevails, the growth of capital depends not at all on a low propensity to consume but is, on the contrary, held back by it; . . . experience suggests that in existing conditions saving by institutions and through sinking funds is more than adequate, and that measures for the redistribution of incomes in a way likely to raise the propensity to consume may prove positively favorable to the growth of capital. (Keynes, 1965: 372–73)

Keynes goes on to state his position even more forcefully:

Thus our argument leads towards the conclusion that in contemporary conditions the growth of wealth, so far from being dependent on the abstinence of the rich, as is commonly supposed, is more likely to be impeded by it. One of the chief social justifications of great inequality of wealth is, therefore, removed. (Keynes; 1965: 373)

Keynes' point, that the taxation of the rich is good for capitalism, is an important one indeed. For it means that capitalism functions better when the rich are taxed and the government invests the money into economic growth areas or socially useful public projects. A minimum tax on the rich, in order to avoid their "skillful evasions," becomes sound economic policy within the Keynesian system. Further, none of the incentives for the rich are removed by such taxation, because they retain enough of a fortune to continue with the excitement of the economic "game," yet they contribute enough in taxation to allow goverment investors to pursue economic programs for the betterment of the middle classes and the poor. Keynes' taxation program is Aristotelian indeed.

Keynes' Theory of Low Interest Rates

Keynes not only believed that taxation of the rich was important for the proper functioning of capitalism, but also that low interest rates were critical for the growth of the economy as well.

There is . . . a second, much more fundamental influence from our argument which has a bearing on the future of inequalities of wealth; namely, our theory of the rate of interest. The justification for a moderately high rate of interest has been found hitherto in the necessity of providing a sufficient inducement to save. But we have shown that the extent of effective savings is necessarily determined by the scale of investment and that the scale of investment is promoted by a *low* rate of interest. (Keynes, 1965: 373–74)

Keynes, of course, was not suggesting an indiscriminate lowering of the interest rates, but rather a carefully calculated lowering. In a given economic situation, Keynes would recommend the lowest possible interest rate. Throughout his general theory he chastises the "classically" oriented economists for keeping the interest rate too high and therefore slowing investment, holding back the economy, and hurting the middle and working classes by thereby reducing employment and income for them.

We will discuss the effects of Milton Friedman's "monetarist" policy, which includes a raising of the interest rates, later on. As we will see, monetarism benefitted the rich at the expense of the middle class and the poor.[20] We will also discuss inflation and Keynes' policies in the modern economic context in the same section.

Keynes on Full Employment

Keynes' program for taxation and interest rates, as far reaching as it is, is hardly radical. However, his program for full employment is more radical, and as such has been more difficult for democratic-capitalist societies to institutionalize.

Remember, however, that Keynes did not want to alter the capitalist economy as it stood, but rather sought to add it to a government sector that would provide the employment that the private sector could not.

We cannot delve deeply into Keynes' regrounding of capitalist economic theory, but it is worth presenting at least some of Keynes' theorizing as it relates to full employment. Keynes explains why he rejects classical capitalist economics in this regard, and why he suggests an expanded government role for the reduction of unemployment.

The classical theorists resemble Euclidean geometers in a non-Euclidean world who, discovering that in experience straight lines apparently parallel often meet, rebuke the lines for not keeping straight—as the only remedy for the unfortunate collisions which are occurring. Yet, in truth, there is no remedy except to throw over the axioms of parallels and to work out a non-Euclidean geometry. . . . Obviously . . . if the classical theory is only applicable to the case of full employment, it is fallacious to apply it to the problems of involuntary unemployment. . . . (Keynes, 1965: 16)

Keynes first tackles the old fashioned unemployment problem that has bedeviled capitalism throughout its pre-technocratic phase, and which is still a problem today. (From his system, a remedy can also be found for today's "structural unemployment" created by automation. We will discuss this later.)

Keynes begins with a rejection of "Says Law"[21] and the basic assumption of Ricardian[22] economics:

Says Law, that the aggregate demand price of output as a whole is equal to its aggregate supply price for all volumes of output, is equivalent to the proposition that there is no obstacle to full employment. If, however, this is not the true law relating the aggregate demand and supply functions, there is a vitally important chapter of economic theory which remains to be written. (Keynes; 1965: 26)

Keynes goes on to write this monumental "chapter" of economic theory:

In a given situation of technique, resources and factor-cost per unit of employment, the amount of employment, both in each individual firm and industry and in the aggregate, depends on the amount of the proceeds which the entrepreneurs expect to receive from corresponding output. . . . Enterpreneurs will endeavor to fix the amount of employment at the level which they expect to maximize the excess of the proceeds over the factor cost. (Keynes, 1965: 24–25)

Keynes' formula (pp. 24–25) shows that since *the employers will reach maximum profit at a point less than full employment, the employers will not attempt to achieve full employment*, unless they are induced to do so through increased investment and increased consumption. The inducement to invest and consume will be brought about through a carefully regulated government program calculated to increase the propensity to consume and to expand investment.

Therefore, while retaining the capitalist economy as the basic system, Keynes added an enlarged governmental sector. This governmental sector, however, was to function according to carefully laid out capitalist principles—even in its public works programs. These principles are new, and different from Ricardian economics, but different in the way quantum physics is different from Newtonian physics—that is, with "revisions" and "special cases" of a basically accepted system.

Finally, in terms of Keynes' theory of full employment, it is important to note that his program of expanded public works is adaptable as a solution to "structural unemployment," or the unemployment created by automation and robotization. Since the new generation is rapidly training for technical, managerial, and white collar occupations (and going to college in ever-larger numbers as part of the preparation for such careers), the newly unemployed—pushed out by automation—could be absorbed through government-directed public works programs (especially in under-serviced areas of our economic system). We will discuss this situation later on; I mention it here to establish that Keynes' system is by no means dated. The vast military sector of the U.S. economy functions precisely along the lines Keynes hypothesized, whereas in Japan, Germany, Holland, and the Scandinavian countries (where the military sector is small), government-directed investment policy (made in partnership with the indigenous giant corporations of these nations) functions precisely in the manner Keynes theorized it would.

Lastly, the expansion of useful, nonmilitary public works programs could absorb a good deal of the unemployed created by the new technocratic economy we are moving toward.

It is worth repeating Keynes biting comments on the proclivity for creating military, but not civic, public works:

Pyramid-building, earthquakes, even wars serve to increase wealth, if the education of our statesmen in the principles of classical economics stands in the way of anything better. It is curious how common sense, wriggling for an escape from absurd conclusions, has been apt to reach a preference for wholly "wasteful" forms of loan expenditure rather than for partly useful forms . . . it would indeed be more sensible to build houses and the like; but if there are political and practical difficulties in the way of this, the above would be better than nothing. (Keynes, 1965: 129–30)

From Keynes' formula, one can see that if military spending is to be cut, there must be a corresponding increase in government-directed spending in other productive areas in order to avoid an economic downturn. This is why the U.S. Congress is talking of military conversion, rather than military reductions alone.

CONCLUSIONS

Keynes' system, though technical and complex in terms of economic theory, is consistent with the principles of equality and democracy enunciated by Rawls and Aristotle. The condition of the middle classes is enhanced, while the rich are induced to contribute of their wealth to the civic good through taxation and government-directed investment in general economic expansion and civic projects. The poor are absorbed into the expanded labor force of both private and public sectors. And all of this, in the Keynesian system, is carefully calculated so as to produce a more efficient, more expansive capitalist sector of the economy.

For Keynes, the reduction of wealth inequalities and unemployment, and the increase in the government role in the economy, would preserve freedom and democracy and individual initiative, promote economic efficiency, and reduce the tragedies engendered by unemployment and poverty.

In my view, a new look at Keynes' total system is critical for any modern program of equality with democracy. Although the technocratic economy of the near future will be quite different than the economy Keynes viewed, nevertheless enough of the capitalist principles of economics will be retained so that both the classic theories and the Keynesian revisions will still be cornerstones of its functioning. In fact, given the "mixed" nature (corporate plus government) of the emergent economies (such as the Japanese and German, and the American as well, if the military sector is included), the Keynesian formulas may become ever more cogent—though, of course, new revisions and additions will continue to modify those formulas.

The Problem of Inflation

Keynes did not address the problem of inflation. He wrote his treatise during the Great Depression when inflation was not a key factor in the British and U.S. economies. Inflation, however, has become a serious issue in contemporary American and European economies.

It should be remembered that inflation was not a serious problem up until the mid–1960s. The rate of inflation did not begin to "accelerate until after 1966; it went up more than 6 percentage points between 1969 and 1973 and nearly 14 percentage points from 1974 to 1975, the final increase lodging the phrase 'double digit inflation' disastrously in American economic terminology."[23]

It must be pointed out that a large portion of the inflation came from the OPEC oil price increase, a factor that has nothing to do with Keynesian economics.

The role of the oil price increase as an inflationary force was recognized [by 1973]. Their exceptional character was made evident in the terminology of the time: the oil shocks, they were called. The increase in the price of oil accounted for perhaps 10 percent of the inflationary effect in these years, but its proclaimed effect was much greater.[24]

The solution to the inflationary spiral engendered by the oil price increases is economically simple, although politically complex: roll back the oil prices to a fair level, somewhere between the cheap oil prices of the 1950s and the high prices of the 1970s. Oil is plentiful. The market price should be lower than it is. Mexican oil has barely even been tapped. Since oil is the base chemical from which so many product lines are developed, this one adjustment would have a profound effect on the inflationary tendencies of the economy.

Turning to another process influencing inflation, we come to the "wage-price spiral." As Galbraith states it:

With industrial concentration, corporations had achieved a very substantial measure of control over their prices . . . and trade unions had achieved substantial authority over wages and associated benefits accorded their members. From the interaction of these entities had come a new and powerful inflationary force: the upward pressure of wage settlements on prices, the upward pull of prices and living costs on wages. This was the interacting dynamic that came to be called the wage-price spiral.[25]

In response to the wage-price spiral, the Kennedy administration (in 1962) and the Common Market nations instituted an informal system of wage–price "guidelines and controls." The wage–price guidelines program—although disliked by the corporations and the unions—worked relatively well during the Kennedy years. The Common Market countries, with more foresight than the United States, institutionalized a wage–price guidelines program that remains effective. However, the OPEC oil price rise hit Europe even harder than it hit the United States, and therefore the inflationary spiral is still quite problematic there. Still, their program is one we should emulate.

In . . . Germany, Austria, Switzerland, Holland, Scandinavia, and Japan . . . steps to limit wage increases to what could be afforded from the existing price structure became normal, accepted policy. In Austria . . . controls on wages and a counterpart system of restraint on corporate prices were put into effect with considerable formality through what was called the Social Market Policy.[26]

The point is that Keynesian policies were not responsible for the inflation that hit the industrial world in the 1970s. The Keynesian program for economic stability and growth with greater equality can and should be pursued, along with the new policies of wage–price controls and lowered oil prices to put the lid back on inflation.

A Note on Milton Friedman's "Monetarism"

We must mention "monetarism" before going on to operationalize the Keynesian theoretical program. The reason for this is that Friedman's monetarist policy advocates the *raising* of interest rates, producing a restriction of loans. High unemployment and economic recession result from it. It is a method for slowing inflation, but its side effects are so dire in terms of economic stagnation and unemployment that the cure may be worse than the disease.

Furthermore, monetarism favors the rich at the expense of the middle class over the poor. Friedman realized this and suggested a negative income tax for the poor. However, the negative income tax, like the whole monetarist scheme, has side effects worse than the cure. The reduction of work motivation it engenders is more problematic than the funds it supplies to the poor.

Let us look more closely at Milton Friedman's monetarist policy, why it was adopted, and why we object to it.

Monetarist policy could be accomplished by the central bank, in the United States the Federal Reserve System, with only negligible staff. No tax increases would be necessary nor any curtailment of public expenditure. . . . It operates against inflation by raising interest rates, which, in turn, inhibit bank lending and resulting deposits—that is, money—creation.[27]

The high interest rates restrict the money supply. Notice: the money supply is not restricted through high taxes, but rather through high interest rates.

High interest rates are wholly agreeable to people and institutions that have money to lend. . . . In so favoring the individually and institutionally affluent, a restrictive monetary policy is in sharp contrast with a restrictive fiscal policy, which, relying as it does on increased personal and corporate income taxes, adversely affects the rich. . . . The applause for professor Friedman from the conservative affluent, which has been great, has been far from unearned.[28]

The blatant favoring of the rich in Friedman's policies is still evident in American income statistics. The number of rich has increased, and their affluence as well, while the poor have fared badly and the middle class finds itself in a state of precipitous decline.[29] Yet the reality of inflation—and the negative attitudes toward wage–price controls—led American and British political leaders to attempt to use monetarist policy to reduce inflationary pressures. As Galbraith puts it:

[I]n the latter part of the decade, by the ostensibly liberal administration of President Jimmy Carter in the United States and the avowedly conservative government of Prime Minister Margaret Thatcher in Britain, strong monetarist action was initiated. The Keynesian Revolution was folded in. In the history of economics the age of John Maynard Keynes gave way to the age of Milton Friedman. . . . Economic expansion was arrested, but the wage–price interaction [spiral] continued. So did the effects of the OPEC cartel. And so did inflation. Another singularly offensive word was added to the economists' lexicon, *stagflation*, which describes a stagnant economy in association with continuing inflation.[30]

The negative effects of "double-digit interest rates" on the economy of the United States were monumental.

The latter curtailed demand for new housing construction and for automobiles and other credit supported purchases. And in 1982 and 1983, they brought a sharp restriction in business investment. With this came a large increase in unemployment—to 10.7 percent . . . also the highest rate of small business failures since the 1930s and severe pressure on farm prices.[31]

If these disastrous economic events were not bad, enough, monetarism hastened a trend that has nearly undermined the American economy entirely, in relation to foreign competition:

[T]he high interest rates brought in a strong flow of foreign funds, which bid up the value of the dollar, curtailed American exports and strongly encouraged imports, especially from Japan. The overall result was the deepest economic depression since the Great Depression.[32]

Thus, monetarism, while it does lower the inflation rate, produces such terrible economic side effects as to make it unacceptable as an inflation cure.

In the present thesis, therefore, monetarism is rejected for both its negative effect on the economy and unemployment, and for its blatant production of inequality. A program of wage–price guidelines and controls, along with oil price reductions, is suggested instead, along with the reinstatement of Keynes' complete program of public works, government investment, full employment, progressive taxation, and low interest rates.

Inflation is a real and pressing issue that must be contained. But the economy must be put on a sound footing through re-investment and industrial development, while at the same time a fair modicum of social justice must be added to our otherwise individualist system.

KEYNES AND THE BUDGET DEFICIT

The question of the budget deficit has always been at the heart of the neo-classical critique of Keynesianism. However, Robert Eisner has recently written in defense of deficits. In his book, *How Real Is the Deficit?*[33] Eisner argues that the deficit can have *positive* effects on the economy, and that current deficits have not been measured correctly because inflation has not been added into the calculation.

Eisner states unequivocally that " . . . federal budget deficits can have great consequences for the economy. Startling as this may seem, these may be good as well as bad. And deficits can be too small as well as too large."[34]

Inflation and the Deficit

One of Eisner's main points is that the federal deficit has been calculated incorrectly since the Nixon years, because inflation has distorted the calculations:

[A]s inflation wipes out the value of money, it also wipes out the value of debt. As it does that, it profoundly alters the significance of conventional ways of measuring the deficit. Accordingly, meaningful correction for inflation can cause a dramatic shift in understanding. Deficits which have appeared to be enormous can turn out to be moderate. Moderate deficits may even be converted into surpluses.[35]

For instance, "in 1973 . . . with inflation accelerated in response to oil price shocks, our adjusted budget was in substantial surplus. . . . But everyone looked at the official deficit. The tricks played by inflation were ignored or never seen."[36] Eisner insists that real budget deficits are beneficial to the economy:

Over the last thirty years . . . we find that the *stimulus effect* of *real* federal deficits are dominant.[37]

. . . deficits in other countries turn out to matter as well. . . . The United Kingdom, with inflation adjusted budget *surpluses*, has had the slowest economic growth. High growth Japan, on the other hand, had had the *largest real deficits*.[38]

Government Spending and Capital Expenditures

Eisner makes a telling point about the nature of "capital expenditures" and their relation to future development. One of the confusions about the deficit had occurred because

[T]he federal government has a strange accounting system . . . every large corporation . . . distinguished between current and capital expenditures. Every individual sensibly managing his own finances must so distinguish. Our official measures of the federal deficit do not.

Why make the distinction? Because it makes a difference whether a family's outgo exceeds its income—a deficit—because of gambling losses in Las Vegas or the purchase of a new home. Business investment in excess of retained earnings is applauded as contributing to economic growth. But by federal government accounting practice, AT&T, General Motors, IBM, and many other companies would be guilty of "deficit managing."[39]

The federal government, alone, does not differentiate between capital and current expenditures.[40]

Eisner insists that the investment in capital expenditures builds our nation's strength, rather than sapping it, as critics of Keynesianism have suggested. There had long been concern that federal deficits pass on our burden to future generations. What we really bequeath the future, however, is our physical and human capital. A "deficit" that finances construction of our roads, bridges, harbors, and airports is an investment in the future. So are expenditures to preserve and enhance our natural resources or to educate our people and keep them healthy. Federal budgets that are balanced by running down our country's capital are *real* national deficits.[41]

Eisner then states unequivocally that capital investment should be directed toward the rebuilding of our economic and social infrastructure.

We may well wish to spend more on investment in our public infrastructure and human capital and less on subsidies and support to those with the most political clout. . . . We may also wish to devote more to our nation's welfare and less to warfare. . . . And we may wish to finance our expenditures with a more equitable tax system.[42]

The Deficit and Economic Theory

The attack on Keynesian theory emanating from the monetarists, the neoclassicalists, and the rational-expectationalists is beginning to subside. It is subsiding because the economic results of these theories have been disastrous. As Eisner puts it:

After reviewing the state of economic thinking on the effects of debt and deficits upon the economy, we can look at the facts. A statistical study confirms that deficits are very important, more important than our old faulty measures indicated. And as a consequence of all this, our analysis has import for much of the disarray in modern macroeconomics theory. Current measures of debt and deficits clear a path through the thickets of confusion shaped by the varying claims of monetarists, supply-siders and the apostles of market-clearing rational expectations. In so doing, they open the way to a new "keynesian-neoclassical synthesis."[43]

We have listened to new monetarists, supply-siders, and the market-clearing apostles of rational expectations. We have been challenged and learned in the process. We can now return confidently to what has been the mainstream of economic thinking. A competitive, market-oriented economy is capable of stunning success. But there remains a major role for government policy to insure the aggregate demand for full employment and maximum growth.[44]

Let us pursue the new "Keynesian-neoclassical synthesis."

KEYNESIAN PROGRAMS AS KEYNES ENVISIONED THEM

Taxation of the Rich

Keynes, like Aristotle, was aware of the political risks of taxing the rich heavily. Aristotle feared political retaliation by the rich if they felt attacked by the poor and middle class. He wished to avoid oligarchic reaction. At the same time, he made it clear that the rich must be encouraged to give of their wealth to the poor and to the civic good.

In terms of the power drive of the rich, as Keynes analyzed the situation, the enormity of the fortunes that would still be derivable from economic activity would still draw the high rollers to the game. With fortunes running to the billions, it is hard to believe that a 25 percent tax would be enough to discourage the players and divert their "will to power" into the political arena. Of course, the rich will try to prevent their own taxation, but they will not pack up their marbles and go home to plot an oligarchic takeover. As Aristotle and Keynes both believed, the gains from diverting such funds from the rich to the poor would be great enough to encourage any society to take the risk.

Second, in terms of the economic problems, the "skillful evasions" of the rich could be prevented through the establishment of a *minimum tax* with no allowable loopholes. Whether the middle class and the poor have the power to pass such a law over the objections of the rich becomes a question that each capitalist country must face separately. However, such a minimum tax, set at a high enough percentage, becomes a long-term solution to the tax evasions of the rich. The rich will always try to evade their taxes; therefore, the middle class and the poor, through the mechanisms of the legal-democratic institutions, must always countervail the rich in such attempts at evasion.

As to the savings of the rich, as necessary for the capital accumulation and expansion of the economy, Keynes turns this problem around, establishing that just the opposite process is good for the expansion and stability of a capitalist economy:

[O]ur argument leads toward the conclusion that in contemporary conditions the growth of wealth, so far from being dependent on the abstinence of the rich, as in commonly supposed, is more likely to be impeded by it. One of the chief social justifications of great inequality of wealth is, therefore, removed. (Keynes, 1965: 373)

Keynes' argument here is one of the foundations for modern day economic theory, even though it is considered outrageous by those adhering to classical economics. Keynes is insisting that the taxation of the rich makes available capital that must be invested by the government into public projects—be they military, civic, or industrial—and that such investment stimulates the growth of the economy.

Thus, from the Keynesian system, a minimum tax set on the rich, which allowed no loopholes, would make available huge amounts of capital that could then be invested into socially useful public projects. Such projects should include industrial development and technological research, as well as career programs for the poor, housing, and so forth.

Corporate Taxation

Following the same logic as that just outlined, one gets the principle from Keynes' system that corporate investment functions best when assisted with the partial "socialization of investment." And it must be pointed out that those nations that have evolved a system of *government–corporate partnership* in investment programs have prospered indeed. Nations such as Japan, Germany, Holland, and Sweden have produced a working partnership in government–corporate investment that has been very effective. As Keynes has pointed out, massive military investment takes on this function in the United States. However, where government investment has been directed toward "industrial policy," rather than military needs, the results of the joint investment process have been more fruitful.

Note carefully that the separation of power between the corporations and the government is maintained, but blurred somewhat. The government does intervene more actively in the investment process. The threat of "statism" does emerge from this kind of government expansion, and this should be taken very seriously. (We will discuss this problem and possible solutions to it in a later chapter.) However, the reader should also be aware of the fact that in the United States the military sector has grown so large that the reality of "statism" is just as real as it is in Germany, Sweden, and Japan. The recent "Iran-Contra affair" should stand as a warning against military statism and its insidious effect on democracy. The political aspects of government-directed investment needs a constant and careful evaluation, whether it be military or civic in nature.

In terms of the economic aspects, however, the data seem to support Keynes' thesis that corporate wealth, if fully retained by the corporations, is less well invested than if it is taxed and this taxed portion of corporate wealth is invested by the government.

For instance, when given huge tax cuts by the Nixon–Ford administration, U.S. corporations did *not* invest this captial into industrial development, R&D, product development, or the introduction of high technology production techniques. Instead they invested it in paper megers, conglomerate amalgamation, and overseas development. The U.S. economy fell into an industrial crisis, while corporate profits soared. The tax break did not achieve industrial expansion, while at the same time, fairly taxed corporations in Germany and Japan (e.g., Mercedes Benz, Toyota, and Sony) made tremendous industrial strides.

From the Keynesian system, corporations should be taxed, and the government should direct the investments gained from such taxation. Again, Keynes would not touch 75 percent of the profits taken by corporations, nor tamper with 75 percent of the investment directed by the corporations and the financial institutions. The capitalist system should function in its free wheeling creative independent way. Keynes simply adds on to it the necessary adjustments to prevent it from careening dizzily into its cycle of boom and bust, through its nonproductive use of excess capital. Government investment is like ballast for a ship that is too light and blows to quickly with the wind.

Taxation of the Middle Class

The middle class must, of course, pay its fair share of taxes. They may be more willing to do so if they know that the rich are paying their fair share. The middle class will be taxed at a progressively lower rate than the rich; they will be taxed enough so that capital is made available for investment in large quantities, but will not be taxed so much as to inhibit their "propensity to consume."

Within the Keynesian system, the middle class must be encouraged to consume in order for the economy to expand. Therefore, a careful balance between fair taxation and ability to consume must be created in each nation, depending on its resources and its wealth. Such a balance has been established within capitalist societies and can be intelligently calculated.

The middle class will always feel overtaxed, but if its propensity to consume is not greatly inhibited, it will support fair taxation. Further, if governmental social services are of a good quality—medical, retirement, educational, and childcare services, for instance—the middle class may be willing to pay into such services (as premiums), even if such payments inhibit their consumption ability to a moderate extent.

For the Keynesian system, however, overtaxing of the middle class is disastrous. The growth and vitality of the industrial economy is dependent on the middle class' ability to consume manufactured goods. Overtaxing the middle class would stultify the economy. Therefore, taxation of the middle class must remain moderate, and the propensity to consume must be stimulated. The cost of social services should be made up by military conversion, taxations of the rich, and taxation of the corporations, wherever this is possible. If the cost of social services runs beyond the society's capabilities, as just outlined, then a crisis develops, and a choice between services or consumption must be made. (We will discuss this in our "Objections to Equality" chapter.) Keynes did not foresee such a dilemma. However, if one looks carefully at military spending, and notes the colossal capital investments, Keynes will seem more wise and less dated than both conservative and liberal prognosticators believe.

One more point on the taxation of the middle class. It is important to note that the mobility potential and consumption style of the upper middle class should not be impeded by taxation. The upper middle class should be taxed fairly, but lacking the vast fortunes of the rich, they should not be overtaxed. Again, a careful balance becomes necessary such that the upper middle class can continue to be upwardly mobile and lifestyle pacesetters, but such that wasteful "conspicuous consumption''[45] is limited. High level consumer spending for mass production products, such as state-of-the-art cars, television sets, and so forth is good for the economy and eventually brings prices down on such goods. However, the buying of luxury items such as jewelry or mink coats does little for the economy and flaunts an unachievable lifestyle in the face of the middle and lower classes. There is a difference between high consumption levels and "conspicuous waste."[46]

Taxation of the Poor

Keynes' progressive taxation program would ensure, of course, that the lower middle class and the poor are taxed at a low rate. Keynes never suggested a "negative income tax," but rather focused his full effort on the creation of employment for the poor. With jobs and careers, the poor could become contributing taxpayers, adding their fair share of tax revenues to the civic good. It is a highly significant contrast that we find in Milton Friedman's program of a "negative income tax" for the poor. Friedman's program assures no job, no career, no property for the poor, yet would provide them with extra money. Friedman's program is inconsistent with the Aristotelian ideal of careers and property for the poor. It creates the "leaky jar" situation that Aristotle warned against. Keynes' program, on the other hand, is fully consistent with Aristotle's ideal, focusing on jobs and careers for the poor and a fair level of taxation.

We will not dwell on taxation of the poor here, but rather present Keynes' program for *full employment*. Employment is what the poor need and want, and absorption of the poor into the middle class and the body politic at large can only be achieved through such an employment program.

Before describing Keynes' program for full employment, however, we must spell out one further Keynesian mechanism that functions for the benefit of the middle classes in particular, and the economy in general. We are referring to the *rate of interest*.

Low Interest Rates

Low interest rates are critical for Keynes in two ways. They stimulate business investment, thus heating up the production end of the economy, and they stimulate consumption by placing increased income in the hands of the consuming public.

Bringing down interest rates on home mortgages is especially beneficial, and a systematic program of lowered interest rates on mortgages should be undertaken. Something like a G. I. Bill may be necessary again if the "American Dream" is to be kept alive for the new generation.

Low-interest educational loans are also critical for college support, as this is a good investment in the future of the nation. Though outright scholarships, as suggested in the chapter on Rawls, are more equitable than loans, if the loan program is retained, it should certainly be instituted with low-interest, long-term provisos.

In contrast with Keynes' principle of low interest rates, we have discussed Milton Friedman's "monetarist" program, which centers on raising interest rates in order to tighten the money supply, create a recession, and thus reduce inflation. Monetarist policy, however, results in expanded income for the rich, restricted income for the middle class, and unemployment for the poor. This is unwise public policy politically, economically, and socially. Further, it results in "stagflation,"[47] inhibiting economic growth without reducing inflation enough to help the average consumer.

Civic Public Works

One of the hallmarks of the Keynesian revolution in economic theory is the concept of government-directed investment in public works. In Keynesian theory, this program stimulates the economy and generates jobs. This "partial socialization of investment" is necessary, because in actual circumstances, large business concerns set their operations at a productive level that ensures the maximum amount of profit, but this productive level does not produce full employment (which could only occur at a higher level of industrial productivity). Thus, left to itself, the capitalist system will not produce full employment.[48] Add to this Keynesian analysis the Marxist one, which focuses on "the reserve army" of unemployed workers as depressing wages, and one can see that the system will not, of itself, provide for anything like full employment.

Keynes therefore suggested a supplementary system for the creation of full employment. Classic economic theory provides for no such corrective, but rather denies that the problem exists, while the socialist corrective of total government employment reduces both work motivation and capitalist efficiency and creativity.

The Keynesian supplementation should, therefore, be evaluated—as it has operated since the Great Depression—as the best actual solution to an endemic problem within industrial capitalism. Let me remind the reader that every capitalist nation has adopted the Keynesian program of massive public works to stimulate the economy and to provide employment. However, especially in the United States, it has been military public works that have been undertaken. "Military Keynesianism" is effective, but "civic Keynesianism" would be equally effective and produce a better society.

This is not to say that military Keynesianism can be phased out, but rather that it can be reduced—civic projects replacing miltiary projects in an evolving progression. No denial of the realities of the Cold War or of the Soviet Union's expansionary-aggressive tendencies is suggested herein. No naiveté or idealism is suggested either. Military preparedness—even military leadership for the United States—will remain necessary. But there are few Americans who are unaware of the colossal waste in the military public works program. Most military analysts believe that the military budget could be cut by at least one third without harming our military superiority. If the Russians become willing to cut their military budget—and it seems that under Gorbachev they are willing to do so—American opportunities to do so will expand.

Finally, who would deny that in the United States today the rebuilding of our economic infrastructure might not be more important than the expansion of our military prowess? Our basic industries have gone to rust, and our railroads, our bridges, our hospitals, and our schools are decaying. It might be better to delay building, say, two atomic submarines and a number of new bombers, and to expand our expenditure on the above-mentioned civic projects instead.

Strength in industrial productivity and an educated citizenry might be a better barometer of the power of a nation than military power alone. In fact, looking at the history of the world since the Industrial Revolution, one should come to the conclusion that industrial capacity has become the main measure of national power.

Military Conversion Programs

Military public works programs are routinely undertaken by capitalist societies. As Keynes wryly pointed out, the governments of capitalist countries spend trillions on military projects, yet are reticent to engage in civic public works of a more useful nature. Such governments also allow for economic waste in military expenditure, but judge civic projects on a strict cost-accounting basis more stringent than corporate standards.

Since military spending and military programs cannot be cut back without a corresponding increase in other public works programs, what programs could be generated or expanded to accomplish such a conversion? We know that nations such as Germany and Japan, with lower military budgets than the United States', have more stable economies than the United States. What kinds of programs do they encourage?

Research and Development

The United States led Germany and Japan in patents in the 1960s and early 1970s. Now, the situation is reversed. A large scale cutback by American corporations in R&D has had ill effects on American products development and industrial leadership. It is only in the high-tech area that the United States has retained a world lead. R&D in science and engineering, through corporate, university, and independent think tanks, should be expanded.

The benefits of such an expansion of R&D to any capitalist industrial economy are very great. Since the days of Thorstein Veblen[49] we have known that the industrial–technological sector of the modern economy engenders dynamics of its own, beyond business principles. Business needs and industrial needs are not always co-extensive. For instance, mergers and conglomeratization may be good business but they may not improve industrial-product capacity in any way.

The expansion of R&D, as funded through government investment, helps bring business and industrial dynamics into closer synchronization by promoting technological advancements and applications that result in more and better industrial products for the consumption market.

Heavy Industry

While the Americans were investing in military production, the Europeans and the Japanese were investing in heavy industry. The production of steel, chemicals, machine tools, container shipping, and so on has slipped away from the United States. Labor costs have risen in those nations, while through automation, robotization, and union give-backs, labor costs have dropped in the United States.

Therefore, it is time to rebuild our heavy industry once again. Industrial leadership cannot be maintained if heavy industry is abandoned. Military power cannot be maintained in the face of a "hot" war if heavy industry is lost. The United States does not need world leadership in this area, but must co-produce steel, chemicals, machine tools, and other basic industrial products with the Common Market and Japan in order to keep our industrial vitality equal to theirs (and maintain our military independence).

Consumer Products Development

The United States leads the world in military product development, commercial aircraft development, and computer development, but we are drifting far behind in the area of automobiles, electronics, small appliances, and household goods. Everything from bicycles to baby carriages are made elsewhere. The computer market is already under competition from European and Japanese brands, and therefore the message is clear. If the American economy is to survive as a modern economy, we must reclaim at least a fair share of the production of autos, televisions, electronics, household appliances, and so on that will make up the consumer market of the future.

The United States cannot allow what happened in Britain to happen here. We cannot simply invest in the maintenance of our overseas "empire" to the neglect of our domestic industrial-productive system. Consumer production is, after all, what industrialization is all about in the end, and without leadership in this area, or at least parity, no industrial economy can maintain itself. Our national power, our national pride, and our national sensibility are all on the line here. Our economy will have to compete in the area of consumer goods production, or decline. In the Keynesian schema, government investment from the military sphere should be diverted and re-invested in our consumer products sector (as well as our heavy industry sector). Together the development of heavy industry and consumer products would create the "re-industrialization"[50] of America which is so sorely needed.

Rebuilding the Economic Infrastructure

Most Americans are painfully aware that our roads, our bridges, our railroads, our shipping, our mass transit system—our infrastructure—are antiquated and in desperate need of repair. Every month, it seems, reports of bridge collapses, road-span breaks, and railway problems are reported in the nightly news.

The diversion of military investment toward the rebuilding of the infrastructure is becoming more and more necessary. An extensive bridge and road repair program is not only economically sound, but morally sound at this point.

The program of modernization of our docks, waterfronts, and shipping, which was begun in the 1960s, has been lagging and needs reinvestment for further modernization. The system of "containerization" needs updating by now, and all across America old and new dock areas remain dilapidated—they are symbols of 19th century industrialization that should be cleaned up and made models of 20th century progress.

Our railroad system and our mass transit system are also neglected areas of modern scientific and economic attention. We have monorails running around Disney World, but not around our cities. The Japanese, French, and other European nations have a few high speed trains in service (we have at least one, between Washington, D.C. and New York), but no nation has many. There is no doubt that with a major program of government investment in this area, faster, quieter, more remarkable systems of mass transit could be invented and made operational.

The Space Program

In the Kennedy years, the government undertook a gigantic expansion of the space program. This is a perfect alternative to military spending since space programs encourage and help develop high technology, along with new frontiers of scientific and technological productivity. In recent years military programs (including military space programs, e.g., "Star Wars") have taken precedence over scientific space programs, with disastrous results for both the society at large and the space program in particular. Many scientifically useful space programs were cancelled,[51] while military programs were pursued.[52]

Rebuilding the "Social Infrastructure"

By the "social infrastructure" we mean: 1), housing, 2) hospitals, 3) schools and culture centers, 4) parks and beaches, as well as 5) shopping areas. Here, military conversion is not necessarily implied and funding would have to be sought from other sources, such as taxation.

Housing

In the United States there is a crisis in housing for the poor and for the urban middle class. (In Germany and Scandinavia there is a crisis in housing for young adults, which those nations are just beginning to respond to.) The trend in the

United States has been toward the construction of luxury condominiums and cooperatives. These are highly profitable; however, they have left the middle class and the poor out in the cold. In the cities, "single room occupancy" (SROs), low-income project sites, and middle-income housing sites have all been converted to luxury housing units. At the same time, the rising price of these luxury units has driven up the price of suburban homes so that they will not be affordable for the next generation of the middle class.

Young middle class individuals cannot find suitable urban rentals or suburban housing. And, as is now known to the world's travelers, America's poor are literally living in our streets. The response of city governments to the lack of housing for the poor is to drag them to dangerous mass shelters to save them from the cold of winter. Wouldn't housing for the poor be a better plan?

What is needed for the middle class? The answer would include the following: (1) Urban middle income apartments and moderately priced condominiums. An investigation in New York City in 1985 showed that middle income housing can still be run at a modest profit.[53] (2) Mortgage assistance is needed for suburban housing—a new "G. I. Bill" offering low-interest mortgage rates and long-term repayments. (3) Rent-stabilization—the compromise between rent-controls and market pricing. Market pricing is too high for the middle class (much less the poor), while rent-control was set too low for landlord profitability. Rent stabilization has produced an honest compromise allowing for landlord profit and affordability. (4) If condominiums are to be the trend, then middle income condominiums should be constructed and partially subsidized, through tax and other incentives, so that they remain within the buying power of the middle class. This trend has already successfully begun, and it should be dramatically expanded.

What is needed for the poor? The homeless poor need housing. They need real housing, not emergency shelters. However, we have learned some lessons since the 1960s. Many large-scale, low-income projects became "vertical slums." We should avoid this problem. The way to proceed is twofold: First, brownstones in the cities and wooden houses in the small towns and small cities should be refurbished and made available to the poor. Much good housing would exist if already standing structures were improved. Second, large-scale, low-income projects should be built, along with vest-pocket low income projects.

Furthermore, the working poor, who are responsible and upwardly mobile, have to be protected from the poor who are into crime, vice, drugs, alcohol, and so on. Can this be accomplished? Partially. Each project, large or small, needs social work services, educational services, day-care services, and job placement services. The projects that work have these facilities.

City slums still exist in most American cities. The rebuilding of such slums, begun in the Kennedy–Johnson era, has been abandoned since then. The South Bronx still sits as it sat, a symbol of our callousness and lack of imagination. Small cities like St. Louis have small slums sitting near beautifully redeveloped "Yuppy" neighborhoods. The Yuppy neighborhoods are interesting—whether they have been developed in St. Louis, Kansas City, Philadelphia, Alexandria, Virginia, or elsewhere. These "gentrified" neighborhoods are very nice additions to most American cities. But, as Keynes would have put it, it is not that the 90 percent of what the capitalist system generates is misdirected; it is the 10 percent it neglects that needs to be attended to. Just so, the slum neighborhoods across our land need rebuilding. Sometimes they need to be rebuilt for the poor, other times as new kinds of neighborhoods entirely—as long as the displaced poor are first moved to good housing in another neighborhood. As they used to say in the 1960s, "urban renewal" should not mean "negro removal"—or the removal of the poor in general.

Hospitals and Community Mental Health Centers

Our hospitals are among the best in the world. However, in our urban areas, they are overcrowded and understaffed. Some shocking statistics have come out of urban hospitals in poverty neighborhoods. For instance, the infant mortality rate at Harlem Hospital is higher than that for many Third World nations. The emergency rooms of these same hospitals are overcrowded and disastrously understaffed. The poor must wait for hours to be serviced. Many rural hospitals are also in need of modernization and staffing.

Our mental hospitals, except for the model few, were in such a condition of overcrowding and under-staffing that a de-institutionalization program was generated as a humanistic alternative to the giant mental hospitals that seemed unable to help their patients. The de-institutionalization program instituted in the United States in the 1970s is, and was, the right idea. But—to de-institutionalize mental patients without creating the corresponding day treatment centers and controlled housing system was crazy (if you will pardon the pun).

The "snake pits" are gone, but the mentally ill are wandering around our cities and small towns. "Bag ladies" and bag men are regular residents of our playgrounds and transit systems. They stagger, vacant-eyed, listening to voices in the middle of our countryside. The "bag lady" has become almost a folk heroine of American life.

What is needed? Day treatment centers—well-staffed and fully funded—to provide treatment and custodial care for the incurable mentally ill during the day—plus supervised housing units for the night. Such day treatment centers and housing units do exist. But not in sufficient numbers. Nobody wants these facilities in *their* neighborhood. However, they must be built—the mentally ill are everywhere anyway. Since we de-institutionalized them, we now owe them modern treatment and care.

Cultural Centers, Libraries, Universities, Schools

In the 1960s, Kennedy–Johnson policy liberated large sums of money earmarked for the buidling of cultural centers, libraries, schools, and university buildings. Under Nixon, such funds were sequestered and then cut-off. Carter and Reagan did not push for funding in this direction. Yet these would be excellent "civic projects" for any modern society.

The worry about "the masses" being uncultured, by anti-democratic intellectuals such as Ortega y Gasset,[54] was partially correct. However the push in the 1960s to bring culture to the middle class and the poor was well received. Thousands attended "concerts in the park," and local theatre groups were booked-up with reservations. The building of music, art, and theatre centers is a good idea for any society, and a very good idea for a democratic society.

In some localities, and especially at some universities, library facilities are overcrowded or antiquated. Money for libraries was lavishly spent during the Kennedy–Johnson era, and such funding for construction and renovation should be brought back. Universities such as Columbia, N.Y.U., C.U.N.Y., and others in the New York area, have libraries that are overwhelmed with users. Whenever this is the case, public works projects for library construction should be encouraged.

In terms of universities in general, even our prestige universities are becoming tarnished and run-down. Yale lacks adequate air conditioning for its summer programs, Columbia's older buildings are in need of renovation, the interior of the classroom buildings in some of Princeton's older halls need sprucing up. State universities lack office space for their faculties and are generally in need of more building and grounds maintenance.

Finally, our public schools should be modernized and rebuilt in the inner cities and in the rural areas. Though suburban schools are in good repair, generally, inner city and rural schools are a mess. Why not hire great architects and make beautiful public schools? Jefferson believed such schools were the backbone of democracy. We have lost faith in our public schools. This could be one way to renew our faith in them (along with the enhanced educational programs for the middle class and the poor that will go on inside of them).

Parks and Beaches

America's parks and beach fronts need more tending than they now get. Both our urban and woodland parks could use much larger labor forces. The East Coast beaches and Western parks are so overwhelmed by tourists that an investment in their upkeep (and expansion) would be wise policy. Programs for the rehabilitation of beaches and parks are pending right now in congress. Such programs could be made part of the job-creation process. We could and should triple our park maintenance staff and expand our park building and beautification program. Land is precious and park land, if well preserved, becomes a monument to our future survival—our gift, as it were, to the next generation.

Shopping Mall "Strips"

Throughout the United States, from New Jersey to California, from Boston to Miami, urban–suburban sprawl areas have become congested and ugly. Areas that were once lovely shopping malls surrounded by landscaping have become urbanized "strips." These are usually made up of old and new shopping malls that have run together to create an asphalt and concrete monstrosity where once park-like malls stood.

Such areas can easily be re-furbished and beautified. The demolition of designated, less-used shopping sites at regular intervals between the better utilized ones, and their subsequent conversion to park enclaves connecting the still used shopping centers can create beauty and environmental improvement where urban-suburban decay is setting in.

Government-Generated Job Programs

Keynes first reaffirms his faith in the capitalist system as the basic job-producing institution of society, and then suggests supplementary governmental programs for those left out of it:

[W]hen 9,000,000 men are employed out of 10,000,000 willing and able to work, there is no evidence that the labor of these 9,000,000 men is misdirected. The complaint against the present system is not that these 9,000,000 men ought to be employed on different tasks, but that tasks be available for the remaining 1,000,000 men. (Keynes, 1965: 379)

Job Retraining and Job Placement

A growing problem in modern technocratic economies is the displacement of industrial workers through automation, robotization, and computerization. This will be an ongoing and burgeoning trend. In the long run it will be a good thing. Few workers enjoy assembly-line work.[55] In the short run, though, industrial workers by the thousands are being pushed out of their jobs.

Job retraining, educational retraining, and job placement programs should be made available to such workers. From a Keynesian point of view, the economy is correctly employing the new generation of technocratically and managerially educated workers. What to do with those left out?

For those workers of any age who successfully return for re-educational skills that allow them entrance into the technocratic work force, financial and educational support should be provided. For those workers who cannot re-educate themselves, job retraining and job placement into available industrial jobs should be actively established. This means government or corporate job retraining programs, along with public or private job placement centers to let workers know in which industrial sectors and in what geographical areas jobs may be available.

For those workers who cannot be placed (and there will be a large surplus of workers) and who cannot be technically re-trained, jobs must be created.

This latter brings us back to the Keynesian principle that for the 10 percent or so who cannot be employed by the market, the government becomes the employer of last resort. We wish to remind the reader, however, that an aggressive and well run retraining, re-educating, and job placement system could provide for the re-employment of a fair percentage of those able bodied workers who had already been employed (and showed a good work record).

One further morbid reminder is also necessary. From among these displaced workers, a very high rate of violence emanates—violence against families, former employers, and strangers. Everyday one reads of an unemployed worker going berserk and killing his own family, a manager or supervisor from his former plant, or strangers in a public place. Keynesian job retraining and job creation programs are better than this.

Careers for the Unemployed in "Under-serviced Areas" of Society

There are sectors of society that go under-serviced in capitalist societies, usually because they are less profitable to run, or part of the public service system. Yet, often they are work sectors that are greatly needed.

In the United States, for instance, the number of police, fire, sanitation, park, and mass transit workers should probably be doubled. New York City, in 1987, has approximately the same number of police as it had in 1950, and fewer park and transit workers. Federal subsidies for such municipal workers would be necessary because of the lack of a tax base existent in most American cities with the movement of the middle class to the suburbs. The suburban exodus did not reduce the need for the city workers, since so many suburbanites work within the cities, and because new immigrants have filled the residential districts that the suburbanites have left. Thus, the tax base left, but the need for the city services usually increased at the same time.

The suburbanization has increased the need for mass transit workers. This is a desperately understaffed area of our society. The very high crime rate in American cities makes doubling the number of police a wise policy—not that this will reduce crime, but it certainly can protect the citizenry and help police departments cope with the desperate situation they find themselves in. As the inner city buildings get older, the number of fires goes up. Therefore, doubling the number of firemen also becomes not only a wise, but an absolutely essential policy.

America has some of the dirtiest cities in the Western industrial world. Our sanitation workers are overwhelmed with the job of garbage removal and street cleaning. We need to more than double the sanitation work force to make America's cities look as clean as their European counterparts.

Along with sanitation workers, we need park workers in our cities, suburbs, and rural areas. Again, American's parks are comparatively ill-kept, unbeautified, untended, compared with their European counterparts. We have not only too few flower gardens and too many untrimmed trees, but baseball fields—our national pastime—untended in our suburbs as well as our cities, tennis courts badly in need of upkeep, rural woodlands strewn with the rusted wreckage of cars and innumerable beer cans and soda bottles. Local communities may not be able to afford such services, but such services are sorely needed.

Not only would the above job program protect people and the environment, but it would also provide jobs for working class and poor men, the groups from which high crime statistics emanate when they are unemployed. (This is not to imply that women ought not to be hired for these jobs as well.)

Would this kind of a job program be effective? Whenever police, fire, sanitation, or transit positions become available, long lines of potential workers form days in advance. Why turn away such workers and then be forced to pay them unemployment insurance for not working, or, worse, pay their prison upkeep ($25,000–$50,000 per year per inmate) instead, if they turn to crime?

Other areas wherein workers are needed include hospitals, nursing homes, childcare facilities, day treatment centers for the mentally ill, schools, and social work agencies.

Within schools, as an example, we do not now have language, science, math, or physical education specialists in enough numbers. Most European schools teach a number of languages to grade-school children. This is the best age to teach children languages. Why not teach Spanish, French, German, Chinese, and other languages to grade school children? Language teachers are needed in every grade school. So too are science and math specialists. Most teachers are not well prepared in these subjects. Einstein, genius though he was, would not have had the background in math and science necessary to excel if he had gone to an American public (or private) school. In his memoirs, he discusses the "mind experiments" he engaged in as a youth in response to questions posed by his grade-school and "gymnasium" teachers in Germany. Most Americans are not exposed to such questions because we do not have enough trained science and math coordinators in our schools.

The physical education programs within our public schools are also quite poor. After-school programs are excellent, but why not have school programs? Most schools have gyms and equipment, but no one to instruct the children. Again, there are some European programs, especially those in Germany and Eastern Europe, that are quite excellent and could be emulated within our schools, or attached to them as after-school programs. We don't have to pressure our children to become Olympic athletes, as they do in Eastern Europe, but we should provide everyday physical education programs within our school system.

Day-care centers need more teachers and more paraprofessionals. Recent sex-abuse scandals have warned us that such workers need to be carefully screened, and that more middle class, rather than lower class, individuals should be recruited for such jobs. Nonetheless, workers are needed in this area, as more and more women take to the work force.

Social workers are needed in three critical areas: day-care facilities for the mentally ill, family therapy agencies (because of the rising divorce rate and the general disintegration of the extended and nuclear family), and in job programs themselves. We have discussed the need for social workers in the section on the poor in our chapter on Aristotle.

Workfare Replacing Welfare

In the section on Aristotle, we have already described the workfare system and why it should replace the welfare system. Nobody wants the welfare system, especially not the poor. It is time capitalist societies gave up the "poor laws" and turned to constructive work programs for the poor.

Do We Need the C. C. C. and Urban Job Corps Again?

There will remain a large number of workers not employed by the job retraining and public service job programs. They will be the most difficult to train, place, and retain, for they will be drawn from the long-term unemployed and the hardcore poor. The unemployed drawn from the hardcore poor will have bad social attitudes, poor work habits, may be on drugs or alcohol, will have illegitimate children (at a young age), and may even be violent at times. Still, a percentage of such workers are redeemable.

Right now the cost of crime and of prisons is astronomical. Our prisons have become our social program for the detention of the hardcore poor. But the prison program is very expensive and it does not rehabilitate the poor. Spending $25–50,000 a year to keep someone in prison, while knowing that upon release criminal behavior is more likely to be exhibited than before detention, is as unwise a social policy as ever a society has devised.

Why not a massive C. C. C. and urban job corps instead? It will be less expensive in the long run and more constructive in the short run. Such programs can be run in quasi-military style and/or in purely social-group-work style. That is, both authoritarian programs with rigid discipline, and group-oriented programs with more democratic norms, can be established. The idea behind the program is to provide jobs with a structured work setting for those individuals who are unable to find work, or keep work, in the private or public service sectors of the economy.

The Problem of Funding

No discussion of job programs can be complete without a discussion of the funding. We wish to suggest a list of potential sources of funding so that the credibility of such job programs is at least temporarily bolstered:

1. Allotment of at least one third of the military budget should provide a great deal of funding for civic projects and job programs.

2. Taxation of the rich and corporations should provide further funding.

3. Welfare conversion to workfare, with its long-term increase in the tax base and decrease in welfare payments, should help.

4. Employment of unemployed workers will reduce unemployment payments and increase the tax base.

5. Decreased prison costs—which are now astronomical—will release funding in the long run, if job programs are successful.

Other Problems Engendered by Public Works and Employment Programs

Along with funding, which is undoubtedly the major stumbling block of all job programs, there are other serious problems that must be overcome. We will discuss these problems in detail later, in the chapter on the neoconservatives, but here we wish to at least forewarn the reader of such obstacles:

(1) The authoritarian and obstructive nature of government bureaucracies is now well known. If job programs create huge bureaucratic monstrosities, they will not only fail in their job-creating intent, but create a greater social problem than they sought to alleviate. Can job programs be structured so as to minimize the inefficient and authoritarian tendencies of bureaucracy? We will suggest ways in which this can be accomplished.

(2) Unions will attempt to obstruct job programs unless they are brought into them and gain, rather than lose, membership.

(3) The hostility and unreliability of the poor and lower class shocked the middle class reformers in the 1960s. We have already suggested that massive social work and educational support systems are necessary in the effort to rehabilitate the poor and find them careers.

(4) Jealousy from the working class and lower middle class must be avoided. Programs meeting their needs must be instituted alongside programs for the poor. Mortgage assistance, college scholarships, educational supports, and so on should be provided to this group so that their jealousy of the poor is reduced. In this regard it might be best to offer universal career and educational programs that benefit all groups in society. In our section on Rawls we suggested this.

(5) The "revolution of rising expectations," especially among the poor, becomes a real problem when job programs fail to meet the short-term expectations of those attempting upward mobility through them. This cannot be fully avoided, and only the long-term success of the career programs can reduce this problem. More on this and the other problems in a later chapter.

PART II

OBJECTIONS TO THEORIES OF EQUALITY

4

de Tocqueville, Weber, and Hayek: The Dangers of Socialism

The flaws inherent in the socialist program, relating to the power of the state and the enveloping nature of bureaucratic organization, were pointed out, remarkably, by two theorists who had never experienced socialism at all! Alexis de Tocqueville and Max Weber based their critique of socialism on their understanding of the monarchical states of France and Germany, which had ruled despotically and smothered individual freedom. It was the fear of a revival of patrimonial-bureaucratic leadership that led de Tocqueville and Weber to warn against any socialist schemas that included the idea of the strengthening of the state.

Both the French and the German royal bureaucracies attempted to control economic and political activities, limiting the scope of entrepreneurial economic action and nullifying or inhibiting the free politics of the budding parliamentary-democratic institution that had emerged. Both de Tocqueville and Weber realized that the despotic state with its centralized bureaucracy might transcend the death of the monarchies. They feared that the socialists, because of their rejection of capitalism and individualism and their distrust of bourgeois parliamentary government, would become prime movers for a program that would inadvertently re-enshrine a despotic-bureaucratic state.

Weber predicted precisely that the Bolshevist program in Russia would produce a new form of the despotic-patrimonialism that it had sought to destroy![1] Hayek, writing after WWII and witnessing the full flowering of the despotic-bureaucratic states of the Soviet Union and China, warned even more adamantly against this brand of social organization.

Hayek believed that even the democratic socialist programs of Scandinavia and Britain would lead to the slow erosion of free institutions, robbing us of our citizenship and leaving us in a condition not unlike that of serfdom.

Let us look more closely at the arguments of de Tocqueville, Weber, and Hayek. Their arguments against socialism stand as a challenge to all programs for equality in the modern world—a challenge that must be met if a more equitable society is to emerge without destroying democracy and freedom.

de TOCQUEVILLE: SOCIALISM AGAINST FREEDOM

Alexis de Tocqueville was one of the first theorists to see that the centralized administrative state developed by the European monarchies would transcend the political and economic revolutions of his day. To de Tocqueville's dismay, the centralized bureaucratic state developed by the kings did transcend the French Revolution and threatened to overwhelm the political freedoms engendered by the revolution. de Tocqueville may also have been the first to see that the economic reformers, in the name of equality, would fix the administrative state as central in their utopian vision. For de Tocqueville, this was tantamount to sacrificing political freedom to attain economic and social equality.

Let us look at de Tocqueville's argument, for it reads as contemporary as any I have ever read. First, he describes the origins of the bureaucratic state under the French monarchy:

When the love of the French for political freedom was awakened, they had already conceived a certain number of notions on matters of government, which not only did not readily ally themselves with the existence of free institutions but which were almost contrary to them.[2]

They had accepted as the ideal of society a people having no aristocracy but that of its public officers, a single and all powerful administration. . . . They therefore undertook to combine an unlimited administrative centralization with a prepondering legislative body . . . the administration of a bureaucracy with the government of electors.[3]

In the centre of the kingdom, and close to the throne, there had been gradually formed, an administrative body of extraordinary authority, . . . its origin was ancient, but the greater part of its functions were of recent date . . . as the superior administrative board, it had to frame the general regulations which were to direct agents of government.[4]

This administrative council was not composed of men of rank, but of personages of middling or even low extraction, former Intendants or other men of that class thoroughly versed in the management of business, all of whom were liable to dismissal by the crown.[5]

As the whole administration of the country was directed by a single body, nearly the entire management of home affairs was entrusted to the care of the single agent—the comptroller general. . . . In each canton was placed below him an officer nominated by himself, and removeable at will, called the sub-delegate. . . . The number of . . . regulations . . . were immense; and they seem constantly to have increased the nearer we approach the revolution.[6]

This centralized administrative state grew stronger and more intrusive, and as it did, it strangled entrepreneurial development, parliamentary legislation, and citizen's participation in France. As it became more rationalized (less traditional), it became less despotic, and yet more smothering in its effect in political and economic freedom.

In proportion as it became minute and more comprehensive, it also became more regular and more scientific. It became more temperate as its ascendency became universal; it oppressed less, it directed more.

The smallest independent body, which seemed likely to be formed without its intervention, caused alarm; the smallest voluntary association, whatever was its object, was considered troublesome; and none were suffered to exist but those which it composed in an arbitrary manner, and over which it presided. Even the great industrial companies found little favor in the eyes of the administration; in a word, it did not choose that the citizens should take any concern whatever in the examination of their own affairs, and preferred sterility to competition.[7]

The whole essence of the then state of France is contained in this passage: rigid rules and lax practice were its characteristics.[8]

de Tocqueville describes the smothering effect of the bureaucratic state upon French society, and then reacts with horror to the utopian dreams of the French economic reformers who wished to use this very administrative state to accomplish their social goals. To de Tocqueville it was obvious that the reinforcement of the all-encompassing administrative state would destroy freedom, citizenship, law, and creative economic development.[9] However, to the economic reformers seeking pure equality, the use of the power and structure of the administrative state seemed obvious.

[A]ll sorts of new systems of government were concocted. The ends which these various reformers had in view were various, but the means they proposed were always the same. They wanted to employ the power of the central authority in order to destroy all existing institutions, and to reconstruct them according to some new plan of their own devise; no other power appeared to them capable of accomplishing such a task. The power of the state ought, they said, to be as unlimited as its rights; all that was required was to force it to make proper use of both.[10]

The point was, then, not to destroy absolute power, but to convert it. . . . In fact, they set no limits to the rights of the state, nor to what it could effect. The state was not only to reform men, but to transform them—perhaps if it chose, to make others![11]

de Tocqueville then, amazingly, gives a name to and describes that form of despotism that would emerge in the modern world:

That peculiar form of tyranny which is called DEMOCRATIC DESPOTISM, and which was utterly unknown to the Middle Ages, was already familiar to these writers. No gradations in society, no distinctions, no fixed ranks—a people composed of individuals nearly alike and entirely equal—this confused mass being recognized as the only legitimate sovereign, but carefully deprived of all the faculties which could enable it either to direct or even to superintend its own government. Above this mass, a single officer, charged to do everything in its name without consulting it. To control this officer public opinion, deprived of its organs; to arrest him, revolutions, but no laws. In principle, a subordinate agent; in fact, a master.[12]

de Tocqueville then links this form of ''democratic despotism'' directly to the socialists, and this linkage is the flaw that the socialists have not been able to overcome. As de Tocqueville put it:

It is supposed that the destructive theories which are designated in our times by the name of socialism are of recent origin; this again, is a mistake; these theories are contemporary with the first French school of economists. Whilst they were intent on employing the all-powerful government, they had conceived in order to change the form of society, other writers grasped in imagination the same power to subvert its foundations.

In the CODE DE LA NATURE, by Mirelly, will be found, side by side with the doctrines of the economists on the omnipotence and unlimited rights of the state, several of the political theories which have most alarmed the French nations . . . community of goods, the right to labour, absolute equality of conditions, uniformity in all these things, a mechanical regularity in all movements of individuals, a tyranny to regulate every action of daily life, and the complete absorptions of the personality of each member of the community with the whole social body.

"Nothing in society shall belong in singular property to anyone". . . . "Property is detestable, and whosoever shall attempt to re-establish it, shall be shut up for life, as a maniac or an enemy of mankind. Every citizen is to be supported, maintained, and employed at the public expense." "All productions are to be stored in public magazines, to be distributed to the citizens and to supply their daily wants . . . at five years of age all children will be taken away from their parents and brought up in common at the cost of the State and in uniform manner."[13]

This description by the early French socialists reads almost like a combination of the state structure of ancient Egypt and the ideology of Plato. As we shall see, Weber feared that modern society might become a rationalized version of ancient Egypt, wherein all economic needs were met, but wherein political freedom would be destroyed and forgotten. We have already discussed Aristotle's cirtique of Plato's theory of pure communism, but here, the early French socialists repeat Plato's ideas on raising children in common and abolishing private property. Karl Popper takes Plato to task for his teachings on this and his rejection of political democracy.[14] Yet, no theorist ever more eloquently or decisively has criticized romantic socialism and its state-centralized program than de Tocqueville.

de Tocqueville ends his diatribe against the socialists with this quip:

Of all the men of their time (1755), these economists are those who would appear most at home in our own; their passions for equality are so strong, and their taste for freedom is so questionable, that we might fancy they are our contemporaries.[15]

Could anyone make a stronger case against socialism? The identification by de Tocqueville of the power of the centralized state and its stultifying effect on society, and also of its antagonism to voluntary associations and independent economic activity, was ahead of its time. Actually, de Tocqueville was ahead of his time because he was behind his time! That is, he could still witness the effect the monarchical-bureaucratic state was having on France. For de Tocqueville, this effect was wholly negative and antagonistic to the society of freedom that the French revolution had championed.

In the modern situation, therefore, any theory of equality can only be put forword with de Tocqueville's warning in mind: the centralized administrative state should not be strengthened or extended, its power should be limited and checked, the legal system and the legislature should be empowered, and economic development should be separated from state control.

In short, freedom should not be abandoned in order to create greater equality. de Tocqueville believed that if the socialists had their way, they would inadvertently destroy political freedom in their quest for equality and community. The socialists did not give credence to the theories of power limitations and power balancing put forth by Locke and Montesquieu; they did not give credence to the theory of constitutional law, nor did they favor an individualist social ethic. The socialists were well-meaning—they wished to eradicate poverty, create community, and reduce the selfishness that comes with wealth and privilege. However, the society that they wanted to create, de Tocqueville showed convincingly, would be no utopia.

For de Tocqueville, the establishment of political democracy was the central issue. Within the context of law and democracy and a power-limited state, the quest for equality could be pursued, but democracy could never be compromised in order to further the goals of equality.

Democracy extends the sphere of individual freedom, socialism restricts it. . . . Democracy and Socialism have nothing in common but one word: equality. But notice the difference: while *democracy seeks equality in liberty*, socialism seeks equality in restraint and servitude.[16]

In his phrase, "democracy seeks equality in liberty," de Tocqueville leaves the door open to a quest for equality within a society guaranteeing freedom. He does not suggest that equality ought not to be a proper social goal. In fact, in *Democracy in America*, he describes over and over the relative equality found in the new nation, as compared with Europe. de Tocqueville was even a little shocked by American anti-aristocratic rudeness—although he basically loved American individualism, independence, irreverence, and the "I am as good as you are" attitude.[17]

Nor was America—wide open, with property for the taking—a land of extreme poverty when de Tocqueville traveled through it. Compared with France, America's rich were modest indeed. Using the budding America as a model, de Tocqueville saw little need for a special program of economic equality.[18] Conversely, the basic problem in his France was the ongoing difficulty in establishing political democracy and the liberation of capitalist energies.

de Tocqueville's analysis of the limited state was remarkably astute, and his desire to see France move in the direction blazed by the United Sates was wise. However, had de Tocqueville lived to see Britain in 1860, with its wretched slums and mass emigrations, he might have developed further his idea of "equality with liberty." In his era, however, the overriding passion was the establishment of democracy, and de Tocqueville saw correctly that the romantic socialists were its enemy.[19]

In this treatise, we will stress the need for increased equality within the constraints of legal-democratic guidelines, but we will do so with de Tocqueville's warnings ringing in our ears. A "new servitude" must not be brought forth by the quest for equality.

Here is the final quote from de Tocqueville—the quote that Hayek repeats over and over again, and which the neoconservatives hold up as the warning of warnings for the new generation of humanists:

[T]he supreme power then extends its arm over the whole community. It covers the surface of society with a network of small complicated rules, minute and uniform, through which the most original minds and the most energetic characters cannot penetrate to rise above the crowd. The will of man is not shattered but softened, bent and guided; men are seldom forced by it to act, but they are constantly restrained from acting. Such a power does not destroy, but prevents existence; it does not tyrannize but it compresses, enervates, extinguishes, and stupifies a people; till each nation is reduced to be nothing better than a flock of timid and industrial animals, of which government is the shepherd.[20]

WEBER: BUREAUCRACY AGAINST DEMOCRACY AND SOCIALISM

If de Tocqueville was the first to see that the monarchical bureaucracy would transcend to the modern world, Max Weber was the first to describe *modern* bureaucracy in detail and to analyze specifically its effects on society.[21] Weber, living in the era of the Bismarckian bureaucratic state, could see, even beyond de Tocqueville's vision, that the bureaucratic state would not "wither away" *even with the establishment of parliamentary democracy*. Weber saw that this was not an either/or situation—that parliamentary democracy and a modern bureaucratic state would emerge together into the new world of modernity; Weber saw, too, that these two sets of institutional forces would be in conflict with each other.[22] As with de Tocqueville, he predicted that socialism would reinforce the bureaucratic state so thoroughly as to overwhelm or destroy the parliamentary-democratic political institutions that had been so painfully established.

Weber spent his life helping to establish democracy in Germany and, like de Tocqueville, looked to America for guidance.[23] Although sympathetic to the humanism of the socialists, he felt they were misguided and hopelessly romantic. He loved his friend Lukacs,[24] but warned him that his dream would become a nightmare.

Unlike Karl Marx and his followers, who offered a quasi-millennial eschatology of hope in the midst of modernity's agonies, Max Weber may be envisioned as a latter day Jeremiah—a prophet of doom concerning the development of modern society. As with the prophets of old, however, his message was meant as a warning, not as a fated, irreversible prediction. Weber's pessimistic analysis of modern society was written with the hope of stimulating future generations of social scientists, politicians, and statesmen to create and develop responsible proposals and programs that would establish possible solutions to the problems that were emerging. While railing against utopianism of any kind, Weber remained passionately committed to political action that could produce *practical* results based on the actual social conditions of modernity.[25]

What exactly was Weber's nightmare vision of modernity, and is there any way out of it?

While the Enlightenment thinkers and Marx based their visions of the future on the analogy of the ancient Greek *polis*, Weber based his on the Oriental empires. He stated his position thus:

History shows that wherever bureaucracy gained the upper hand, as in China, Egypt, and, to a lesser extent, in the later Roman empire and Byzantium, it did not disappear again unless in the course of the total collapse of the supporting culture. In contrast to these older forms, modern bureaucracy has one characteristic which makes its "escape-proof" nature much more definite: rational specialization and training. . . . Wherever the modern specialized official comes to predominate, his power proves practically indestructible since the whole organization of even the most elementary want satisfaction has been tailored to his mode of operation. . . . Together with the inanimate machine it is busy fabricating the shell of bondage which men will perhaps be forced to inhabit some day, as powerless as the fellahs of ancient Egypt. . . . An "organic" social stratification, similar to the Oriental–Egyptian type, would then arise, but in contrast to the latter it would be as austerely rational as a machine. *Who would want to deny that such a potentiality lies in the womb of the future?*[26]

What Weber saw as an ideal typification of bureaucratic organizational structure was *a new form of despotic domination.* This form of domination is subtle in that it controls decision making and negates civil liberties without resort to a secret police or conquering army. The hallmarks of democratic government—citizens' participation in decision making and leadership choice, the limitation of the power and tenure of leaders, and lawful procedures for rule making and rule enforcement—are replaced by an administrative megamachine controlled from the top down and insensitive to individual needs.[27]

For many years, socialism stood out as an alternative to capitalist democracy. With the oligarchic elements removed from society, socialists believed that true democracy and dramatically increased equality should emerge. Weber, however, doubted that this could be the result; rather, he stated flatly that socialism would demand even more bureaucratization than capitalism. He further claimed that this bureaucracy would be fully fused with the politico-military might of the state, hence increasing the tendency toward despotic control:

State bureaucracy would rule *alone* if private capitalism were eliminated. The private and public bureaucracies, which now work next to, and potentially against, each other and hence check one another to a degree, would be merged into a single hierarchy. This would be similar to the situation in ancient Egypt, but it would occur in a much more rational—and hence unbreakable—form.[28]

Furthermore, in a bureaucratic economy, workers' control is a utopian dream which will collapse before the reality of control by managerial officials:

What would be the practical result? The destruction of the steel frame of modern industrial work? No! The abolition of private capitalism would simply mean that also the *top management* of the nationalized or socialized enterprises would become bureaucratic. [T]here is even less freedom, since every power struggle with a state bureaucracy is hopeless and since there is no appeal to an agency which as a matter of principle would be interested in limiting the employer's power, such as there is in the case of a private enterprise. *That* would be the whole difference.[29]

[Thus] this would be socialism in about the same manner in which the ancient Egyptian "New Kingdom" was socialist.[30]

Though clearly favoring capitalism over what he argued would become stultifying bureaucratic socialism, Weber was not an apologist for capitalism. He did not excuse the selfishness of the rich, nor did he believe that capitalism served the needs of the workers. It simply was clear to him that if an economic planning bureaucracy were fused with the military and police power of the state, the emergence of a despotic system of government would increase in likelihood. This is precisely what he predicted for the Soviet Union shortly after the triumph of the Bolsheviks—a transformation of the dictatorship of the proletariat into a "dictatorship of the bureaucrats."[31]

Weber presents us with a picture similar to that of de Tocqueville's, except that he warns that even without socialism, the state—overgrown with modern rational bureaucracy—might overwhelm political freedom and individual citizenship: "For the last stage of this cultural development, it might well be truly said: 'specialists without spirit, sensualists without heart; this nullity imagines that it has attained a level of civilization never before achieved'."[32]

Then Weber throws down the gauntlet and leaves us with this challenge:

Given the basic fact of the irresistible advance of bureaucratization . . . how can one possibly save any remnants of individualist freedom in any sense? After all, it is a gross self-deception to believe that without the achievements of the Age of the Rights of Man any one of us, including the most conservative, can go on living his life. . . .[33]

HAYEK: THE WELFARE STATE AGAINST DEMOCRACY

de Tocqueville and Weber never lived to see Fascism and Communism emerge as new forms of despotism. Hayek, however, did. His warnings against the power of the State took an even greater urgency then that of the aforementioned thinkers.

Hayek, along with Karl Popper, in *The Open Society and Its Enemies*,[34] reacted not only against the Fascists, Nazis, and Stalinist-Communists, but also against the Social Democratic parties of Europe, which they believed contributed to the rise of fascism and communism by their structure and ideology.

That is, the Social Democratic parties, as Michels[35] pointed out, while pledging to work within the legal-electoral-democratic system, organized their membership into a very authoritarian, elite-dominated, hierarchical party structure that contributed to the overall anti-democratic ideology and practice of the European nations.

Furthermore, the Social Democrats advocated government ownership of the means of production and a centralized planned economy. According to Hayek, although the motives of the Social Democrats were good, they inadvertently contributed to the emergence of the worst despotic governments in history. Totalitarianism itself, according to Hayek and Popper, can be partially laid at their doorstep.

For Hayek, *any* program that would seek to increase the power of the State in *any* sphere of life would lead us down the "road to serfdom." He therefore makes laissez-faire economics and minimal government the cornerstones of his program.

In *The Road to Serfdom*[36] and *The Constitution of Liberty*,[37] Hayek has written perhaps the most influential critique of socialism of the modern era. Hayek's argument follows from that of de Tocqueville and Weber in that he believes that the structurally inevitable trend set in motion by socialism will destroy political freedom. That structural trend is, of course, government ownership of the means of production, centralized planning of the economy, and State intervention in the society for the purpose of creating greater equality.

If Hayek had ended there, he would have added nothing new to the argument. However, Hayek goes on to analyze democratic socialism and the welfare state, as they emerged after World War II. His critique of socialism becomes all the more devastating because of his view that even democratic socialism and welfare-statism can lead to despotism and to a stultified society. His basic arguments were not set against the Marxist-Leninists, but against the European Social Democrats, English Laborites, and American New Dealers. His arguments have been used more often against such works as Wooten's *Freedom Under Planning*[38] (a blueprint for democratic socialism in England), than against Lenin's five-year plans.

In later volumes, such as *The Constitution of Liberty*, he develops his argument further yet, opposing any and every attempt to create equality or regulate the economy. Hayek not only opposes welfare state programs, but progressive taxation, city planning, or any program that would interfere with laissez-faire economics.

He does, however, in the end, yield on certain grounds, such as: the establishment of generally good living standards for the majority of the population, safety net programs for retirement and disability, and monetary policies for the control of inflation[39] and the business cycle—but little else.

Let us look carefully at Hayek's position, for it is the most extreme modern expression of the tradition of "European liberalism" and British "Whig-liberalism," and it has been zealously adopted by the American "neoconservatives."

Obviously, in my view, no program for equality can stand unless it comes to grips with Hayek's warnings and avoids the dire results he predicts.

Hayek makes it clear in a new introduction written for *The Road to Serfdom* that his critique of socialism extends beyond the Soviet model and includes not only Democratic Socialism, but also welfare statism and the New Deal.

I recognize that the hot socialism against which [this book] was mainly directed—that organized movement toward a deliberate organization of economic life by the state as the chief owner of the means of production—is nearly dead in the Western World.[40]

It is now even widely recognized that democratic socialism is a very precarious and unstable affair, ridden with internal contradictions and everywhere producing results most distasteful to many of its advocates.[41]

Hayek goes on to warn against welfare statism, as well as Democratic Socialism,[42] and here he sounds exactly like a contemporary neoconservative:

That hodgepodge of ill-assembled and often inconsistent ideals which under the name of *the Welfare State* has largely replaced socialism as the goal of reformers needs very careful sorting out if its results are not to be very similar to those of full-fledged socialism. . . . A full understanding of the process through which certain kinds of measures can destroy the basis of an economy based on the market and gradually smother the creative power of a free civilization seems now of the greatest importance.[43]

Hayek then implores the reader to think toward the future, for he believes that the process of the erosion of freedom and creativity will be a slow process, not so readily visible as yet, but overwhelming once a certain structural preponderance has been reached. He defends his views against those who insist that nothing negative has happened in those nations where Democratic Socialist programs have been adopted.

Of course, six years of socialist government in England [and more in Scandinavia, Germany and France] have not produced anything resembling a totalitarian state. But those who argue that this has disproved the thesis of *The Road to Serfdom* have really missed one of its main points: that the most important change which extensive government control produces is a psychological change, an alteration in the character of the people. This is necessarily a slow affair, a process which extends not over a few years, but perhaps over one or two generations.[44]

Perhaps I should remind the reader that I have never accused the socialist parties of deliberately aiming at a totalitarian regime or even suspected that the leaders of the old socialist movements might ever show such inclinations. What I have argued in the book . . . is that the unforeseen but inevitable consequences of socialist planning create a state of affairs in which, if the policy is to be pursued, totalitarian forces will get the upper hand.[45]

Mirroring de Tocqueville and Weber, Hayek goes on to say, "It [becomes] a despotism exercised by a thoroughly conscientious and honest bureaucracy for what they sincerely believe is the good of the country."

Hayek then concludes, " . . . the defeat of the onslaught of systematic socialism has merely given those who are anxious to preserve freedom a breathing space in which to re-examine our ambitions and to discard all those parts of the socialist inheritance which are a danger to a free society."[46]

This is a statement of reprieve that we should take quite seriously. Hayek then goes on to state what has become a principle of democracy not fully appreciated by previous generations of theorists, a principle that is undoubtedly one of the central foundations upon which democracy rests. That principle is this: The separation of the economic sphere from governmental control means that those who pursue power in the economic sphere do not have direct access to the power of the State. Hayek emphasizes the meaning of this for democracy. Weber and Keynes made the same point.[47] Hayek states it this way:

The power which a multiple millionaire, who may be my neighbor and perhaps my employer, has over me is very much less than that which the smallest "functionaire" possesses who wields the coercive power of the state and on whose discretion it depends whether and how I am to be allowed to live or to work. . . . *The evolution of private capitalism with its free market has been a pre-condition for the evolution of all our democratic freedoms.*[48]

What our generation has forgotten is that the system of private property is the most important guarantee of freedom. . . . It is only because the control of the means of production is divided among many people acting independently that nobody has power over us. . . . If all the means of production were vested in a single hand . . . whoever exercises this control has complete control over us.[49]

There is much truth to these observations by Hayek. Democratic processes and legal protections did grow out of the commerical culture of ancient Greece, and later, post-feudal Europe.[50] The decline of this culture and its carrying classes should be cause for concern. The growth of bureaucratic structure and state power could produce a despotic structure. The fusion of economic and political power demanded by the Marxist socialists has produced despotism. Therefore, the maintenance of private property and the separation of the economic sphere from the power of the State remains central for the preservation of democracy. Hayek's theory and Hayek's warnings in this regard must be taken deadly seriously.

Looking at the modern scene, Hayek does give in a little against this strict laissez-faire formula. He knows that the Great Depression has occurred, and he knows that not everybody fares well under laissez-faire. Therefore, he allows for certain programs to be established to ensure the health and well-being of the individual within a free-market society, and for programs to help stabilize the otherwise violent fluctuations of the business cycle.

As long as the State stays out of the process of planning and economic control, it can, according to Hayek, provide services and establish minimum standards of living.

> Two kinds of security are [necessary]: first, security against severe physical privation . . . and second, the security of a given standard of life. . . . There is no reason why in a society which has reached the general level of wealth which ours has attained that the first kind of security should not be guaranteed to all without endangering general freedom. . . . There are difficult questions about the precise standard which should thus be assured.[51]

One can see that health insurance, retirement insurance, and a decent standard of living ought to be provided to individuals within Hayek's system—though obviously, private programs would be preferable to State-run programs. Here is Hayek's position again, and in this quotation he even concedes that the State could provide such programs as long as it keeps out of the business of economic planning and economic control.

> Nor is there any reason why the State should not assist the individuals in providing for those common hazards of life . . . such as sickness and accident . . . and the case for the State's helping to organize a comprehensive system of social insurance is very strong. . . . There is no incompatibility in principle between the State's providing greater security in this way and the preservation of individual freedom.[52]

This latter is a major concession from Hayek, which allows for the creation of a social "safety net" within a free market society. For Hayek, as long as the separation of the economic sphere from governmental control is maintained, as long as the government does not interfere with business, safety net programs may be established.

To be sure, any programs that increase government bureaucracy and power would be seen as negative within Hayek's system—and rightly so. But he does not suggest that we therefore ignore basic needs and basic living standards. He is not an advocate of some new form of callousness. He does remember the days of the Great Depression and does not wish to throw us back upon such a situation.

> There is, finally, the supremely important problem of combating general fluctuations of economic activity and the recurrent waves of large scale unemployment which accompany them. Many economists hope, indeed, that the ultimate remedy may be found in the field of monetary policy which would involve nothing incompatible even with 19th century liberalism. Others, it is true, believe that real success can be expected only from the skillful timing of public works undertaken on a very large scale.[53]

Hayek obviously favors the monetary solution, which is fully consistent with his laissez-faire liberalism. However, he does not close the door on Keynesian public works solutions to the unemployment and business cycle problems of modern free market economics. If monetary solutions failed to provide for greater employment, stability or a sufficient standard of living, public works programs could be acceptable. Such projects would increase the size and power of the government and would be avoided where possible, yet they are not ruled out by Hayek.

There are all kinds of public amenities which it may be in the interest of all members of the community to provide by common effort, such as parks, and museums, theatres and facilities for sports—though there are strong reasons why they should be provided by local rather than national authorities. . . . There is little reason why government should not also play some role, or even take the initiative, in such areas as social insurance and education, or temporarily subsidize certain experimental developments. Our problem here is not so much the aims as the methods of government action.[54]

Hayek is by no means advocating a welfare state, and he remains utterly opposed to any redistributary programs. However, he does not oppose safety net programs, he does not fully oppose public works, and he does support economic tinkering that can somehow correct the boom and bust cycle that laissez-fiare continues to engender, even under modern conditions of production.

Finally, and for this treatise this is central, Hayek warns against allowing for the conditions that produce a disempowered, alienated middle class. Hayek lived through fascism and nazism, and remembered correctly that the impoverishment of the middle classes in Italy, Austria, and Germany opened them to the appeals of the fascist parties and their charismatic leaders.[55] "It should never be forgotten that the one decisive factor in the rise of totalitarianism . . . is the existence of a large recently dispossessed middle class."[56]

This factor is correctly cited by Hayek, but he offers no theory for, and no program for, the nurturance and protection of the middle class. This is a flaw in his theory, if we take his own warnings about fascism seriously. We have provided, and will further justify, the theory that does have at its core the expansion and nurturance of the middle class.

For the moment, however, let us emphasize Hayek's warnings.

SAFEGUARDING DEMOCRACY FROM STATISM AND BUREAUCRATIC DESPOTISM

Any program for achieving greater equality in the modern world must successfully meet the objections presented by de Tocqueville, Weber, and Hayek.

The expansion of the power of the state and the creation of giant bureaucratic organizations must not be a by-product of programs for equality. The market economy, though corporate, oligopolistic, and conglomerative, must not be impeded in its entrepreneurial creativity. Nor should the economic sphere be fused with the state into a monolithic bureaucratic centrally-planned "leviathan." Government programs run by giant bureaus should not be allowed to extend their "tentacles" into the everyday lives of citizens. The right to privacy must be protected, and private initiative encouraged. In short, political and economic freedom should not be compromised in order to achieve equality.

Can programs for equality be established that will not lead us into bondage? Can a modicum of equality be achieved without violating the guidelines set forth by de Tocqueville, Weber, and Hayek?

We will attempt to operationalize a set of guiding principles and innovative safeguards that could create a structural framework within which programs for equality could be actualized without endangering or compromising individual freedom, law, or democracy.

Before answering the question—"Can greater equality be achieved without destroying democracy?"—a prior question must be answered: "Why establish any programs for equality at all? Wy not leave things as they would be in a society with a legal-democratic government and a corporate-capitalist market economy?"

The answer to that question is given by another set of questions: Do we want "Dickensesque" poverty, such as the situation with the homeless in the United States today, to mushroom? Do we want the rich to lose their commitment to the civic good, avoiding taxation and developing an amoral disconnection to the society with which they are enmeshed? Do we want the middle class to become divided, disempowered, and confused as they became in Italy, France, Germany, and Austria during the fascist period? Should we live with such a high rate of crime and violence emanating from among unemployed men? Do we want the stock market dizzying us with its soaring surges and sudden crashes? Should financial "insiders," "corporate raiders," and chief executive officers become fabulously rich, while the corporate economy declines, the middle class loses its stock holdings, and the poor collect in our railroad stations?

The "invisible hand of the market" does not, by itself, create economic well-being for the greatest number, and democratic stability cannot be maintained in the face of a polarizing class structure. If history tells us that we must help stabilize the corporate-capitalist economy and that we must nurture and expand the middle class in order to safeguard democracy, then we must adapt our theories to these realities. As Keynes put it, writing after the Depression and the rise of fascism, if we have a theory that parallel lines never meet, but in fact they tend to do so, we cannot merely "rebuke the lines." Rather we must improve and expand the theory to cover the reality of the actual situation. Thus, in the capitalist-democratic world, as it exists, we do need theories and programs for the creation of a greater relative equality.

However, if the reality of history also tells us that the expansion of the power of the state and the growth of giant bureaucracies threaten our freedom and could destroy forever the fragile legal-democratic system we are so proud to hold before the world, then theories, principles, and guidelines for the control of "statism" and bureaucratic authoritarianism must also be institutionalized.

We have already acquainted the reader with a set of theories and programs for the establishment of greater equality. These theories: (1) establish law and democracy as the only acceptable form of government; (2) oppose a centralized monolithic state; (3) accept a market economy; and (4) allow for a wide range of economic inequality.

None of these theories demands perfect equality, or state intervention to bring it about. All of these theories, however, warn that marked inequality can lead to political instability, violence, lawlessness, and the ruin of democracy. And all of these theories warn that completely unregulated market economics leads to excessive greed and selfishness, economic instability, and amorality in civic affairs.

Having established the need for theories and programs of *relative equality*, now let us establish the guidelines within which they must function in order that democracy be preserved, statism avoided, and bureaucracy controlled.

OPERATIONALIZING de TOCQUEVILLE, WEBER, AND HAYEK: "THE DOCTRINE OF LEAST HARM"

In order to operationalize the critique presented by de Tocqueville, Weber, and Hayek, let us establish a set of principles that will set the guidelines within which any modern program for equality—operating within the constraints of the legal-democratic system—would be limited.

First Principle

A. *Avoid programs so instituted as to increase the power of the state.*

The central warning emanating from the works of de Tocqueville, Weber, and Hayek is that "statism" will destroy a democratic, open society. Even the statism created to serve good intentions, such as the socialists and the welfare state advocates recommend, will have this overwhelmingly negative effect. Therefore, the avoidance of statism becomes absolutely essential if an open, democratic system is to be preserved.

This does not mean that social justice and social fairness must be abandoned. Even Hayek agreed, grudgingly, that a basic modicum of well-being ought to be a goal for any modern society. If such well-being could be created without state intervention, all the better.

Taking the warning against statism as a basic principle, *social programs should be designed so as to avoid statism wherever possible.*

The example of housing should help to illustrate how this principle should be operationalized.

Government planned, built, and administered housing should be avoided. Government housing is usually not only boring, uniform, and inadequate, but also contains within it the tentacles of control over population movement (and the possibility of reward and withholding for political purposes). Where the market, however, *cannot* provide adequate available housing—as, say, in the

United States now in terms of the lower middle class and the poor—such housing must be generated through governmental initiative.

The government initiative need not be statist in its structure. For example, after World War II, on Long Island, Levitt—a private builder given government incentives—created thousands of middle income suburban homes. He did so with government subsidies and got tax abatements for himself as a builder (and with G. I. Bill—and other—low interest, long-term mortgage assistance for the middle class buyers).

This kind of middle income housing program does not create the kind of government housing bureau whose bureaucracy could stultify the housing construction market, control family movement, or invade the privacy of home buyers.

In the same way, middle income condominiums and cooperatives could and should be generated. Examples of successful middle income programs abound throughout the nation.

In terms of low income housing the problem is more difficult, because low income housing requires more regulation and increased monetary subsidies. Regulation becomes necessary to protect the tenants from crime, vandalism, juvenile violence, vice, and drugs. Social work support teams, after school and pre-school programs, and extensive policing are usually necessitated in low income housing areas. Further, profit is not forthcoming from such housing.

What is the alternative? Increasing numbers of homeless poor accumulating in our cities and the expansion of emergency shelters—built and run by the city and state governments. Which is more statist and bureaucratic: emergency shelters, or housing projects for the poor?

To sum up our housing example, if housing is left to purely market forces, luxury housing tends to be overbuilt, middle income housing underbuilt, and low income housing ignored entirely. On the other hand, where government has taken over the process of creating housing, as in Eastern Europe, the housing has tended to be boringly uniform, poorly constructed, and inadequate in size and in quantity. Worse, the state has controlled population movement. Even in Sweden, where government housing is beautifully built and well planned, a housing shortage has continued to exist, and the building of individual houses has been inadequate.

The best alternative is a *modified market approach* utilizing government generated incentives, private builders, and private banks, to stimulate the market such that middle and low income housing becomes profitable and remains attainable.

The principle is clear, however. Avoid statism at all costs. Where social programs are necessitated, structure them—whenever possible—so that government initiatives are carried out by private organizations.

Some social programs, however, cannot be carried out by private organizations, but must be administered by the state. The collection of taxes falls into this category for instance. How can statism be contained in such cases?

B. *If a program for equality must be administered by the state then*:

1. a suitable checking institution, such as an ombudsman or a congressional watchdog committee, must be instituted along with it (and external to it);
2. legal limitations on its scope and the power of its officials must be clearly delineated at its inception.

There are certain programs, such as taxation and public education, which will be administered by the government. Statist control and harrassment definitely can emanate from such programs. Yet, since these programs cannot be dispensed with, they should be established with carefully empowered checking institutions set against them.

The Swedes have pioneered the ombudsman system, while the Anglo-Saxon countries have established the power of the courts in opposition to the power of the executive and legislative branches of government.

Later we will discuss both the ombudsman and court systems as "power-checking" institutions. Here we wish to establish the principle that whenever a social program must be established through the state, it must be checked in its power and scope by a countervailing institution. Along with the courts and the ombudsman, congress (parliament) should expand its watchdog role in this regard. Specific watchdog committees could be established—with the usual bi-partisan composition—to safeguard citizens' rights within government-administered social programs.

For example, both the tax bureau and the public schools have functioned reasonably well as state-administered programs. As disappointing as the public schools may seem, they have helped to establish the reality of modern mass democracy as a political system. And of course, as anxiety-producing as the tax bureau is, it provides the financial underpinning without which modern society cannot exist.

Such homilies aside, both government agencies contain within them the potential for authoritarian control and political harassment. In my view, citizens are insufficiently protected from, or represented in, either institution. As for the tax bureau, the citizen trembles with fear of an audit, and with the basic feeling that somehow the system is unfair. The fear generated by the tax bureau and the rigidity and mediocrity generated by some (though not all) public schools stand as a warning against government-run programs of any kind.

However, within a democratic system, even government programs can be checked in their power and can be improved in their delivery and service potentials. The Canadian Health Insurance Program is really quite excellently administered, for instance, while some public schools are remarkable in their educational and cultural impact, and even the tax bureau (I.R.S.) can be fought in the courts. The principle we wish to emphasize here is that further safeguards against statism need to be established wherever a social program is government-administered.

Second Principle

A. *If a program can be instituted either through the state or through private organizations, then it should be instituted through private organizations.*

In keeping with Weber on this issue, the principle should be followed that private organizations are more vulnerable to the courts and to union pressures than are governmental bureaucracies. This rule has not necessarily proved to hold in all cases, as corporate authoritarianism has grown over the years. (Cases of black-balling and surveillance have increased over the decades.[57]) Still, in these cases the legal-democratic government itself acts as the check on the private organizations, whereas checking the power of government agencies is a more complicated political affair.

It is worth mentioning here that private organizations are not necessarily more efficient than government bureaucracies. For instance, the Canadian Health Insurance agencies, run as provincial-government bureaus, have been as efficient, perhaps more efficient, than some of the U.S. private insurance companies, such as Blue Cross/Blue Shield. However, the principle still holds in terms of political power and the mushrooming of statism, that private organizations separated from government are the safer way to establish social services.

B. *Programs for equality administered privately must be universal in their reach and nondiscriminatory in terms of race, ethnicity, religion, creed, class, sex, or age.*

One of the problems with privately administered programs is that they tend toward exclusivity. Programs so administered, therefore, must, by law, service all citizens in terms of access and quality of services. For instance, if one compares the Canadian Health Insurance Program with the American private ones, one finds a shocking disparity. While the Canadian system provides excellent health care to all its citizens, the American system discriminates against the poor and the lower middle class, and service for the middle class varies from excellent and fully funded to mediocre and non-funded.

If a program such as health insurance is to be privately provided, then the legislature must make certain that it is provided well, and to all, and with equitable financial outlay for the citizens.

The principle of privately instituted progams will not be accepted if universality and equity of services cannot be established through it.

Third Principle

A. *Avoid the creation of new bureaucracies wherever possible; dismantle bureaucracies wherever a service can be delivered in another way.*

It is important to establish the principle of avoiding and dismantling bureaucracies. For once they are created, they often take on a life of their own, beyond the service for which they were created.

There is consideration at present in New York City of dismantling the Board of Education. Some think the public schools would function better without it. If they could, then they should.

Social programs can sometimes be established with a minimum of bureaucratic administration. For instance, housing and scholarship programs for the middle class would necessitate no increase at all in administration. While progressive, minimum, and luxury tax programs could be administered by the bureaucracies as they stand. Even universal health insurance programs, if established with computer-card, doctor-recipient reimbursement, could develop while keeping bureaucracy to a minimum.

Further, with a proper social policy, ill-designed bureaucracies could be dismantled. For instance, if careers and education for the poor are established, the odious welfare bureaucracy could be dismantled in the United States. So too could clinics for the poor be dismantled if a system of private doctors and insurance reimbursement for those doctors were established in place of those officious, demeaning, overcrowded facilities.

If educational and career programs for the poor and the unemployed working class are successfully established, prisons—those most repressive of state-run bureaucratic organizations—could slowly be dismantled as well. Furthermore, a system of community-based small scale mental health agencies (and supervised dwelling places) could allow for the abandonment of the giant state-run mental hospitals, whose reputation as "snake-pits" speaks for itself.

Social programs for the attainment of greater equality need not depend on the kind of giant bureaucratic structuring of society that Weber believed would create a "shell of bondage" from which the modern individual could never escape. Alternative, non-bureaucratic, locally based, or technologically administered programs can be conceived and established. A greater modicum of social fairness can be achieved while the "iron cage of bureaucracy" is avoided.

B.   *Where bureaucracies must be created and sustained—whether public or private—they must be*:

1. checked by a suitable external institution, such as an ombudsman, or checked by the legislature (or both);
2. the power of the elite managers of such bureaucracies must be balanced internally by a democratically elected board of directors;
3. those impacted by such a bureaucracy must be legally protected by a newly extended "Bill of Rights" applying to those affected by government, service, and corporate bureaucracies.

It is obvious that public bureaucracies not only can, but often do, act in an authoritarian manner toward the citizens they are supposed to be servicing. By their very existence, they increase the power of the centralized state. It is less obvious, however, that private bureaucracies can also act in an authoritarian manner. Ira Glasser, in *Doing Good*,[58] presents the case of nursing homes that took over the lives and the wealth of the elderly-infirm in their care. It took years of litigation[59] to begin to prevent these abuses. Paul Rosen, in *Bureaucracy Against Democracy and Socialism*,[60] presents the case of a private hospital that through case records defamed the reputations of patients who questioned procedures.

Whether a bureaucracy is public, such as the public schools or the department of highways, or private, like most of the nursing homes or institutions for the care of the mentally ill, its impact may be despotic.[61] Therefore all giant bureaucratic organizations should be checked by external institutions.

Many scholars and legal activists have been writing on the question of controlling the despotic tendencies within giant bureaucratic organizations. The consensus among them is that in order to limit the power of bureaucracies and protect the citizens from them: (1) A national and local ombudsman system should be established. The ombudsmen would act as the "people's defender" against bureaucracy. Donald Rowat[62] has written extensively on the system. The ombudsman would be empowered to investigate and prosecute bureaucratic organizations that violate the rights of citizens. Furthermore, by law, the elite managers would be held responsible for authoritarian or illegal activities. (2) Public, quasi-public,[63] and private bureaucracies would have to have a democratically elected board of directors[64] that would hold the power to hire and fire elite managers. And (3) the Bill of Rights would be extended to cover individuals employed by, or serviced by, public or private bureaucracies.[65]

Hopefully such a program, if institutionalized, could protect us from the kind of despotic control that de Tocqueville, Weber, and Hayek warned could, and would, emerge from both state and private bureaucracies.

Finally, in terms of the creation of, and administration of, social programs to create greater economic equality within democratic societies, the "doctrine of least harm" should be followed. That is, as delineated by Ira Glasser in *Doing Good*,[66] a social program should be so instituted as to create the least harm to the civil liberties of the citizens impacted by that program, and every effort should be made to extend our constitutional safeguards to the citizens involved with that program. Lastly, if a program—no matter how well meaning—unintentionally stifles the democratic rights of the citizens impacted by it, then that program should be dropped, no matter how humane its original intent.

This latter embodies the message of de Tocqueville, Weber, and Hayek to the modern democratic world. And the "doctrine of least harm" leads us away from the "road to serfdom."

A NOTE ON NONSOCIALIST SOURCES OF DESPOTISM AND SAFEGUARDS AGAINST THEM

de Tocqueville, Weber, and Hayek have alerted us to the despotic potential inherent in socialism. However, despotism can emanate from other sources. The power of the state can be enhanced and directed against the people through the expansion of institutions not at all connected to the creation of greater equality.

Obviously, the expansion of the power of the military sector of the state has in the past led to military despotism, while the executive branch of a polity has more often taken the form of a despotic kingship or dictatorship than a power-limited presidency. Further, the use of organized police and espionage power against the people has as often characterized states as not.

The point is that if we are serious about protecting democracy from the despotic potential of socialism, we should extend this analysis to cover the worrisome and expanding despotic potential inherent in the military, spy, police, and executive sectors of the state.

Fascist totalitarianism, for instance, though helped into existence by the socialist rejection of "bourgeois democracy," did not come into being as the result of the establishment of socialism. The turn toward militarism, the desire for a dictatorial executive to create "order," along with the rise of a charismatic-led mass movement (aided and abetted by a paramilitary organization) entrenched fascism in Italy and Germany (although socialist symbolism was used to recruit the people to its banner).

In today's world, the power of the state is being dramatically enhanced through nonsocialist sources. Every year, it seems, there is a scandal concerning the overuse of power by military, police, and spy bureaucracies. And, as is well known by now, the "imperial presidency," extending itself beyond constitutional bounds (through the control of ever-larger appointed staffs of functionaries) has become a reality of the modern mass democratic state.

Clearly, if we wish to maintain the laws and freedoms guaranteed to us by our constitution, we will have to create new power-checking institutions directed at controlling these expanding sectors of the modern state.

I have written of this elsewhere, in *The New Middle Class and Democracy*,[67] but in this context, I merely wish to make the point that if the socialist dream can become a "Brave New World"[68] nightmare, the expansion of the state through nonsocialist sources can lead us toward Orwell's bad dream.[69] The year 1984 may have come and gone, but "Big Brother" may still be waiting to watch over us.

The technology for surveillance and computer-compiled dossiers has lent the military, police, spy, and executive branch (and even private corporations) a terrifying new system of authoritarian control. Orwell's predictions could easily become reality given the new technology available for espionage.[70] Beyond the state, private corporations and service bureaus have been increasingly overstepping the bounds of the law in this regard.[71] Following this analysis out, a set of institutions should be developed to check the growing power of the military, policy, spy, executive, and private bureaucracies.

For instance, in Germany, building on institutions created in Sweden, three ombudsmen systems have been created.[72] The military ombudsman oversees citizen's complaints about military-authoritarianism, while the political ombudsman oversees the machinations of the executive branch, and the corporate ombudsman investigates complaints against private organizations. Each ombudsman system is set up like a federal court system, but possesses the constitutional power to investigate and prosecute cases for the protection of citizens' rights.

In conclusion, then, we wish to establish that the warnings of de Tocqueville, Weber, and Hayek on the threat to democratic processes emanating from state-administered programs of the socialist variety should be extended to other state-administered programs, and even to programs emanating from private bureaucracies. The power, size, and despotic potential of these nonsocialist sectors of the modern state and society has grown (along with the socially-oriented sector) as a threat to freedom, democracy, and law.

5

The Neoconservatives: Against Government Programs

The neoconservative position, on its theoretical level, is a defense of Enlightenment liberalism, which takes as its premise minimalist government, market economics, and competitive individualism. We have discussed liberalism in terms of the work of de Tocqueville and Hayek. In this vein, the works of Hobbes, Locke and J. S. Mill were revived, and the works of de Tocqueville and the contemporary Hayek were enshrined for their anti-socialist, pro-liberalist arguments.

However, the neoconservatives have produced modern works of their own as well. Scholars such as Robert Nozick[1] and Milton Friedman[2] have revived the theory of liberalism, and gone beyond it in their models. For instance, Nozick, writing to defend the minimalist state, utopianizes on the possibility of the *ultra-minimalist* state, or the "night watchman" state—a state with the barest functions of order and defense left to it. Friedman, for his part, wishes a return to laissez-faire economics—a laissez faire so complete as to rule out Social Security, the Federal Reserve Board, and even public schools.[3]

Theoretically, then, the neoconservative position begins with classic liberalism, but then attempts to extend it to its logical limits. In this project, the neoconservatives flirt with utopianism (Nozick even uses the term "utopia" in his title). And, as I shall suggest in the next chapter, utopian thinking, while abstractly interesting, can lead to serious problems, for the application of theory to social reality must deal with social *reality*, not with utopian *fantasy*. Ironically, this is the very pit the romantic socialists fell into (and that the neoconservatives are so quick to warn against when referring to the socialists).

The neoconservative revival of "Whig" liberalism did not occur in a vacuum—it was not generated by an abstract intellectual exercise. Rather, it arose in direct reaction to the tumultuous events of the 1960s, which threatened the foundations upon which this nation was built. The neoconservatives were reacting to the demands of the black civil rights movement, the sexual revolution of the new "hippy" youth culture, the women's movement, the gay-rights movement, and finally, to the revival of radicalism (and the new anti-Americanism) that occurred as the Vietnam war heated up the "Cold War" into a hot war.

Not only did the neoconservatives react against the disruptions created by these events themselves, but also against the responses to these events by the Kennedy–Johnson administrations (and by the Supreme Court). The neoconservatives did not favor the direction of governmental policy during this era, and worked mightily to change that direction.

It should be established that many of the neoconservatives were *not* conservatives in the usual American sense, as epitomized, let us say, by Barry Goldwater, and Robert Taft before him. Although they joined with the conservatives in their attack on the social policies of the late 1960s and early 1970s, many of the neoconservatives were actually anti-socialist liberals. Though opposing the programs developed by the Johnson administration (and pushed by the courts of the Johnson era), many of the neoconservatives do favor certain other social programs—especially programs designed to engender greater equality of opportunity.

What the neoconservatives do share in common is a deep commitment to: individualist competitive striving and meritocratic reward[4]—the American dream of working hard and raising oneself up by one's own bootstraps; minimalist government—or "that government which governs least"; and a stern rejection of the Johnson programs that attempted to redress the grievances of groups that had been left behind in the competitive race for success in American society. Affirmative action programs, court-ordered quotas, and government programs geared to redressing the past grievances of blacks, women, and other minorities were vehemently criticized by the neoconservatives (for reasons we will describe shortly).

Among the most prominent of the neoconservatives are Irving Kristol and Norman Podhoretz, both scholars and journalists well known for their anti-socialist positions.[5] They continue to espouse a hardline conservativism on social and foreign policy issues.[6]

During the crest of the neoconservative tide, Daniel Patrick Moynihan, now a U.S. senator, but also a sociologist and Harvard academic, and Nathan Glazer (also a sociologist) authored and co-authored a series of books, articles, and studies lambasting the affirmative action and quota hiring programs initiated by the Johnson administration and continued into the Nixon administration. Nathan Glazer published an entire volume against the quota hiring systems,[7] while Moynihan's "The Moynihan Report"[8] (on the black family) and *Maximum Feasible Misunderstanding*,[9] along with his policy alternative—"benign neglect"[10]—became the rallying cry for the entire neoconservative movement.

Moynihan and Glazer, however, while sharply criticizing the Johnson programmatic efforts, do favor strong governmental programs for the improvement of the condition of the poor. As we will see, Moynihan and Glazer favor precisely the programs that we have made central—especially the "Aristotelian" career programs for the poor. In fact Moynihan is sponsoring the "workfare" bill in the Senate (1988).

Seymour Martin Lipset[11] and Daniel Bell,[12] academic sociologists at Stanford and Harvard, respectively, wrote articles and books opposing the governmental policies of the late 1960s and early 1970s. Both wrote in the spirit of "Whig" or Enlightenment liberalism and with a background of anti-Marxist criticism. But Lipset and Bell never characterized themselves as conservatives, "neo-" or otherwise. Bell, especially, bristles at being termed a neoconservative and strongly favors government programs directed toward the improvement of "equality of opportunity" for the lower classes.

However, like it or not, Bell's "Coda for the Future" in his best selling book, *The Coming of Post Industrial Society*,[13] has been oft-quoted by the neoconservatives, for it contains a powerful theoretical argument against the principle of "equality of end result" and against compensatory hiring and university admissions programs.

Finally, after a decade of neoconservative assault on the "War on Poverty" programs of the Johnson era, a book appeared that summarized, supported, and backed with data, the whole of the neoconservative argument. That book is *Losing Ground*[14] by Charles Murray.

Murray asserted that the poor were not helped by the programs of the "War on Poverty," and that, in fact, their condition was made worse by these governmental efforts. In *Losing Ground*, Murray produced the most devastating critique of the social programs of the post-Kennedy era written in our time. His book became the "bible" of the neoconservative movement. From the point of the publication of this volume onward, the advocates of governmental programs for the solution of the social ills of poverty had to, and have to, answer to Murray's critique.

Any argument *for* governmental social programs will now have to come to grips with Murray's data and his powerfully presented neoconservative policy positions. With Murray, we do not have an abstract theoretical critique, such as that of de Tocqueville or Hayek, but rather a direct hands-on criticism of the specific programs undertaken during the Johnson–Nixon eras.

Since, in this volume, we have argued for social programs designed to help balance the class structure in the direction of an expansion of the middle class, and since this includes a raising up of the poor, we will have to come to grips with Murray's position (as it embodies the entire neoconservative critique). Let us turn to this task now.

CHARLES MURRAY: *LOSING GROUND*

If any single book epitomizes the neoconservative critique of the social policy of the 1960s, it is Charles Murray's *Losing Ground*. Murray mounts an assault on the Johnson–Nixon job and educational programs, showing rather convincingly that they failed to help the poor rise to middle class status.

Murray's criticisms fall into three major categories:

1. Welfare payments, the negative income tax, food stamps, and other programs which give *money* to the poor, discourage work motivation and encourage dependency. In the long run, they fail to help the poor.

2. Programs that facilitate equality of opportunity should be established and perfected. However, programs attempting to create equality of result—such as affirmative action hiring and educational quotas—are dangerous and misguided. They push the unqualified poor ahead, and destroy the success-through-merit spirit of the "American dream."

3. Job-training and job-creation programs, though in principle correct, have in reality failed. Employment rates for the poor declined under their impact, and the status of the working poor dropped as well.

Let us look at each of these observations by Murray in turn. For, if programs for the poor are to be successful in the future, they must avoid the mistakes of the past.

Work vs. Welfare: No More "Leaky Jar" Solutions

Murray points out correctly that the welfare system, in its present form, was inherited from the New Deal. However, the New Dealers had intended it as a temporary support system for widows with children. Such widows, in the 1930s, would by and large become re-absorbed into the extended family. Long-term dependency on welfare payments was unusual.

The New Deal sponsors of AFDC (Aid for Dependent Children) had intended to help the widow with small children. The support she received would tide her over in the interim between the loss of her husband and the day when the children were old enough to take over support. . . . From this innocuous beginning AFDC evolved into the bete noire of the social welfare system.[15]

After WWII, however, the welfare system spread in rural and urban poverty areas, becoming a long-term—even inter-generational—dependency system. The massive emigration from rural to urban areas, along with the black migration from the South to the North, inadvertently produced a new structural situation.

By the fifties it had become embarrassingly, outrageously clear that most of the women were not widows. Many of them had not even been married. Worst of all, they didn't stop having babies after the first lapse. . . . This had not been part of the plan.[16]

The New Dealers had not intended the welfare system to arise as a permanent support system, nor had they intended to discourage work. Yet the welfare system, as it evolved, not only discouraged work but also encouraged family disintegration. These latter phenomena must be understood within the context of urban poverty and racial exclusion from dwindling union jobs. Nonetheless, the results were disastrous, as Murray stresses.

The very existence of a welfare system was assumed to have the inherent, intrinsic, unavoidable effect of undermining the moral character of the people. Not working is easier than working; not saving is easier than saving; shirking responsibility for parents and spouses and children is easier than taking responsibility. . . . By the late fifties, widespread dissatisfaction had developed with this state of affairs.[17]

The Kennedy administration's response was, in my view and Murray's, the correct response. The Kennedy advisors (in "Aristotelian" fashion) decided to shift the emphasis from welfare dependency to work and independence.

Kennedy recognized . . . the disgruntlement with the welfare system. The essence [of his response] was expressed in the slogan . . . "Give a hand, not a handout". . . .

By shifting the focus of welfare policy away from the dole and *towards escape from the dole*, Kennedy brought the federal government into a role that it had barely considered in the past: not maintaining a WPA as an emergency measure to relieve unemployment, but instead taking a *continuing responsibility* for helping Americans to help themselves.[18]

Murray is pointing out two factors here. One, that the Kennedy administration program was correctly directed toward work, not welfare—and this Murray favors. But two, that the Kennedy administration wrongly established the idea of long-term government involvement: Having worked on the first pilot project of the new Kennedy program, "Mobilization for Youth," I can relate with vivid remembrance both the feeling of elation generated by the "job-independence" idea, and the feeling of despondency engendered by the size of the population that needed help, and most of all, the degraded condition that we found them in.

It was these latter factors—the immense size of the poverty group and their shocking social condition—that fostered the long-term view. This did not emerge from a policy principle, as Murray seems to suggest. Actually, the Kennedy people were *very hesitant* about the long-term aspect of this attempt but, given the enormity and severity of the problem, moved ahead with caution.

The Kennedy premise was that: most of the able-bodied on welfare would work if given the opportunity. Their program: Train the chronically unemployed, train the youngsters growing up without skills or resources, help them get that first job. Their promise: The able-bodied will be on their way to permanent self-sufficiency.[19]

Before these programs got off the ground, Kennedy was assassinated, and a cataclysm of social disruptions altered the course of events. The Kennedy programs might have failed, but we will never know because the social situation and the political leadership changed. Murray recognizes this.

Through 1964, the rationale for new social action programs was the one set by Kennedy: The government should take a more active role in helping people get on their feet. Then new agendas, new assumptions, and a rush of events (not the least of them Vietnam) complicated the situation.[20]

At first, it looked as if the Kennedy program would simply be implemented and expanded by Johnson.

Johnson lost no time in implementing the Kennedy rhetoric. . . . The bill was a faithful attempt to follow the "hand, not a handout" script. It provided for job-training, part-time jobs for teenagers and college students, community anti-poverty projects, loans to low income farmers and businessmen, and the establishment of VISTA, the domestic Peace Corps. There was not a handout in the lot. . . . Johnson was careful to point out that . . . "The days of the dole in this country are numbered."[21]

Then, everything changed. The black civil rights movement became militant; riots swept the northern cities and the horrors of ghetto life were described by a new generation of black writers. Jobs for blacks in the administrative aspects of the government programs were demanded, and "the system" in the North was denounced as racist like its Southern counterpart. "White backlash" against this "black anger" had hardly been absorbed when the Vietnam war was dramatically expanded by the Johnson administration.

And, in the midst of the turmoil of demonstrations and counter-demonstrations generated by the new hot-war in Vietnam, the youth rebellion, the sexual revolution, and the women's movement erupted. A social revolution of monumental proportions tore the fabric of American society asunder before a cautious job program initiated by the Kennedy administration to replace the welfare system could be truly tested, adjusted, or improved.

The job program had barely been begun—the actual career-line jobs had never even been established—and no real evaluation of the program could occur. As Murray correctly observes:

From 1964 to the end of 1967 . . . social policy [changed] . . . a social program could hardly be constructed on grounds that simply guaranteed equality of *outcome*. A hand was not enough.[22]

Militant blacks, and then Latins, and finally women, demanded more than just jobs and job training. They demanded redress from a system that had denied them opportunity for a century or more. Whether this demand was justified or not, it produced a shift in policy that would polarize American society. For while there was little reaction against the job programs, there was tremendous negative reaction against the "affirmative action" programs.

Affirmative Action was destined to be one of the most highly charged legacies of the Great Society. . . . The disadvantaged were to be given something more than just an equal chance, they were also to be given a leg up. It was a sensible and just response to a history of exploitations, in the view of its advocates, race discrimination in reverse, according to its critics.[23]

Since this shift from the job programs of the Kennedy era to the affirmative action programs of the Johnson years was, and is, so controversial, before analyzing the fate of the job programs we should look further at this issue. For it was, along with the Vietnam war, one of the major factors that produced the neoconservative reaction.

Equality of Opportunity vs. Equality of End Results

Opposition to job programs existed, but it was slight compared to the earthquake of reactions against hiring quotas based on race, sex, or minority group status. Liberals, such as Theodore White and Daniel Patrick Moynihan, who had been staunch Kennedy supporters, turned against the Johnson programs. Anti-socialist liberals such as Irving Kristol, Daniel Bell, Seymour Martin Lipset, and others, joined with conservatives in condemning the affirmative action ideal.

As Murray describes this opposition:

Theodore White (among many others) describes the shift from "equality of opportunity" to "equality of outcome" as a fundamental change. [By 1965] Lyndon Johnson was proclaiming the . . . battle "not just for equality as a right and theory but equality as a fact and equality as a result." A few months later, Executive Order 11246 required "affirmative action." By 1967, people who opposed *preferential measures* for minorities to overcome the legacy of discrimination were commonly seen as foot-draggers on civil rights if not closet racists.[24]

Daniel Bell, in his best-selling *The Coming of Post-Industrial Society*, would add an entire section, in his chapter, "A Coda for the Future," analyzing what he believed were the negative effects of affirmative action programs on American society.

[W]ithout public debate, an entirely new principle of rights has been introduced into the polity. . . . The principle has changed from discrimination to representation. Women, Blacks, and Chicanos are to be employed as a matter of right, in proportion to their number, and the principle of professional qualification or individual achievement is subordinate to the new ascriptive principle of corporate identity. . . . Furthermore, quotas and preferential hiring mean that standards are bent or broken . . . [25]

Bell, like most of the neoconservatives, is opposed to discrimination of any kind, and favors programs for equality of opportunity.

If there is discrimination—on the basis of sex, or color, or religion, or any category extraneous to the stated one of professional qualifications—there is no genuine equality of opportunity.[26]

For Bell, and for most of the liberals who joined with the neoconservatives in their rejection of affirmative action, programs for the implementation of equality of opportunity reinforce the American dream of competition, hard work, and success, whereas affirmative action programs, by pushing ahead the less qualified and recognizing *group* categories (rather than individual merits), distort the process of free competition and upward mobility.

As a principle, equality of opportunity denies the precedence of birth, of nepotism, of patronage or any other indicator which allocates place, other than fair competition open equally to talent and ambition.[27]

Bell goes so far as to predict that the institutionalization of affirmative-action, quota-oriented hiring could destroy the entire order of American society. This position has been reiterated by Moynihan, in so many speeches, and by Podhoretz, Kristol, Lipset, and others, in so many journalistic articles.[28]

In short, can the principle of quota representation in the polity, defined along communal or particularistic lines, escape either the polarization or the fragmentation of the polity and the fact of ataxia for the society?[29]

Having established his dislike and distrust for affirmative action, Bell then reaffirms his commitment to equality of opportunity. I quote this because it is the credo of the liberals-turned-neoconservative:

The idea of equality of opportunity is a just one, and the problem is to realize it fairly. *The focus, then, has to be on the barriers to such equality.*[30]

Murray reiterates this neoconservative credo as forcefully as it can be stated:

Billions for equal opportunity, not one cent for equal outcome—such is the slogan to inscribe on the banner of whatever cause my proposals constitute. Their common theme is to make it possible to get as far as one can go on one's merit, hardly a new ideal in American thought.[31]

We will have more to say about equality of opportunity and the neoconservative commitment to it later. Now, let us present Murray's most devastating critique—that the job programs of the Johnson era failed.

The Job Programs Fail

The job programs initiated by the Kennedy administration were supposed to replace the welfare system. However, Kennedy was killed, and his programs had barely three years of operation. The welfare system was, of course, not phased out, nor were the job programs ever fully or properly phased in. Though it was hoped by the Kennedy followers that Johnson—the master legislator—

would pass the Kennedy programs and expand them, this did not occur as expected. The Johnson programs, though seeming to follow the Kennedy guidelines, were: (1) phased in through politicians, rather than social science professionals—the politicians, where honest, usually did not fully understand the intent or scope of the programs, and where dishonest, simply used the programs for local patronage; (2) administered through community action organizations, rather than universities, unions, or corporations—the career and socialization goals of the original programs were lost sight of, while the maintenance and leadership of the community-based organizations became the issue; and (3) these Johnson programs came to focus on everything *except* career-line job mobility for the poor in under-serviced spheres of society.

Thus the major focus of the Kennedy effort was lost sight of in the Johnson years. This is why the Johnson program produced such meager results. Murray observes that,

Each project had its own tale to tell about why it failed—an ambitious city councilman who tried to horn in, a balky banker who reneged on a tentative agreement, and so on. There were always villains and heroes, dragons and maidens. But failure was very nearly universal.[32]

The case of Oakland is typical and can illustrate just why the job programs failed.

The course of the projects followed a pattern. To see how this worked in practice, we have the example of . . . the urban development program in Oakland. . . . The program was an assortment of community-run economic development projects bankrolled by the government . . . *2,200 jobs* were to be provided, and more were to follow from "spinoffs." These jobs would go to the unemployed residents of the inner city.

As far as its national publicity told the story, the program was a great success. A book (*Oakland's Not For Burning*) was in the bookstores by 1968, claiming that the program "may have made the difference" in preventing a riot in Oakland . . . [33]

I must comment at this point that it may very well have been that the Johnson urban projects *did* prevent riots, and not just in Oakland. But, as we shall see, they did not provide career-line jobs for the poor.

It was not until a year after these stories had appeared that the *Los Angeles Times* printed a follow-up story revealing that [the program] had never gotten beyond the planning stage. *All told, only twenty jobs had been created.* . . . The authors of the case study . . . concluded that the effect of the project on "despair and disillusionment" among blacks was probably to have made matters worse.[34]

This last is the key: The actual jobs promised by the urban community projects never really materialized. Since the jobs were not provided, can we really call these job programs?

I remember two projects I was associated with. One was Haryou-Act in New York City, the other Model Cities in New London, Connecticut. Both programs were riddled with conflict between black and white administrators. Both were inefficient to the point of paralysis. And one, Haryou-Act, became graft-ridden and corrupt as New York City officials grabbed for a portion of the generous funding from Washington. What is critical is that neither program provided career-line jobs for the poor as they were supposed to. With the Kennedy advisors and social workers gone, nobody in the Johnson programs seemed to know that stable jobs were the intended goal for the projects in their attempt to help the poor!

In New London, in the Model Cities program (to which I became a consultant), a number of able black leaders were found to head the program, but *no* jobs were created beyond these three administrative positions themselves! The black leaders used the project to launch their political careers, and they were effective as politicians. As for the poor blacks, aside from being dragged into occasional community meetings and encouraged to express their hostility and outrage at the conditions in which they lived, their job needs were never even addressed nor was a job-training or job-placement program ever undertaken for them.

Thus, from Oakland to New London, from Phoenix to Atlantic City, the Johnson poverty programs, although well-funded, did not provide work or socialization support—the mainstays of the Kennedy ideal.

Furthermore, as Murray goes on to show, the job-training programs were also a failure. Many of these Johnson job-training programs were well-staffed and seemingly well-run. Why were they so much less effective then expected?

The failure of the training programs was a greater surprise still. These of all programs were expected to be a sure bet. . . . The programs were seldom disasters, they simply failed to help many people get and hold jobs that they would not have gotten and held anyway.[35]

The problem with the job-training programs was that the Johnson people were naive about the conditions and attitudes of the poor. Whereas the Kennedy programs had been administered by social workers, provided by the leading social work schools, such as Columbia University School of Social Work,[36] and N.Y.U.,[37] the Johnson programs were administered by city politicians, government bureaucrats, and black-activist leaders.

The Kennedy programs recognized at their inception that the poor might be: educationally disadvantaged, on drugs, unreliable in work habits, hostile, teen-pregnant, involved with criminality, vice, and gang violence. This is why social work-administrators were brought in. The re-socialization of the poor to middle class work habits and interaction patterns was a taken-for-granted part of the job-training process, given as central a role as the inculcation of job-related skills.

I remember some of the social workers at "Mobilization for Youth" in New

York City romanticizing the poor for their "spontaneous expression of sexuality" and "unrepressed expression" of rightful "hostile feelings." But few were naive about the condition of the poor socially, educationally, or morally. The Johnson bureaucrats seemed to know nothing of this.

It was quickly learned that people on welfare do not necessarily enroll in job programs once they become available. Those who enroll do not necessarily stick it through to the end of the program. Those who stick it through do not necessarily get jobs. And, of those who find jobs, many quickly lose them. Sometimes they lose them because of their lack of seniority when layoffs occur. Sometimes they lose them because of discrimination. Sometimes they lose them because they fail to show up for work or don't work very hard when they do show up. And—more often than anyone wanted to admit—people just quit, disappearing from the evaluator's score card.[38]

Another problem with the Johnson programs was that they focused largely on teenage youths for their training programs. Yes, these young men needed the jobs most, but they were also the most hostile, violent, sexual, and difficult population among the poor. Again, the Kennedy programs included a massive street-worker involvement in the pacification of these youths, before and during the training process.[39] And again, the Johnson programs usually dispensed with this kind of social work support. As Murray points out, " . . . the effort was concentrated on . . . disadvantaged youths in their late teens and early twenties . . . they were supposed to be the most trainable. . . ."[40]

Of course this group turned out to be the most difficult group to succeed with. I should point out—and Murray fails to point this out—that teenage girls were much more trainable than the boys. They did continue to get pregnant, but even with this, they socialized more quickly to middle class behavior and dress standards (some of the girls becoming quite stylish in a sophisticated, rather than a street, way), and they picked up job skills quickly. In general, the girls were less resistant and less hostile than the boys.[41]

Nonetheless, Murray is correct about the difficulty with the boys, and the girls did continue to get pregnant at a very early age. The teenage "gang" kids turned away from the Johnson bureaucrats, who couldn't really deal with them and seemed not to be providing them with the jobs they had expected to receive, or the skills that would allow them to find jobs on their own. Murray is correct that

in the late 1960s—at the very moment when the job programs began their massive expansion—the black youth unemployment rate began to rise again, steeply, and continued to do so throughout the 1970s. . . . If the 1950s were not good years for young blacks (and they were not), the 1970s were much worse.[42]

As we have pointed out, and as Murray makes central, the job and job-training programs of the late 1960s and 1970s simply did not train and enroll poor workers in long-term, career-line jobs. Failing this, the young poor turned toward other forms of survival—that is, crime, vice, drugs, and welfare. We were back to square one.

Aristotle pointed out centuries ago that the poor turn to "petty crime" if not provided with careers and property and integrated politically into the society. America's ethnic immigrant groups, in their early phase of assimilation at the turn of the century through to the 1940s, in fact turned to crime wherever their legitimate mobility was blocked or slowed.[43] One need only view the George Raft and Edward G. Robinson gangster–prison movies to bring back the image of the hero–mobsters who turned to crime as a way of "making it big, quick" in America.

Because in the late 1960s the job market and the job programs were failing to absorb the poor youth, they, like their ethnic predecessors, turned to crime with a vengeance. The drug trade was expanding and opportunities to push drugs, as well as the need to support a drug habit, drew the poor into crime. Drug pushers and drug dealers are seen as so heroic in poverty neighborhoods that the electronic "beeper"—used by drug dealers "on call," like surgeons and physicians—has become the symbol of success in the urban ghetto.

Furthermore, the middle class was newly accumulating expensive high-tech luxury goods, such as high performance cars, stereos and video equipment, ten speed bicycles, and so on—and these were ripe for stealing and fencing.

People survive. Large and increasing numbers of young persons in the 1960s were no longer in the job market, or were in the job market only intermittently, or were unsuccessful at finding a job when they tried. Large numbers of them were functionally illiterate and without skills that the larger society values. . . . One of the ways they were surviving was through crime. In the mid 1960s . . . the number of people engaging in criminal activity— and the number of their victims—increased explosively. The people who suffered most from this change were urban blacks.[44]

The crime rate soared. Crimes of violence along with petty theft went "off the charts" as compared with the other industrialized nations of the world.

[A]t 1970 levels of homicide, a person who lived his life in a large American city ran a greater risk of being murdered than an American soldier in the Second World War ran of being killed in combat. If this analysis were restricted to the ghettos of large American cities, the risk would be some order of magnitude larger yet.[45]

As Murray goes on to point out, "the most conspicuous local success stories were drug dealers, pimps, and fences."[46]

Since the job programs were never properly institutionalized and failed to provide large numbers of career-line jobs, and since poor youths do not have the educational skills to qualify for the expanding technocratic and white collar job world, crime and welfare, once again, became favorable alternatives for survival.

In the day to day experience of a youth growing up in a black ghetto, there was no evidence whatsoever that working within the system paid off. The way to get something from the system was to be sufficiently a failure to qualify for help, or to con the system.[47]

THE NIXON–FORD–CARTER YEARS: BACK TO THE "LEAKY JAR"

With the job programs in disarray and with the Vietnam war draining away the monetary resources needed to create jobs, the poverty programs regressed toward "leaky jar" solutions. It was during the Nixon years that massive amounts of money and in-kind services were provided to the poor, increasing their dependent conditions.

As ineffective as the Johnson program was, it was at least pointed in the right direction. With the coming of Nixon, Ford, and Carter, the programs became misguided, and the massive funding—although humane in its short-term effect—was wasted. The ironic part of this is that much more money was spent during these years than during the Johnson years.

In terms of real expenditures on social programs, the Johnson years were more like the Kennedy and Eisenhower years than they were like the Nixon, Ford, and Carter years. . . . Using constant 1980 dollars . . . we find that during the five Johnson years (fiscal 1965–1969), the federal government spent a total of $6.6 billion on public aid. This was $30 billion more than was spent during the five preceding years. . . . But in the five years immediately after Johnson, public aid spending rose by $80 billion.[48]

Following the theoretical framework we have been outlining, it is not surprising that during the years when money and services were given to the poor, progress in reducing poverty declined, and the poor were left in a situation where "the act of taking" simply left them in a situation where they then had "to ask for more."

It was 1972 when progress on net poverty slowed. . . . Thereafter, net poverty failed to sustain additional reductions. In 1979, net poverty stood at 6.1 percent of the population, compared with 6.2 percent in 1972, despite more than a doubling of real expenditure on in-kind assistance during the interim. . . . *Huge increases in expenditures coincided with an end to progress.*[49]

Most of the programs initiated during the Nixon–Ford–Carter years were humane programs undertaken to improve the everyday condition of the poor, but they were not designed to move the poor out of poverty. The food-stamp program, the Medicaid program, and the expansion of welfare allotments were all initiated by good people concerned with the deteriorated condition of the poor.

The food stamp program under Lyndon Johnson began with 424,000 participants in 1965. When Johnson left office, it served 2.2 million people. In the first two Nixon years, that number doubled. By the end of the next two it had quintupled. By 1980, the number of participants had grown to 21.1 million—fifty times the coverage of the original Great Society legislation.[50]

Along with the food stamp programs (and an expensive, yet still inadequate medical program), a "welfare rights" movement succeeded in increasing the welfare allotments in AFDC and other welfare categories. Ironically, this "welfare rights" movement was initiated and organized by Richard Cloward, Francis Fox Piven, Sherman Barr, and other social workers originally attached to the Kennedy job programs. As they watched the job programs become distorted and the job-placement program evaporate, they demanded that the poor not be abandoned altogether. If the poor were not going to be provided with jobs—and it seemed that they were not—then their welfare coverage should be expanded to include warmer clothing for their children, telephone service, more nutritious food, toiletries and medical necessities, and so on.

The "welfare rights" advocates were correct that the welfare allotments were too meager to sustain even a poor quality of life. They saw children who were cold and hungry, adults who had no razor blades to shave with, no disinfectant to put on a cut. These facts were true and were shameful in an America famous for its over-production of food, clothing, and pharmaceuticals.

But—these advocates for the poor inadvertently shifted the base of the funding toward programs that could provide little or no long-term improvements in the living conditions of the poor. Poor children were now more likely to show up at school well dressed and healthier—which is good, who can say this is not good? But these children were just as likely to drop out and drift into crime, vice, and welfare as before.

And worse, these humanitarian intellectuals, by pressing for an expansion of welfare benefits and by publicizing this demand, inadvertently fueled the backlash against the poor that would eventuate in the curtailment of the very funding they were pressing for.

Further, by abandoning the job, career, and educational orientation of the Kennedy programs in favor of the demand for more and higher welfare payments, these liberal intellectuals confused the public and the politicians. For now, liberals became identified with the welfare system—the very system the liberals had said should be replaced. And conservatives, who opposed the Kennedy job programs, now demanded that the poor be put to work! Confusion reigned for years, and is only now yielding to a newly focused view of the problem.

The Reagan reaction against the welfare rights advocates was, in part, justified, although we will show that taking welfare programs away from the poor is no more a solution than increasing welfare payments. Before we get to the Reagan years, however, we must discuss another "leaky jar" solution suggested during the Nixon years. This program was advocated by conservative intellectuals. To show just how misdirected the effort to reduce poverty became during the Nixon—

Ford–Carter years, a description of the experimental "negative income tax" program is illustrative.

Murray calls the negative income tax "welfare for working people," because instead of establishing government funding payable for *work* beyond wages earned during regular hours, or payable for *merit* promotions within the job ladder, the negative income tax simply provides funds—with no work-increase proviso—for those earning incomes below the poverty line.

Strangely, Nixon, who had always been a vehement critic of welfare, became enamored of the negative income tax after coming under the influence, not of the liberal-humanists, but of Milton Friedman, a conservative economist, whom we have discussed in our chapter on Keynes.

Nixon had lambasted the Great Society during his 1968 campaign. His administration promptly set about dismantling its appurtenances (for example OEO). But it was Nixon who, only six years after the first antipoverty bill, introduced the Family Assistance Plan (FAP), a form of negative income tax. . . . Conservative economists, not liberal reformers, had first advocated a negative income tax as a replacement for the existing welfare system.[51]

The FAP program was not actually passed by congress, but pilot projects all over the nation were initiated. There were experimental programs established in New Jersey, Pennsylvania, Iowa, North Carolina, (Gary) Indiana, (Denver) Colorado, and (Seattle) Washington.

In each site, a sample of low-income person was selected and randomly split into two groups. . . . [T]he experimental group were told that for three years they would receive a floor put under their incomes . . . the members of the control group received no benefits.

With vigor and enormous detail, the scientists validated not the sponsors hopes, but their fears. . . . The key question was whether a negative income tax reduced work effort. The answer was yes.[52]

The negative income tax, then, is not a good program for the poor. However, it should be pointed out that it could be linked to work motivation. That is, government subsidies could be offered to the working poor in the form of overtime or merit payments. The situation would be the same as that in any union-organized arrangement, except that employers would be subsidized to make such payments. Such a program could increase work incentive and reward the working poor for their extra efforts.

However, such a program would also cause jealousy and backlash from regular union workers if it were not extended equally to them, even though their salary base-pay is much higher than that of the working poor. Therefore, while I have argued for progressive taxation in this treatise, the negative income tax idea is just simply too riddled with difficulties, too counter-productive in its effects, to be successful in the American context.

Finally, the negative income tax, as it was proposed under the Nixon administration (the Family Assistance Program) should not be confused with the European and Canadian "Universal Family Allowance Program." This latter program supplies government funding to families in order to help defer child-rearing costs. Low fertility rates in Germany, France, Scandinavia, and Canada prompted the passage of this child-support program. The Universal Family Allowance Program, which provides a small monthly allowance for each child, paid to the mother, has been well received in Europe and Canada and has not been problematic in terms of work-motivation (though it has not stimulated the birth rate).

Such a program, if introduced in the United States, could be similarly instituted as in Europe for the American middle class, but would be more effective for the poor if given as in-kind payments, such as subsidized day-care, pre-school, school, and college scholarship programs (this latter to retain consistency with our principle that you don't just give money to the poor).

Before analyzing Murray's position and attempting to operationalize his program, one more topic central to the neoconservative critique of the programs of the late 1960s and early 1970s must be discussed. Let us examine education—the key to the door of opportunity in America, and one of the central areas of debates between liberals, conservatives, and neoconservatives.

EDUCATION: STOPPING THE "REVOLVING DOOR"

The educational gap between the poor and the middle class is monumental, and the gap between the black poor and the middle class is greater yet. Liberal educationalists took note of this in the early 1960s. They saw that both the rural and the urban poor did badly in the public school system, as it was structured at that time. Further, the public schools were deficient for the middle class children as well: compared with their European counterparts, American middle class children were learning far less (catching up only in the later college years, if at all).

The liberals tried to reform and improve the schools through a kind of "Summerhill"[53] approach—a small-group, democratic—discussion, nonauthoritarian, "open-classroom" approach. In fairness to the liberal educators, they also attempted to bring math and science into the curriculum through new and innovative programs.[54] They also brought literature, art, theater, music, and cultural enrichment programs to the schools.[55]

The nonauthoritarian approach was not a total failure with middle and upper middle class children coming from nonauthoritarian families. However, this "Summerhill" approach did lead to a kind of laxity that eventuated in a decline of the performance levels of the middle class children on high school and college entrance exams.

If the liberal reforms were mildly unsuccessful with middle class children, they were completely unsuccessful with lower class children. Poor children, in many cases, simply ran wild in the school's hallways and yards. And, while the open-classroom groups were geared to each child's developmental level, most poor kids were so far behind ("educationally deprived," as we used to term it) that they could not catch up. Many of them began to withdraw, became truant, and eventually dropped out.

To make matters worse, the liberals believed that to leave a child back was to socially stigmatize that child, and therefore they pushed children ahead even though they could not do the work. Although seemingly psychologically sound, this policy served to reduce the motivation of children who could have pulled through with long-term effort. The attitude instilled was, "Why bother, I'll be promoted anyway."

The liberal experiment in helping the poor failed. The drop-out rate reached epidemic proportions. The test scores of poor children, and especially black poor children, on grade school examinations and college entrance tests dropped precipitously in the 1970s. As mentioned, SAT scores for middle class children also declined.

The message was clear. The schools had to be improved for both the poor and the middle class—but especially for the poor, for whom the system, as it stood, was a colossal failure.

[A]s of 1980 the gap in educational achievement between black and white students leaving high school was so great that it threatened to defeat any other attempts to narrow the economic differences separating blacks from whites. . . . As of 1980, the mean SAT score of blacks was 330 for the verbal test and 360 for the math test, more than 100 points lower in each test than the mean for whites.[56]

Murray is correct that a re-emphasis on basic reading and mathematics became necessary, along with a re-imposition of school authority and promotion by merit. And it is interesting that it has been *black* educators around the nation who have pressed for a tougher, more tightly controlled school structure and merit promotions.[57]

It should be pointed out, however, that Murray does not criticize the pre-school or college "prep" programs that were generated by the liberal reformers of the 1960s. These programs worked. The college prep programs, which are now being revived both privately[58] and publicly,[59] have been succeeding with a very high ratio of the students they service.

The pre-school program's results are harder to pin down, because the gains can be lost if follow-up support is not supplied to the children once they are in grade school. Conservative ideologues did attack "Headstart" and "Higher Horizons" and all of the educational enrichment programs of the 1960s. However Murray and other neoconservatives wavered on this, and now (1988) recognize the potential benefit of these programs.[60]

It is important to point this out, because part of the liberal program of the 1960s was well conceived, while other portions of it were ill conceived and produced negative effects. The "permissive" atmosphere engendered by the school restructuring of the 1960s did not work well for the poor or the lower middle class children. Cutting and truancy rates skyrocketed while "sliding by" with the least amount of work became normative.

While the children of the middle and upper middle class enjoyed the nonauthoritarian atmosphere and in general functioned quite well within it, their reading and math scores, and their general pre-college preparation level, deteriorated. I can remember my own son, who loved the "open classroom" public school he went to, complaining when he went to junior high school that he had hardly learned anything in the fifth and sixth grades. He felt cheated, because he knew that he could have learned so much more. I will have more to say about this momentarily.

But first I want to make it as clear as possible that the pre-school, cultural enrichment, and college prep programs were more successful. If my son felt cheated in his fifth and sixth grade learning experience, he certainly did not feel cheated about singing in an opera directed by a member of the Metropolitan Opera company, or having his school receive a $10,000 prize from the Rockefeller Foundation for this event. Nor did he feel cheated by the newly instituted college-prep oriented junior high that rapidly brought the children (white, black, and Latin) up to, and beyond, college entrance standards. Murray, Bell, Moynihan, Glazer, and other neoconservatives are now advocating these programs, within a context of tight school discipline and merit promotions.

This combination of pre-school, extra-school, and college prep programs linked with the "tight ship" discipline advocated by the neoconservatives could be the best approach to educational uplift for the poor. Two warnings need be mentioned before leaving this subject, however.

One, a large percentage of the poor children—perhaps even as high as one third—may be forced out of the school system because they simply cannot abide by its authoritarian rules. This has happened in the schools where strict discipline has been enforced.[61] The two-thirds who remain do better—but the neoconservatives, at this moment, have no program for those poor children who "fall between the cracks." These kids will end up in crime and in prison. We will have more to say about these children later in the next chapter.

Second, the middle and upper middle class children have not needed an authoritarian structure. They have needed "gifted programs," or programs heavy with advanced academic content. The neoconservatives were among the leaders in pushing for programs of academic excellence for "gifted" children. These gifted programs were opposed by many liberals on the grounds that they were "elitist." As it turned out, these programs have not become "elitist"—almost any middle-class child—black or white—can get into such a program, and do well, simply because their family interaction pattern gives them the verbal and logical base with which to succeed in the academically advanced programs.

However, the programs, if not elitist, are "class-ist." The lower class children don't, as yet, come into the schools with the background for entrance into, or success in, these programs. The programs, thus, are not really programs for the gifted, although gifted kids do benefit greatly from them. They are, in fact, advanced academic-track programs for the middle and upper middle classes, from which the lower class will be excluded unless they are somehow brought up to middle class verbal and logical standards.

One last point related to the position of the neoconservatives: the middle class children in these "gifted" programs are succeeding in an atmosphere that, although academically disciplined, is nonauthoritarian, friendly, nurturant, and rather democratic in its relational structure.[62] Thus, though the discipline question may be answered one way for the lower and lower middle class children, it may be answered another way for the middle and upper middle class children.

Nonetheless, Murray's position on schooling for the poor should be taken seriously, and school reforms for the poor should be structured within the guidelines suggested by the neoconservative critique.

We have not discussed the neoconservative program of school "vouchers" and the privatization of the school system. However, we will discuss the "voucher" issue in the next section, and we do touch on the voucher program in the section in this chapter on the neoconservative principles as they apply to the rich.

At this point, let us stop, and look at the neoconservative message, as summarized in Murray's *Losing Ground*, and see what it means to operationalize their critique of the social programs of the Johnson–Nixon–Ford–Carter era.

OPERATIONALIZING MURRAY

On first perusal of Murray's argument, one might come away with the idea that Murray wants us to do *nothing* concerning the poor. After all, he asserts that the programs generated to help the poor actually caused them to "lose ground." However, this is not the case. "Benign neglect" is not Murray's, nor the neoconservatives', position now. Rather Murray, and the neoconservatives he speaks for, want something done—but they want it done in such a way that it reaffirms the general American morality, while providing for upward mobility. As Murray states it:

My arguments might seem tailor-made to relieve us of responsibility for persons in need. But I believe just the contrary: That the moral imperative to do something to correct the situation of poor people and especially the minority poor is at least as powerful now as when Lyndon Johnson took office.[63]

Murray and the neoconservatives do not actually oppose social programs, so long as those programs follow certain guidelines. Here are the guidelines that Murray insists on:

- Premise #1: People respond to incentives and disincentives. Sticks and carrots work.
- Premise #2: People are not inherently hardworking or moral. In the absence of countervailing influences, people will avoid work and be amoral.

• Premise #3: People must be held responsible for their actions. Whether they *are* responsible in some ultimate philosophical or biochemical sense cannot be the issue if society is to function.[64]

Now, in these premises, Murray is not "blaming the victim"[65]—which many of the hardline conservatives do. He is insisting that the poor must be treated as responsible citizens—in terms of schooling, work, and family responsibilities, and that they must be rewarded for good citizenship and punished for bad. Most leaders of the poor, the blacks, and the Latins also insist on this, because the dignity of the poor person is degraded if they are not held responsible for their actions, and sociopathic behavior is encouraged as well.

In asserting that the poor, and their liberal advocates, cannot go around "blaming the system," he is not asserting that "the system" is working for, or has been fair to, the poor. He is asserting that both liberals and conservatives have to stop blaming and start engineering[66] programs that provide the possibility for upward mobility and equality of opportunity, while pressuring the poor toward work, family responsibility, and good citizenship.

Murray does *not* oppose programs, and the transfer-funding necessary for the support of those programs, *if* the transference of funds succeeds in producing upward mobility and a better life for those targeted for help. Murray correctly insists that we ask these questions:

Did the transfer reach the people it was intended to reach? . . . did the transfer have the intended effect? . . . did the transfer, in the long run, add to the net happiness in the world?[67]

If the transfer-funding and the programs generated by it truly aid the poor, Murray would have no objections to them.

If the transfer is successful, I, the donor, can be satisfied on either of two grounds: general humanitarianism ("I am doing good") or more self-interested calculations that make transfers not so different from police service or garbage collection. For the sake of my own quality of life, I do not want to live in a Calcutta with people sleeping in the streets in front of my house.[68]

It is worth repeating Murray's dictum affirming programs to facilitate equality of opportunity and merit achievement, but rejecting programs for equality of result.

Billions for equal opportunity, not one cent for equal outcome—such is the slogan to inscribe on the banner of whatever cause my proposals constitute. Their common theme is to make it possible to get as far as one can go on one's merit, hardly a new ideal in American thought.[69]

It will clarify Murray's position even further if we look at his position on the race issue. For here the neoconservative position is at its clearest—whether one agrees with it or not. Programs geared to improving educational success and establishing work for blacks are favored, while programs favoring blacks, based on racial identity, rather than merit, are opposed.

My proposal for dealing with racial issues in social welfare is to repeal every bit of legislation and reverse every court decision that in any way requires, recommends, or rewards differential treatment according to race.... Race is not a morally admissible reason for treating one person differently from another. Period.[70]

This strong statement could lead one to believe that Murray and the neoconservatives, therefore, favor doing nothing to improve the situation of blacks in America. This, however, is not at all true. In fact, Murray recommends that we do everything in our power to guarantee that:

The two critical conditions for a young black person to escape from the ghetto have been met: [that is] white society [should be] rewarding those who have a good education, speak standard (white) English, behave with middle class social graces, and otherwise play within traditional white rules. And social policy is, in a purely technical sense, providing the wherewithal for even the poorest youngster to acquire these assets. The best universities actively seek to enroll capable inner-city students and government programs for poor students provide generous help from college through graduate school.[71]

I don't know if the case could be stated any better. Although this neoconservative position is seriously flawed because it refuses to recognize the impact of racism (and sexism and other barrier-creating prejudices), nonetheless, in itself, it does provide the framework from which socially acceptable programs beneficial to blacks, and the poor in general, can emerge.

For instance, work programs for welfare mothers fit this criterion. Murray contrasts the dependent woman-on-welfare syndrome—so rejected by American society—with the situation that would emerge from a workfare program. Murray creatively describes how the "workfare" woman would present herself to American society, and why she would be accepted (where the welfare woman has been rejected).

The workfare-woman says: "Help me find a job and day-care for my children, and I will take care of the rest." In effect, she puts herself into the same category as the widow and the deserted wife—identifies herself as one of the most obviously deserving of the deserving poor.[72]

The alteration of "welfare-mother" to "workfare-mother" is a critical change fitting in with our Aristotelian criterion, and, of course, with the American work-ethic morality.

Having affirmed the neoconservative critique of the social programs of the post-Kennedy era, and established the guidelines through which the neoconservative approach can be operationalized, we must now analyze another set of critically important data before our operationalizing process can be considered complete. These new data are derived from the period of the Reagan rollback of the social programs of the late 1960s and early 1970s. During the Reagan era the last vestiges of the Johnson "War on Poverty" were eliminated. Yet the results, in terms of the Reagan administration's effect on the poor, were not heartening.

Losing More Ground

Before concluding our discussion of Murray's work and that of the neoconservatives he represents, a critical set of new information must be examined. That is, in the 1980s, with the impetus of the neoconservative critique, the "old conservatives" gained legislative, judicial, and then executive power. Peaking with the election of Ronald Reagan, the old conservatives and neoconservatives joined forces to dismantle the social programs of the Johnson era. The "Great Society" programs were phased out—either fully terminated or drastically reduced. Educational programs such as Upward Bound and Higher Horizons were all but eliminated; Headstart was reduced enough to limit its impact; loan and scholarship programs were severely cut; job programs were phased out, while job-training programs were dramatically reduced. Affirmative action programs directed toward job and university entrance were circumvented or reversed in their priorities.[73] Low and middle income housing funds were first sequestered, then terminated. In other words, the elimination of the social programs that Murray and the neoconservatives deemed counter-productive, un-American, and anti-democratic basically occurred.

But, what were the results? Left to the "benign neglect"[74] of the Reagan era, the conditions of the poor deteriorated even further than during the Johnson–Nixon years. *More* poor males dropped out, turned to drugs, crime, and vice. Prison populations swelled. The number of black and Hispanic males entering prison and/or dropping out of society increased.[75] More poor women ended up on welfare, and the number of those living below the poverty line increased frighteningly.[76]

With housing starts for low income families all but eliminated, and luxury condominium construction gentrifying previously poor neighborhoods,[77] the homeless poor began living in our streets, parks, and railroad and bus stations. New York has become like Calcutta—just what Murray supposedly did not want to occur. From D.C. to L.A., the homeless have accumulated in our city streets.[78]

Now what does all of this mean? Murray and the neoconservatives blamed the Johnson–Nixon programs for the failure of upward mobility among poor and black Americans, insisting that we "lost ground" by implementing programs that reduced work motivation and encouraged dependency and sociopathic behavior. Yet, when the programs were dismantled and terminated, the result was a further loss of ground for poor and black Americans.

The puzzle is really not as difficult to solve as it appears. The conservative–

neoconservative juggernaut gained so much momentum and power that it swept away or weakened most of the programs geared to the poor. Many of these programs *were* ill-conceived and counter-productive programs that reduced work motivation, encouraged the poor to "con" the system, allowed the poor to pass through the school system without gaining an education, and so on. *However*, other of the programs were beneficial to the poor, either in terms of increasing their upward mobility or maintaining their level of income.

For instance, a program such as Upward Bound was succeeding with approximately 50 percent of the high school students it was preparing for college,[79] while the loan program was enabling these successes to make it through the college years. Removal of these programs resulted in a dramatic drop in the number of poor entering and completing college.

What the new statistics show us is that the neoconservatives may have thrown out the baby with the bath water.

Actually, this new situation, tragic as it is, could be the most seminal event of our lifetime. For, as Hayek put it, it gives us a "breathing space"[80] during which we can step back and evaluate which programs failed and which programs succeeded. Both the Johnson and the Reagan eras are over, and both the "war on poverty" and "benign neglect" have failed. The poor lost ground, and now they have lost more ground.

Let us use this "historic moment" to evaluate the programs, and the lack of programs, as they impinged on the condition of the poor.

APPLYING THE NEOCONSERVATIVE CORRECTIVES TO SOCIAL PROGRAMS

First, I would not have dwelt on the viewpoint of the neoconservatives if I did not believe that a good deal of what they argued was true. What we should learn from the neoconservatives is that:

• Programs that reduce work motivation and encourage dependency and sociopathic behavior are wrongly designed. So, for instance, the welfare system, no matter how generous, will have negative effects on upward mobility and family stability.

• Job programs that create large-scale administrative structures, but which do not provide jobs, confuse the issue. Job programs must provide jobs. And the jobs provided must be long-term career-line jobs—jobs that will allow the poor to gain mobility out of poverty.

(In some instances, such as housing and transit guards, nursing and nursing-home aids, positions are so desperately needed by our society that they may not require *any* specially created administrative structure for their implementation. In the case of the rehabilitation of the hardcore poor, such structures are needed, but jobs must still be forthcoming or the structure will be useless.)

• Job training programs *will not succeed with all their applicants*. A large percentage of the "hardcore" poor will drop out, or prove unreliable in their work habits, or lack the basic literacy and job skills to do a minimally passable job, or be on drugs and into vice and crime.

Knowing this, we must structure the job-training programs so as to place and reward the meritorious and hardworking members of the poor so that they become role models for the rest.

Knowing this, we must realize that the remaining hardcore poor will be extremely difficult to rehabilitate. The rehabilitation efforts for these hardcore poor entail far more than just job-training. *Long-term social work support*, as begun in the Kennedy years, becomes necessary. *Carefully supervised job units* become necessary as well. In short, ordinary job programs will not work with the hardcore poor.

• Educational practices that push children through the system, even though they cannot read, write, or do simple arithmetic, are wrong in their theoretical orientation.

• "Permissive" and "democratic" structures within the school system may not work for the poor. The poor may need a tighter authority structure and more clearly specified limits than the children of the middle class.

• Finally, in terms of affirmative action hiring quotas, the neoconservatives are correct in two ways. First, that unprepared and unskilled individuals should not be brought into job situations where they know, and their co-workers know, they cannot meet the standards of the job, And, second, that rigid hiring quotas—if *permanently* introduced into American society—would destroy the competitive individualism and meritocratic mobility system that has made America a beacon to the world.

Having given the neoconservatives their due, we must now turn to what we have learned from the Reagan years. Since the poor have lost more ground, we know that the neoconservatives were not completely correct. Obviously, many of the social programs were helpful to the poor in terms of both their upward mobility through schools and jobs, and in terms of their material well-being.

What we should learn from the Reagan years is that:

• Job programs that open up real jobs for the poor are effective. For instance, when cities from Philadelphia to San Diego open up police, fire, sanitation, park, or construction jobs, lines form for days in advance; people sleep on the sidewalks waiting for applications. Wouldn't it be wiser and cheaper to provide the money for such job slots than to build more prison cells?

• If job programs for the hardcore poor are eliminated, then even greater percentages of poor males end up in prison, and more women end up on welfare.

• As "Headstart," "Higher Horizon," "Homework Helper," "Upward Bound," and other educational enrichment programs were phased out, poor children did considerably worse in grade school and high school. The drop-out rate increased, and along with the cuts in college loans, college applications decreased.

• In terms of affirmative action hiring quotas, what have we learned from the Reagan years? We learned what we already knew, but which the neoconservatives seemed to minimize: that prejudice is real. Racism, sexism, and ethnic hatred exist, and they lead to exclusionary practices in jobs, schools, and neighborhoods.

If a rigid, permanent quota system is un-American—and the neoconservatives are correct that it is—*some* system geared to the inclusion of all individuals on a fair basis needs to take its place. Persuasion is not enough.[81] There must be a system with teeth in it—a system of legal recourse for those to whom prejudice presents a barrier to upward mobility.

Further, in order to reduce the conflict between competing groups, such as blacks and whites, men and women, old and young, more *opportunities* should be opened up. We need to expand the career market—through re-industrialization and re-investment in research and development at the upper end of the job spectrum, and through job creation and job-training at the lower end of the spectrum. Conflict between competing groups would still exist, but its intensity could be greatly reduced wherein the opportunity structure was more open.

Finally—and neither the liberals nor the neoconservatives are sympathetic to this group—perhaps we need to "extend a hand" to the white working class. This group is most closely in competition with poor blacks and Latins in the job and college worlds, and white working class males are in competition with working class females, who usually surpass them in school success.

The white working class has been moving upward "on its own," and when asked, claim they want and need no help. However, within this group family violence is rampant—especially wife and child abuse; drug abuse is very high and alcoholism rising (for adults and teens); teen suicide rates are skyrocketing; and, homicidal violence from previously employed, but then laid-off, male workers fills our T.V. news shows and tabloids.

The white working class needs pre-school and school programs. They need college prep programs. They also need family therapy and teen support-groups. It would be wise policy, while widening the opportunity structure for blacks, minorities, and women, to expand those opportunities for the white working class as well.

During the Reagan years, the condition of the poor has declined, and so, too, has the condition of the white working class. Social tensions between these two groups have worsened,[82] and the resulting violence, deviance, and retreatism (drug addiction, alcoholism, and suicide) have not been a pretty sight for Americans to view, nor has it raised our reputation among the world's nations.

To sum up, then, at this moment in history we have a breathing space, a chance to evaluate our actions of the recent past, and a chance to turn to a new beginning. We lost ground and now we are losing more ground in our efforts to raise up the poor and shore up the middle class. There is much agreement emerging on which programs we should keep and which we should discard. Where there is agreement we should move forward.

Before suggesting an overall approach to such forward movement, one last aspect of the neoconservative position must be analyzed. How do the neoconservative guidelines help us in our programmatic efforts concerning the rich?

Applying the Neoconservative Principles to the Rich

The neoconservatives have been concerned largely with the poor. However, the principles they have established concerning work motivation and educational achievement can be applied to governmental policies and programs directed toward the rich. If we do apply the neoconservative principles to such programs, we discover an unhappy phenomenon. That is, in the era from Nixon to Reagan, the rich have been pressured in the "wrong" direction by a set of governmental policies and programs intended by conservative economists[83] to improve the economy.

The government programs for the rich—which had good intentions behind them, just as the Johnson programs for the poor had—are as misguided in their effect as the welfare system is for the poor. The Nixon–Carter–Reagan policies for the rich pushed them away from industrial productivity and encouraged instead a sociopathic attitude toward the system. Just as the poor have found it more lucrative to "con" the system and/or turn to crime rather than to productive work, so too the rich. Under the impetus of current government programs they find it more lucrative to turn to these alternatives rather than engage in productive enterprise. The Nixon–Carter–Reagan programs have sapped the moral fibre of the rich as surely as the Johnson–Nixon programs sapped that of the poor.

The Nixon–Carter–Reagan programs have encouraged the rich to drop out of productive enterprise altogether and concentrate their efforts on quasi-legal, illegal, and nonproductive financial dealings. A whole generation of our leading college students has been pressured, not toward engineering and science and research and industrial production—as they were during the Kennedy years— but toward finance. Today's American economic heroes are not the "captains of industry," but the "captains of finance," to borrow some phrases from Thorstein Veblen, who, before the Great Depression, warned against policies that neglected technology and industry in favor of finance.[84]

The neoconservatives insist that work-motivation and middle class morality should be the goals of government policy directed toward the poor. Yet, under the pressure of specific government programs undertaken during the Nixon– Carter–Reagan years, what kind of behavior has emanated from the rich?

• Motivation to work toward industrial production has been undermined, while financial wheeling and dealing has been reinforced and highly rewarded.
• Stripped of work motivation directed toward productivity, the rich have turned either to crime or "conning" the system. By crime we mean outright

stock manipulation and embezzlement, and by "conning" the system we mean arbitrage insider trading and "green mailing" (on the financial side), and the arranging of "golden parachutes," million dollar bonuses, and the padding of expense accounts (on the managerial side).[85]

Vice, too, has become part of the everyday amorality of the rich, such that call-girl charges and expensive massage parlor charges sometimes become included in expense account allowances for clients of financial or corporate institutions.

Further, in terms of crime on the corporate side, the policies of Nixon and Reagan especially encouraged the rich to knowingly violate safety and environmental standards,[86] and offered these rich offenders a governmentally-supported rationale for what had heretofore been considered illegal and immoral behavior.

If we follow out the neoconservative logic, "stock chiselers" have become as commonplace as "welfare chiselers" and environmental polluters as dangerous as urban muggers.

• In education, through a system of very expensive private schools, especially the boarding schools, the rich have been pushed along and allowed entrance into the elite colleges,[87] even where they have not shown any academic hard work or intellectual excellence. Whereas the children of the middle class must work exceptionally hard and show prodigious intellectual ability in order to attain entrance into a private school or elite college, rich "preppies" may slide along and make it through with the help of wealthy parental donations, connections to powerful alumni, and aggressive guidance counselors in the employ of the prestigious private secondary schools.

None of this latter encourages hard work or "middle class morality" among the rich, nor does it lead to meritocratic selection for top positions within the society at large. "Equality of end result" is guaranteed for the rich, rather than "equality of opportunity." This runs counter to the core of the neoconservative principles.[88]

What are the policies and programs under Nixon–Carter–Reagan that have undermined the productive orientation of the rich and encouraged their sociopathic bent?

First, Nixon and his economic advisors took us off the gold standard[89] and allowed the dollar to float on the international market. This led to a flurry of speculation in both dollars and gold,[90] and fueled the boom in international financial speculation.

Then, "monetarist" policy was introduced, establishing very high interest rates in an attempt to restrict the money supply to reduce inflation.[91] The high interest rates inadvertently produced a tremendous advantage for any institution or individual lending large amounts of money.[92] Financial institutions became over-capitalized. On the other hand, institutions or individuals borrowing money were put at a tremendous disadvantage. Thus, corporations wishing to expand their productive or research capacities and consumers wishing to raise their living standards, were put at a disadvantage.

Government decontrol of industry followed (pushed by Carter as much as by Reagan). This policy was intended to increase free market competition and, hopefully, bring prices down. But the result of this wide-open competition was an increasing rate of business failures leading to corporate break-ups, sell-offs, and reorganizations.[93] This eventuated in a rash of takeovers by successful corporations, or of partial takeovers of sold-off segments of failing corporate conglomerates by other conglomerates. Furthermore, although consumer prices went down in the airline and other specific industries, the prices of industrial products, such as cars and appliances, continued to climb, as did the prices of food and other basic commodities, such as clothing and housing.

In this kind of unstable situation, with corporations failing, segmenting, and re-consolidating, financial borrowing—both for debt repayment of failing corporations, but more importantly for financial takeovers by successful corporations—escalated dramatically with interest rates set at such unusually high levels by monetarist policy, financial institutions gained windfall profits.

Armed with enormous amounts of capital, the financial institutions themselves began "raiding" the weakened, indebted corporations by buying up their depressed stock. Corporate "raiding" cliques, such as that headed by Carl Icahn, became legendary. Corporations, and/or segments of conglomerates, were bought and sold with no concern for industrial production, but only for financial profit.[94]

"Junk bonds" were used to finance these industrially senseless, but financially profitable, deals. "Green mail" was paid by weakened corporations to suddenly super-powerful financial institutions in order to prevent them from buying out corporate stock. Corporate managers, threatened at every moment by the specter of buy-outs and consolidations that would eliminate their positions, protected themselves through the institutionalization of "golden parachutes" (huge severance pay-offs in case of managerial retrenchment). Top corporate management further insured their security by skimming off huge "bonuses" (paid to themselves even from companies failing to show a profit)[95] to protect themselves from the prospect of future career loss through corporate collapses.

Therefore, the combinations of corporate de-control with monetarist high interest rates (and the international flurry of trade in dollars and gold) shifted the balance of power away from the industrial corporations and toward the financial institutions.

All of this occurred just as the dramatic increase of industrial competition from Japan, East Asia, and the European Common Market was occurring. The kind of industrial planning and R&D necessary to meet this new and formidable competition was impossible given the proclivity for financial manipulations and the rejection of industrial production that occurred.

If this situation were not bad enough, inflation, which was supposed to be brought down by decontrol and monetarist high interest rates, went up. It went up because oil prices skyrocketed—and this, of course, had not been part of the economic equation. But inflation also went up because the policy of decontrol encouraged the corporations to abandon the wage–price guidelines that had been established by the Kennedy economic advisors.[96] Further, the high interest rates forced the corporations to raise their prices to cover the increased costs of borrowing.

Although Nixon tried for a short time to institute wage–price controls, he gave up rather quickly and allowed the whole economy to inflate dramatically.[97] It was during the Nixon years that inflation rose sharply, not during the Kennedy–Johnson years.

These Nixon policies were continued through the Carter and early Reagan years, and the result was a decline in emphasis on industrial production and a growing concentration on finance.

At the same time, the Nixon–Carter–Reagan tax policies de-emphasized the progressive nature of the income tax. Loopholes for the rich were widened and increased—the growth of real estate deductions, for instance, attracting wild speculation and encouraging the building of luxury dwellings instead of moderate priced dwellings.

As a result of these regressive tax policies, the rich, as rich individuals (rather than as corporate entities), became over-capitalized. As Keynes warned, if the investments of the rich are not channeled into industrial production and civic projects, these investments will tend to be directed instead toward short-term profit-making schemes led by the "high rollers" or "lead players" among the rich, or withheld from the market entirely in "safe" savings accounts.[98]

The phenomenon of "high roller" short-term financial schemes and safely hidden Swiss bank accounts was staged inadvertently by misdirected government programs that led to the unproductive, sociopathic behavior of the rich that has now become the subject of government investigations,[99] criminal indictments, and movie, television, and newspaper exposes.[100]

Finally, during the Nixon and Reagan years, government programs were forcefully initiated that overturned or reversed previous government attempts at maintaining safety standards on the job and protecting the environment from corporate pollution.[101] These policies encouraged the sociopathic, amoral behavior that had already been set loose by the financial juggernaut.

Jut as the Johnson policies had set the poor on the wrong course and caused them to lose ground, so the Nixon–Carter–Reagan policies set the rich on the wrong course and has caused America to lose ground to its industrially-oriented competitors.

On the topic of educational programs, the meritocratic elite of our society—the future generation of leaders of industry and government—had been watered-down and siphoned off. Siphoned off because government policies have pushed them toward financial get-rich-quick careers, rather than toward industrial development or scientific research, and, watered down because the children of the rich are allowed to coast through the educational system, taking their place in high economic and political positions without the expertise, knowledge, or drive of those who have risen through the educational meritocracy competitively.

Just at the point in history when America's private and public schools and colleges *were* becoming more meritocratic in selection and promotion practices (in terms of the upper and middle class, but not the poor), this trend was reversed. It was reversed by a combination of the windfall of financial riches, which accrued to the rich, and by a new governmental orientation favoring private schools and private colleges.

The ideal of moving away from public schools entirely, and toward a system of private schools based on payments through "vouchers,"[102] though never actually instituted, served to legitimate private school education and de-legitimate public school education.

An elitism, based not on merit, but on wealth, replaced the meritocratic trend, which Daniel Bell,[103] Daniel Patrick Moynihan, and other neoconservatives were heralding. Tuitions soared to such remarkable heights as to raise the private schools and colleges beyond the reach of the meritorious members of the middle class. With tuition so high, the unmeritocratic children of the rich were welcomed and given entrance to the private schools and colleges.[104]

Government policy encouraged this, for it urged everyone to go private. It encouraged the working class to go to private religious schools—Protestant in the South and Midwest, Catholic in the Northeast—to avoid the "permissive" atmosphere that was condemned (and we have suggested that such a permissive atmosphere did exist, and was somewhat problematical), and to avoid the blacks, who were blamed for their educational and social unpreparedness[105] (and we have suggested that the blacks *were* unprepared educationally).

Government policy also encouraged the upper middle class to go private, to spend their last penny—not for a high level educational experience for their children, but to gain access to the elite connections based on wealth. This ideological climate helped re-institutionalize and re-legitimate the wealth-determined nature of elite selection that had been declining in favor of the more democratic meritocratic elite selection of the 1960s.

The government policies of the Nixon and Reagan years, by attacking the public schools and re-legitimating the success-by-wealth standard of the elite private schools, has pressured the rich away from meritocratic, competitive advancement and toward the kind of "old-boy," "gentleman's 'C' " automatic entrance into the elite that is counterproductive for the educational system, detrimental to the nation, and debilitating to the rich themselves, who are not encouraged to achieve their potential.

As a principle, equality of opportunity denies the precedence of birth, of nepotism, of patronage or any other criterion which allocates place, other than fair competition open equally to talent and ambition.[106]

Meritocracy may be in our future, as Daniel Bell suggests; however, present governmental policy is inhibiting it by weighting the rules toward wealth-selection rather than merit-selection in the educational system. The "voucher" system might have been an interesting one, but it never materialized. The middle class and the poor never got their vouchers, while the rich and upper middle class bought their way through the educational system without them.

To sum up in terms of the neoconservative principles and the rich: government programs should be so oriented as to pressure the rich toward the utilization of their wealth and talent in industrial production and research. Economic policies should be followed that constrain financial dealings and reward industrial productivity. In education, government programs should reward science, engineering, mathematics, and the scholarly pursuit of the humanities, not finance and business management. Nor should educational advancement be based on one's ability to pay high tuition costs.

We must upgrade our rich, just as we have to raise up our poor. We don't want our rich committing suicide as they did in 1929 (and as our poor do now on drug-overdoses), and we don't want our rich in prison (anymore than we want our poor there). If we want our poor working and paying taxes, and living by middle class standards of social morality, so too do we want our rich. If we want our poor educationally prepared, so too do we want our rich. If we extend Murray's principle, it becomes: "No more welfare chiselers and no more stock chiselers."

We have an historic "breathing space"; let us begin again.

PART III

TOWARD A COMPREHENSIVE THEORY OF EQUALITY WITHIN A FRAMEWORK OF LAW AND DEMOCRACY

The goal of this work is to establish the theoretical principles and practical programs through which a greater degree of equality may emerge in capitalist-democratic societies. The safeguarding of democracy remains primary, and becomes the limit beyond which the theories and the programs must not stray. It is our central thesis, however, that within the limits set by the preservation (and extension) of legal-democracy, the expansion of economic equality should be actively pursued.

It is our position that the reduction of extreme wealth inequalities and the expansion of the middle class helps to stabilize and strengthen legal-democracy; that in fact such processes tend to reduce oligarchic and tyrannical tendencies within the polity.

Furthermore, we will attempt to establish that the theories and programs instituted to engender a greater degree of equality can improve the functioning of the modern technocratic-capitalist industrial economy.

Finally, we will argue that the programs (and pressures) for greater equality, if even partially successful, help to ameliorate the social ills engendered by capitalism, and in so doing, reduce the moral dilemma accompanying competitive individualism.

WHY DO WE NEED GREATER ECONOMIC EQUALITY WITHIN CAPITALIST-DEMOCRATIC SOCIETIES?

The reason that greater equality is necessary in capitalist-democratic societies is that liberalism alone does not guarantee the stability of the polity or the economy. Liberal theory provides the essential first step of a two step process for political stability and economic productivity.

In terms of the polity, we have illustrated and we will attempt to establish that the *Aristotelian corrective* is necessary in order to establish and maintain the class balance needed for the stability of the legal-democratic state. We will argue that this is an *essential second step* in the maintenance of democratic political processes and that the liberal program alone cannot ensure these processes. We will also show how the Rawlsian revision of liberal theory brings it into consonance with the Aristotelian corrective.

In terms of the economy, we will attempt to show that—although capitalism provides the undergirding for the legal-democratic state and its processes—the theory of capitalist economics, qua economics, is also a first step theory in need of the Keynesian modification and other correctives. The efficient functioning of the capitalist economic system in its modern technocratic form cannot be assured through laissez-faire theory and program.

If bureaucratic-socialism has failed, it is *not* pure capitalism that has replaced it as the best practical economic system. With the "rationality," efficiency, and entrepreneurial creativity of capitalism taken as the first step of the economic program in the modern context, the second step will consist of a series of modifications of capitalism that retain its strengths, while reducing its weaknesses. I will attempt to show that it is *modified capitalism* that is already leading the way in world economic productivity, rather than pure capitalism, and that the attempt to return to laissez-faire is as destructive a romantic illusion as that of socialism.

6

The Polity: Classical Liberalism as an Incomplete Political Theory

THE TWO-STEP THEORY FOR LEGAL-DEMOCRATIC STABILITY

The first step in the establishment and maintenance of legal-democracy is the liberal step. The liberal program consists of these essential institutionalized processes: government by law—including constitutional constraints on the democratic representative process, and the establishment of law-courts with jury trial; electoral procedures for choosing legislative representatives and executive offices; inalienable rights guaranteed to the citizen (over against the state); the limitation of the power of the state (against the citizen); the separation of the economic sphere from governmental control; and the separation of powers within the state between the legislative, executive, and judiciary.

Liberalism establishes the basic structure of the legal-democratic state in its modern form. This is the great gift of liberalism to the world, for it established this viable form of democracy, beyond the Polis, for the mass nation-state.

If this is so, why can it not stand alone? Why is the Aristotelian (Rawlsian) step also essential?

The answer is that left as it stands, the liberal program may not result in a class structure in which the middle class becomes the majority class. And, if the class structure becomes skewed toward the rich or the poor, then political instability may result and the liberal political structure may be drawn toward oligarchy or extreme democracy, or worse, toward tyranny (spearheaded by the rich or the poor).

The Aristotelian dimension must not be forgotten, for it undergirds legal-democracy as surely as does the liberal institutional structure.

Perhaps it would be helpful to illustrate our point of view with a hypothetical example, and then a set of actual historical examples.

Suppose we were able to establish the liberal political institutions—constitutional representative government and laissez-faire economics—in a nation where the majority of the citizens were quite poor, and where the rich were few but very wealthy, and the middle class was very small and weak. What would be the likely outcome in such a situation? Would it not be most likely that the liberal political institutions, in and of themselves, would not lead to the establishment of legal-democracy? Would it not be very likely that legal-democratic political procedures would be undermined by a lack of commitment to them by the poor, and overridden by a lack of commitment to them by the rich? Isn't it most likely, though not absolutely certain, that the polity would be drawn toward tyranny in the name of the poor or oligarchy of the rich, and that further, this polarization could lead to revolution and counter-revolution, eventuating in a dictatorship of the poor or the rich?

This, of course, is the Aristotelian scenario, but where is the explanation to be found for this in the logic of liberal theory? After all, according to liberal theory, once the ''social contract'' is entered into and the legal-democratic institutions are established, everyone should live happily ever after. Property should be developed, and the more enterprising gain a larger share; elections should establish representation of the citizens in political decision making; citizens' rights should be articulated and protected against the power of the state— all this should occur, and yet few would predict such an outcome, given the structural circumstances outlined in this hypothetical case.

I will present some actual historical examples in a moment to support the view derived from our hypothetical structural situation. First, let me assert that the reason for the inability of liberal theory to assess the effect of the social structure on political action has to do with liberalism's logical starting point: individuals in a state of nature. With such a logical starting point—and this starting point has enormous merit as a philosophical device illuminative of the liberal political processes—it becomes impossible to assess the class balance necessary for the maintenance of the glorious political institutions engendered by the liberal philosophical construction. From Lockian state of nature theory, competitive individualism, the limitation of the power of the state, and the private development of property should be enough to safeguard and support the legal-democratic political system.

Yet it is not enough. Rawls warns that the original logic of state of nature theory is already flawed and in need of revision. That as it stood, the ''social contract'' would never have been entered into by its hypothetical citizens, because the possibility for differentials of property wealth would have been viewed by these original citizens—endowed, as Locke endowed them, with reason—as too great.

From the Aristotelian positions we come to the same conclusion. And, in all honesty, would not *most* contemporary social analysts predict that in a situation where the vast majority of a society is wretchedly poor, the rich few and powerful, and the middle class barely developed, the liberal political institutions and processes would collapse and give way to despotic ones?

Let us look at some actual historical examples that approximate the hypothetical case. These examples will be complicated by cultural and historical factors of great complexity, of course. However, if we focus on our two spheres of analysis—the legal-democratic institutions and processes promulgated by liberalism, and the class balance of the particular society in question—we can still gain a deeper understanding of the political dynamics of the nation in question.

The case of Venezuela and its leader Simon Bolivar[1] is illustrative here. Bolivar, imbued with the ideals of the Enlightenment and charged with the principles of liberalism emanating from the United States, Britain, and France during his lifetime, attempted to establish liberal-democracy in all of Latin America.

After years of warfare, the Spanish colonial "empire" was finally defeated. Bolivar, flushed with the joy of victory, set about establishing legal-democratic institutions in his beloved Venezuela. However, these institutions did not take root. Just a few years after their establishment, they collapsed, leaving Bolivar—"the George Washington of Latin America"—broken-hearted. Bolivar died a dispirited man, watching everything he had fought for disintegrate into a cycle of revolution and counter-revolution, and finally into an anarchy[2] that engendered more violence than had the wars against Spain. For almost a hundred years, Bolivar's dream eluded Venezuela.

From the liberal theoretical perspective, the establishment of the legal-democratic state (and constitution), along with the unfettering of an expanding commercial economy, should have been enough to set Venezuela on a new political course. Bolivar, having absorbed liberal ideology, believed this. Yet it did not occur. The vast majority of Venezuelans were poor and uneducated to liberal political and economic ideas, while the rich were the feudal-oriented descendants of the *Conquistadores*—using wealth for aggrandizement rather than capital accumulation or industrial development (and retaining military power outside the control of the newly established liberal state).[3] The middle class, on the other hand, was commercial, was educated, was committed to liberal political ideals, but was small and comparatively weak in relation to the feudal-rich. The middle class *was* powerful and numerous—within the few major cities of Venezuela, and therefore they made their revolution against Spain. But once the Spanish were gone, the power of the feudal-rich and the numbers of the countryside poor overwhelmed the liberal program. Although a liberal constitution existed in print, *in reality* the politics of oligarchy and tyranny alternately dominated the Venezuelan political process.

Today, with the dramatic growth of the middle class and a steady absorption of the poor, along with a rapid decline of the feudal, land-holding rich, legal-democratic political processes—although still fragile—are slowly gaining stability and legitimacy.

The case of the Philippines is another historical example that illustrates the necessity of a two-step theory for the establishment and maintenance of the legal democratic polity.

In the Philippines, after centuries of Spanish semi-feudal rule, the United States attempted to establish a legal-democratic polity. American motives were noble politically, if not economically (we were openly interested in the raw materials of the Philippines). Unfortunately, as in Venezuela, the vibrancy of the liberal-democratic political institutions was not sustained.

The poor—a vast wretched majority, enormous and degraded even in comparison with the poor of Venezuela—drifted toward revolutionary activity. At first this activity was unfocused and diffuse, but after WWII it became spearheaded by a well-organized Communist leadership. The landed rich were brought into the new American-directed commercial economy, but used their newly acquired wealth for fabulous personal aggrandizement, rather than industrial development. Threatened by the revolt from the poor, the rich preferred a tight military dictatorship that overrode the limited powers of the liberal-democratic state.[4]

Again, as with Venezuela, although the middle class maintained its commitment to the legal-democratic polity, it was tiny and its influence remained confined to Manila and a few smaller cities. Again as with Venezuela, when the middle class grew numerous and prosperous, demands for the re-establishment of legal-democracy grew as well. Today, with a majority poor (who are still very poor) and a powerful rich (who are still quasi-feudal in their use of wealth), but with a growing well-educated middle class, liberal-democracy has been re-institutionalized, and is hanging by a thread.[5]

Notice, again, that the liberal political and economic institutions by themselves are not enough to maintain the stability and vibrancy of the legal-democratic state.

With the indulgence of the reader, I should like to present just a few more historical examples before extending the analysis on the necessity of the two-step process for the maintenance of legal-democracy.

It is so well known and thoroughly accepted now, but what a surprise it was then, that in the British and French colonies of Africa the withdrawal of the colonial powers after WWII was not followed by a period of African democracy. Instead, and to the consternation of the colonialists and the African leaders they had selected, in most (though not all) of the African nations, the legal-democratic institutions did not last long enough even to keep them in memory.[6]

The poorer the nation, the more quickly the collapse into despotism. Cold War machinations, to be sure, have had a devastating effect on much of Africa, eliminating whatever fragile chance there may have been for the successful establishment of legal-democracy. Such nations as Ghana and Ethiopia are cases in point here.

However, it is interesting that in two nations at least, Kenya and Senegal, where a vibrant and growing middle class exists next to a relatively prosperous stratum of village-agriculturalists, and with the absence of a class of ultra-rich landowners, democracy seems to have taken root. With the absence of the wretched poor, who populate so many Third World nations, *and* the absence of the ultra-rich, unusual again, the growing middle class (commercial and white collar) of these nations has given substance to the democratic doctrine left by the British and French colonialists.

In most African nations—termed "basket cases" for the plight of their majority poor—democracy is seen as a luxury for those with a "full stomach."[7]

Two more cases are necessary before we move back to the development of our line of argument. These cases are India and Germany. India must be discussed because it seems to contradict the Aristotelian theory.

India certainly has a majority poor—and the poor are very poor. Calcutta is the example used when one wants to call attention to poverty at its most horrifying level.[8]

Yet what is usually not understood about India is that it possesses a huge and relatively prosperous middle class. An affluent commercial middle class preceded British rule and was entrenched for centuries. Under British occupation this class was almost undermined. Eventually, however, especially by mid–20th century, this class came, not only to prosper, but to expand dramatically. It expanded further yet as a result of the establishment of a British-style civil service, to which thousands applied, and from which a well-educated officialdom emerged.

By the time of independence—which, remember, came after WWII—the middle class was not only prosperous again, but expanding, well educated, and deeply committed to British liberal ideals. The English language itself, with all its symbols of law and democratic procedure, became the language of the educated middle class.

By independence, the Brahmin religious literate,[9] although still very much an upper caste, had become very British in their political orientation. The British rule, emphasizing the law and reason and debate, rather than military violence and political domination, was quite consonant with the Brahmin life-orientation, since the Brahmins were not a feudal-military stratum of war-lords.[10]

Further, the majority poor were locked into caste relations and isolated in their far-flung rural villages. As such, they could not be easily mobilized either to act or to feel as a corporate class in their political orientation. Rather, the rich Brahmins joined with the commercial and civil service middle class for the support of, and maintenance of, the legal-democratic processes inherited from the British.[11]

To be sure, there was a violent and terrible revolt of the poor, just after independence—one of the most spontaneous and explosive outpourings in history. However this revolt was a religious phenomenon. The Hindu poor and Moslem poor (with the middle class drawn in) slaughtered each other, and dissipated the power of the poorer castes in the emerging political situation.

I only mention the case of India because it would surely be used as an example against the Aristotelian principle. And I cannot, in this context, adequately discuss the complexity of this case. However, I do wish to assert, and this is critical for us here, that the middle class of India is enormous and prosperous by Third World standards, that it is numerous and spread throughout most of the regions of India, and that the middle class is well educated and deeply committed to liberal political processes.

The case of Germany shows most clearly that the liberal political institutions and a capitalist economy are necessary conditions for the establishment of the legal-democratic system, but are not sufficient to sustain such a system.

As is well known, German capitalism did spawn a large, prosperous middle class. Toward the close of the 19th century, with the decline of the feudal classes (which still existed in Prussia and other rural sectors of Eastern and Southern Germany[12]), and the growing irrelevance of the monarchy, pressure to establish a legal-democratic state mounted.

After WWI, a legal-democratic state was established, and the "Weimar Republic" enjoyed the support of the middle classes and the rich capitalists who were emerging as newly powerful figures in the German realm.[13] The remnants of the feudal classes did not support the legal-democratic state, seeing it as weak and indecisive. And a good portion of the working class, along with many intellectuals, also did not support the democracy. The workers and intellectuals either dreamed of romantic socialism,[14] or harked to the "teutonic horns"[15] of the German military past—and with great emotional outpouring, demanded a new militaristic state.

As long as the middle class was growing and prosperous, the legal-democratic state remained intact and the parties favoring legal-democratic government maintained their majority. The socialists, communists, and fascists (Nazis), however, were well organized, highly disciplined, and had substantial followings.

The Great Depression and the unfavorable settlement terms ending WWI altered the political situation in Germany. The middle classes were devastated by the economic collapse. Small businessmen and shopkeepers were losing their clientele as German currency lost its value and the people lost their ability to purchase goods. The civil servants, who had been attached to the Prussian monarchy, feared that the democratic state would let them go. Soldiers, dismissed after the war, found themselves unable to find work and blamed the newly established legal-democratic government. Big business was hit hard by the reparation provisions of the Versailles treaty and began to struggle to survive.

Through all this, the majority of the middle class continued to vote for moderate candidates and support the democracy. However, as their condition declined, they began, in ever larger numbers, to turn toward the non-democratic extremes. The socialists and communists spoke out mostly for the industrial workers, but the fascists (Nazis) touched a chord in the middle classes.

First the soldiers, then the civil servants, went over to the Nazis. Then, small businessmen and shopkeepers, housewives, and boy scouts began to be carried away by the Nazi vision of a return to Germany's past military glory and the tight societal discipline that undergirded it.

Finally, the Jews became the scapegoats for the German failures, and the rest is well known history.

For us, in this treatise, the point must be made indelibly that the decline of the middle classes threw Germany into a condition of political instability and violence in which the liberal institutions of government were abandoned in favor of dictatorial alternatives.

One could make the point that the liberal political institutions in Germany were not really established. After all, Germany was a monarchy until WWI. I would agree with this. In the United States the Great Depression engendered a charismatic leader (with an emergency economic program) *within* the legal-democratic system. Lacking a feudal-military-monarchical traditional structure, fascism did not emerge with any mass appeal, even as the nation collapsed economically. Socialism did gain dramatically among unemployed workers and impoverished farmers, but it never drew anything like the support it gained in Europe.

The New Deal, it should be remembered, although failing to cure our economic ills, temporarily employed enough American workers and middle class to defuse what could have become a more extremist situation. WWII then intervened.

The United States not withstanding, the case of Germany remains as a warning that the destabilization and decline of the middle class may send the society violently lurching toward tyranny of the right or the left. The case of Germany teaches us that the more technologically advanced a nation is, the more terrible the results of tyranny may be. Tyranny does not recognize law. And, as Aristotle said centuries ago, without law in human politics, one sets loose the character of the beast.

The point that I have tried to make with the aid of these historical examples is that the establishment of liberal political and economic institutions, in and of themselves, is not enough to ensure their stability and longevity. The second step—the establishment of a large and prosperous middle class—is also necessary if the situation is not to degenerate into oligarchy or tyranny. The middle class must be nurtured and expanded and the poor raised-up, while, of course, all classes must become educated (in general) and socialized (in particular) to the virtues of democracy and law for the adjudication of political differences.[16]

Why would eminent Enlightenment-imbued liberal theorists—conversant, line and verse, with Aristotle—miss this second step? Why do modern liberal theorists still miss this second step?

The answer is two-fold: either liberal theorists blatantly accept and attempt to justify oligarchy (legal-oligarchy, to be sure) and the poverty that usually accompanies it,[17] or they drift into romantic utopian thinking.[18]

In order to fully understand why liberal theorists turned to justification and utopianism, a journey back to the historical and structural origins of liberalism is necessary.

THE COMMERCIAL REVOLUTIONS AND THE BIRTH OF LIBERALISM

The history of the transition from feudal–monarchical society to capitalist–industrial–democratic society is controversial. Libraries have been written debating the role of religious, economic, and political factors "causative" of this transformation.[19] However, after years of debate between the followers of Weber and Tawney, Marxists and anti-Marxists, enough consistencies have emerged so that this important historical period can be understood. This period of history is critical for us, because it is during this transition that liberalism—both its ideas and its institutions—emerged.

All over Europe feudalism was declining and the centralized kingly state was gaining in power. Free trading cities, existing outside the bounds of feudal restrictions were growing in prosperity and population, and funding the kings against the errant knights of the countryside. At first the commercial classes and the monarchies were allies against feudalism—the kings gaining money-revenue from the city-merchants and in return granting them land for commercial development. This commercial development of the countryside weakened the knights and displaced thousands of peasants.[20]

As the commercial classes of city and countryside gained in strength and the monarchies expanded, they came into conflict with each other.[21] The kings demanded too much tax revenue to finance their wars and began to interfere in the economic activities of the trade-merchants. Conflict between the former allies intensified to the point where the kings sought alliance with the feudal lords, whom they had heretofore greatly weakened. In some nations, this conflict eventuated in violent revolutionary activity by the commercial classes against the monarchies and their feudal allies. In Holland, Britain (and by extension in the United States), and France these revolutions by the commercial classes were eventually successful. Whereas in Spain and Germany, where the kings and feudal lords were very powerful and the commercial classes weak,[22] the revolutions were muted and the actual conflict would not occur until the 20th century. (The case of Italy is a special one, since this conflict occurred centuries earlier in a different structural and historical context.[23])

In the nations where the commercial classes were successful in their revolt against the monarchy and its feudal allies, liberalism was born. Liberalism is the credo of the trade-capitalist commercial classes of city and countryside. It then transcended its origins and became the theory of representative-democracy for all the world and for all time. However, the historical and structural context in which it emerged set the agenda for liberalism as a political and economic theory.

The kingly-bureaucratic state was a despotic state ruling through traditional legitimacy[24]; therefore the trade-capitalists (city merchants and landed gentry) developed the idea of the limitation of the power of the state.[25] To counteract the idea of traditional authority, wherein each "estate" had its ascribed and immutable position, the ideas of the "state of nature" and the "social contract"[26] were created. Through these latter, humans entered into society anew, as equal individuals, with inalienable rights, guaranteed by law (rather than feudal tradition).

Further, the attempt to control economic activity by the monarchy and its bureaucracy generated the counter-idea of laissez faire—that government should keep its hands out of business transactions, and that private enterprise was superior in efficiency, creativity, and energy to governmental monopolistic control.

Finally, against the claim that the king and his courtly functionaries had the legitimate right to rule, the idea of representative government was put forth.

Representative government already existed in the post-feudal system. Kings had met with representatives of the city merchants in regional parliaments throughout Europe for many years. Representatives of each "estate" (including king, clergy, lords, merchants—and even peasants, in Scandinavia) met on a regular basis. The parliaments of this "estate-state" (*standestaat*)[27] period formed the basis from which the representative government of the legal-democratic nation-state would evolve.

Where liberalism triumphed, the representatives became, above all, lawmakers. Rational constitutional law superseded the rule of men, and the representative institution, parliament, became the central political institution of the limited-power state.[28]

The development of the political institutions carried by the merchants of the free cities and the commercially oriented gentry[29] of the countryside took centuries. However, once developed, as mentioned, they transcended their origins to become the universal institutions of modern legal-democracy in the mass nation-state. The theorizing developed to justify the institutions also took centuries to develop, but again transcended its origin.

Thus liberalism, in its Enlightenment form, has become the theory of legal-democracy for the modern world, accompanying the institutions it supports. A passion for limited government, and political freedom, for economic freedom, for lawful political procedures, and political rights are liberalism's great gift to the world.

This legacy is so powerful, so wonderful, so irreplaceable, and so fragile, that to criticize it seems almost sacrilegious. I mean this in all sincerity. Who wants to utter a dissenting note against a crystalline perfection that could be shattered by the slightest vibration of the first voice raised against it?

Yet, utopia alludes us. No set of ideas and institutions are perfect in themselves. The ideas and institutions of liberalism were born with one flaw—if left to their own inner-dynamics, they generate wealth differentials too great to sustain the class balance necessary for the stability of the democratic polity (which they embody and legitimate).

I would like to illustrate the reality of this flaw with one further historical analysis: The history of Britain exhibits both the splendor and the squalor that emanate from liberal theory.

Before beginning our historical analysis, I must say that it is a terrible task to criticize Britain, for Britain is that nation from which modern democracy and the reverence for law sprang first. It is the nation that became a model for Western Europe and then the world. But, as with Karl Popper,[30] who was saddened by his critique of the works of Plato and Marx, which he admired but which he felt had contributed to the emergence of the fascist horrors in Europe, I feel that the events in Britain must be criticized because of their contribution to the perpetuation of the liberal flaw.

LIBERALISM IN ENGLAND: THEORY, REALITY, AND THE JUSTIFICATION OF OLIGARCHY AND POVERTY

From the very beginning of the expansion of the city merchants into the countryside, with the widespread conversion of the land from feudal to commercial use, large numbers of peasants (and small numbers of knights) were displaced from their land.[31] The knights accumulated at the kingly court and became involved in every kind of intrigue before exploding into counter-revolutionary activity. They then slowly disappeared into the dead pages of history.

The poor peasants, displaced from their lands, were absorbed in small numbers into the flourishing artisan trades of the free cities. However the majority of them could not find work in the cities or the countryside. In Britain, and later in France, they accumulated as vagrants and vagabonds living in squalor in both urban and rural settings.

Already, before the liberal program had been institutionalized, a large class of impoverished individuals was accumulating in the midst of "the great transformation"[32] of the economy and the polity.

In the meantime, the transformation of agriculture from feudal to market production was so successful that a class of wealthy merchant-gentry arose to replace the feudal knights.[33] Along with the gentry, a class of small successful commercial farmers also emerged. These "yeoman," as the British called them, were fully commercial in their orientation, totally committed to the legal-democratic state, and violently opposed to monarchism and feudalism.

In the cities, a class of wealthy trade-merchants became more numerous and more prosperous. It was from this class of trade-merchants that the countryside gentry originally arose and expanded. Alongside the merchants, a class of small merchants, shopkeepers, and artisan-producers expanded.

Taken together, the gentry and yeoman, the merchants, and artisans made the revolution against the monarchy and the vestiges of feudalism.[34] These new classes developed the political institutions and ideas that would replace kingship and feudalism.

The new classes were fueled in their quest by Calvinist protestantism,[35] which had emerged in the free cities and spread to the countryside. Calvinism was adopted fanatically in Holland and Britain and carried to the United States—those most commercial and least feudal Atlantic trading nations—and served to legitimate individualism, economic entrepreneurship, money usage, and the ideal of political independence and self-rule. Whether Calvinism spawned commercialism or commercialism spawned Calvinism is for Weber, Tawney, and Marxian scholars to debate.[36] For us, it is enough to know that they emerged together[37] as a mighty force against monarchy and feudalism and elevated law, democracy, and free economic enterprise to a holy plane.

In Britain this led to the "Great Civil War," or revolution, against the kingly state.

The revolution against the kingly-state and the feudal lords was successfully led by Cromwell. His army of yeoman farmers, lesser gentry, and artisans, financed by the merchants and passionately undergirded by both puritan fanaticism and the liberal ideal, fought successfully. The feudal forces underestimated their opponents and failed to recognize their zeal and their wealth. Having lost the majority of their peasants over the years, their forces collapsed more easily than expected in this British revolutionary/civil war.

However, Cromwell's victory and the very first establishment of the liberal political institutions already revealed the flaw that was to plague it for centuries.

The king was beheaded when he refused to take on a limited executive role—how could a "divine" king do so? The parliament was established as the central political institution of state. However, the question of representation and voting rights immediately emerged. Should everyone have the right to run for and sit in parliament, and should everyone have the right to vote?

The rich gentry and city merchants claimed that only they had the right to run, sit, and vote; that they—the rich—would represent the yeoman and the shopkeepers and the artisans—the middle class—in the parliament (as they had done in pre-revolutionary days when they met with the king, clergy, and feudal nobility as the "third estate"). As for the poor—the displaced peasants—they were not even considered part of the polity.

The rich sat in the parliament and refused to allow the middle class or the poor their political rights. "Legal-oligarchy" was established. Legal, because the rule of law was heavily legitimated by the commercial rich; oligarchy, because rule by the few-rich was claimed to be rightful over rule by the people.

Because they claimed their right to rule, and their legitimation, from the possession of property and money wealth, not from feudal traditional authority, political reaction against this claim was inevitable.

From the moment of its victory, liberalism engendered its nemesis, socialism. Arising against the oligarchic parliament, a group of yeoman, shopkeepers, and artisans, calling themselves "the Levellers,"[38] sought to create a system of communal land distribution that would equalize wealth differences and therefore allow everyone a chance to sit in parliament and vote for its representatives.

The Levellers rose up from Cromwell's army. They had fought the King and the Lords, now they would fight the "Gentleman" farmers and merchants. Their program was legal-democracy politically, but pure communism economically. This was similar to the ancient Greek Phalleus' plan for Athens,[39] and, of course, it was what Marx's dreams were made of in his early years.[40]

But this dream, too, is flawed, for it leads away from the liberal program of free commercially oriented economic development, and demands—not in its dream, but in its reality—government intervention in the distribution process.

Whether the Levellers' idea of legal-democratic government with pure communistic economics could have become, or should have become, reality is a moot question: the Levellers were crushed by Cromwell. One can hardly call the Leveller uprising a revolt, for the Levellers so revered Cromwell—their charismatic hero[41]—that they protested, more than they revolted. And Cromwell, for his part, feeling great loyalty to these men who had fought the revolution against the monarchy at his side, executed but one Leveller leader and jailed a few others, among them Lilburne,[42] chief spokesman for the Leveller cause.

The day of the Levellers was not at hand, nor would their program come to fruition. With wide open, unfettered commercial development undergirding the political and economic revolution against feudalism and kingship, how could a turn toward small farming on tiny, but equal, plots carry the future?

Cromwell, however, of middling origin himself (lesser gentry, as Trevor-Roper emphasizes[43]), produced a temporary compromise between the rich and the middle class. He convened a parliament that included representatives of both the rich and the middle class. He counterbalanced the power of the rich with the power of the army he still controlled. In order to maintain even this small compromise—the inclusion of the middle classes in the legal-democratic process—he had to declare himself "Lord Protector" of the realm (temporary dictator) and actually use the power of the army to maintain the place of the middle classes in the parliamentary process.[44] The displaced poor were never included.

But Cromwell was a mortal man. He may have been "God's Englishman" but God claimed him after all. With the death of the charismatic military hero, the power of the army was diluted, and the power of the rich reasserted. Legal-oligarchy with a stringent property qualification was established again.

With the middle class relatively weak, the rich very strong, and the condition of the poor peasantry declining, legal-democracy did not emerge, although the institutional and ideological program of liberalism was fully established.

Legal-democracy would occur in America, as Lord Acton[45] and Seymour Lipset[46] would point out, completing the British revolution at last. But in Britain, legal-oligarchy would last for many years.

Fearful of a further revolt from the yeoman, artisans, and displaced peasants, the rich gentry and merchants restored the kingship, in limited form of course, in 1688. The "Glorious Revolution" of 1688 was, from this viewpoint, a disgraceful counter-revolution,[47] re-establishing enough of the bonds of traditional authority to re-entrap a large segment of the population into quasi-feudal servility. Those who stayed came to treat the king and the gentlemen with a mixture of feudal deference and the "resentment" of revolution defeat. Many drifted into religious cult groups, like the Shakers and the Quakers, and retreated[48] into religious fanaticism and asceticism. Others left for the New World, looking for the property that could buy them the political freedom they had fought for and were cheated of. (Remember that in Britain, the right to vote and the right to sit in Parliament would not be extended to the lower classes until 1867, after the "Chartist Movement."[49])

All of this occurred *before* the industrial revolution. And, of course, these events (along with the religious transformation) ushered-in the industrial revolution.[50]

The industrial revolution brought with it new hope and new dreams, but it also widened the problem that already plagued liberalism. The factory system, with its machine production and assembly line efficiency, looked like the remedy for the liberal problem: the displaced peasants could be absorbed as factory workers, make money-wages, and raise themselves out of poverty. This would be the long-term result, but it would not occur automatically out of the inner-dynamics of the industrial system, and it would not occur for almost two centuries.

In the earlier years, the industrial revolution served to *ruin* the artisans and small shopkeepers of the cities and provided nothing for the yeoman farmers in the way of wealth or mobility. The middle class *declined* under the impact of the industrial revolution, and would not expand anew (in white collar, professional, and small business form) until the turn of the 20th century. This is why Marx, living in England until his death in 1886, believed that the Aristotelian middle class could not stabilize capitalist-industrial society or assert a democratic influence. This is why he believed that the split between the rich and poor would inevitably end in revolutionary violence.[51]

As for the poor, the factory system and machine production did not improve their condition. Entrepreneurial factory owners were creatively productive and *did* innovate the marvels of production that energized our brave new world. Half inventor, half business entrepreneur,[52] the "captains of industry" were like heroes of war, leading us to a new epoch of conquest over nature. But they were also capitalists working for a profit. They developed efficient productive methods to maximize that profit, and they were guided by market forces in the pricing of their products. However, one need not be a logician to realize that the lower the wages they paid to the workers, the higher their profit would be. And one need not attempt to decipher Marx's complex "labor theory of value"[53] to come to the conclusion that the workers were underpaid and overworked.

So intent on profit were the entrepreneurial capitalist-industrialists that they not only underpaid men, but also women and children, who were pressed into the hard labor of factories and mines. And whereas the hard labor of women, children, and men in the outdoors of the farms of old had been healthful—though tedious and exhausting—the indoor work in the factories and mines was destructive to the health of the overworked and underpaid industrial labor force.

The "Dickensesque wretches" were emerging as a social type—the twisted and maimed, the pocked and scarred, the coughing with black lung and emphesema, the birth-defective and the diseased, the economically deprived and socially depraved—with the miserly "scrooges"[54] of the business world emerging at the other end of the economic spectrum.

These figures are hardly characters from Adam Smith's dream, and all but the economically and politically privileged would have refused to enter into Locke's "social contract." As Rawls has so incisively pointed out, the "state of nature" would have to be revisited and the liberal program amended before the parties would have agreed to this new hypothetical "social contract."

The industrial revolution was engendering a massive class of impoverished individuals even worse off than their displaced-peasant predecessors had been in the days of the commercialization of agriculture. And the middle class, in its newer white collar, professional, and modern-small business form, had not yet arisen to alter the class balance in a democratic direction.[55]

Theorists such as John Stuart Mill saw that liberalism was worthy, but in need of modification or addition. He began to toy with the idea of workers' cooperatives.[56] Other theorists, such as Jefferson (in land-rich America) saw that education and a modicum of property might improve the position of the poor and middle classes, and help stabilize a truly democratic, lawful polity.

If liberal theory had followed the lead of Jefferson and Mill, socialism, as a counter-ideology, opposed to and disgusted with liberalism, might never have gained the credence that it did.

However, the major thrust of liberal theorizing—and this is still true today—flows in two different directions (different from Jefferson and Mill). The first direction of theorizing *accepts oligarchy and poverty* as inevitable and justifiable. Inevitable in terms of the competition between men with unequal abilities—this from Aristotle's conception of "proportional equality"; and justifiable in terms of Calvinist protestant theology, and later on, social Darwinism.

The second direction of liberal theorizing drifts toward *utopian thinking*. The utopians would theorize that, if only the system would be allowed to function in its ideal form, the best of all possible worlds would be produced.

THE JUSTIFICATION OF OLIGARCHY AND POVERTY BY LIBERAL THEORISTS

The first justification comes straight out of trade-capitalism and the commercial culture it spawned. That is, whoever works harder and more successfully at money-making activities deserves more wealthy and the greater power that wealth confers. The rich, in this view, are more deserving, and therefore, following

Aristotle's theory of proportional equality, they should be rewarded with high offices and more political power.

Aristotle did not limit his higher political rewards to those with wealth alone, but to those who showed civic excellence. However, within Aristotle's schema, those who had a better education could contribute more to the civic good, and wealth could buy a better education. Therefore, equipped with the best education money could buy, the rich of Britain could claim that they were the "excellent" to whom Aristotle referred. The gentry of Britain claimed superiority of education and wealth as their justification for exclusionary oligarchy, and liberal theorists tacitly supported this justification. Even John Stuart Mill, leaning toward true representative democracy, suggested allowing greater representation for the better educated.[57]

But I have suggested that Aristotle never advocated oligarchy of the rich, but rather a mixed polity with a middle class majority. Nor did Aristotle ever denigrate the poor as lazy or uneducable. Why did the British liberals view the poor in this way when Aristotle believed the poor to be redeemable through property and careers?

Vulgarized Calvinist Protestant Theology and the Justification of Wealth and Poverty

From the vulgarized doctrine of puritan theology—not the doctrine actually written by Luther and Calvin, but that which the people came to believe (this difference is brilliantly analyzed by Max Weber in *The Protestant Ethic and Spirit of Capitalism*[58]—a justification for oligarchy and poverty emerged that had ominous overtones. In vulgarized protestant theology, those who worked hard in their "calling" (profession or trade) were "good," whereas those who were lazy or slothful were "of the devil." The protestant "work-ethic" is well known: working hard is the road to salvation; not working is the road to hell. But there is more to this theology.

The vulgarized notion derived from Calvin's theology of predestination said that if hard work led to the accumulation of money-wealth, that wealth was a "sign of grace"—a sign that you were among the "elect" who would go to heaven. Of course, Calvin's corollary doctrine of "inner-worldly asceticism" inhibited the use of money-wealth for the buying of luxury goods or leisure— these would corrupt your soul. Thus money itself, its accumulation and its reinvestment for the sake of making more money, became the sign of "heavenly grace." This is Weber's thesis of Calvinism and its relationship to the "spirit of capitalism."[59] What is important for us is that those who accumulated money-wealth were considered to be among the "elect"—this was God's sign.

In Calvin's theology only God was supposed to know who went to heaven and why (and God was inscrutable). But in the vulgarized doctrine the "sign" of money-wealth was the revelation. Conversely, if you worked hard, but did not gain wealth, you were not among the "elect." You still had to work hard in order to avoid hell and gain the right to purgatory, but you were not among the elect.

Those gaining wealth were "God's stewards on earth"—they deserved their power, their privileges, and their wealth. Given this theology, of course, those with wealth should rule. Those less fortunate in their wealth accumulation had to keep working and trying, but were clearly undeserving, while those who did not work at all were lost—they were among the damned. The moral was: Do not reach out to them, do not give them alms, do not create charities for them, do not take them into your family. They are the damned, they deserve their fate, they should rot in their living hell.

Who can deny that this vulgarized protestant doctrine influenced liberal thinking? How else can we imagine a great theory of law and democracy and inalienable rights and individual accomplishments accepting a large portion of its citizenry living in a condition so deteriorated and degenerate?

This vulgarized protestant theology still persists in Britain and the United States (and to a lesser extent in Holland and Germany). Very little sympathy for the poor emanates from the rest of the citizenry in these realms. For instance, in the United States today, although millions are spent on the retarded—they are even provided with a "special olympics"—little is spent on housing for the homeless or jobs for the poor. Why is the spending of millions for the retarded considered noble and wise, while spending for the poor is considered misguided and ignorant?

Thus, a justification of legal-oligarchy and the acceptance of poverty received strong impetus from a theological current damning the poor and idealizing the rich. This is a far cry from Calvin's original intent, and of course, it is very different from the ideas of Aristotle.

Vulgarized Biology and the Justification of Oligarchy and Poverty

If the poor are of the devil, perhaps they are not "fit" to survive. It is an easy jump from protestant theology in its vulgarized form to "Social Darwinism." Darwin, like Luther and Calvin with protestantism, never said any of the things attributed to him by the Social Darwinists.

Social Darwinism became an ideological doctrine justifying the power of the rich and the neglect—nay, the annihilation—of the poor.[60]

In its vulgarized form, Social Darwinism pictured the world as a jungle "writ red in tooth and claw"[61] where every species, every race, every individual, was in competition with one another for survival. Nature was not a kindly place. The fitness of the species and race depended on the "natural selection" of the "fit." It was best, in this view, if the "unfit" died off.

It is so easy from this logic to view the rich and well-educated as fit, and the poor and illiterate as unfit. The British Social Darwinists, vulgarizing the doctrine to the utmost, viewed their own lower class—who in their enduring conditions of poverty had developed ill-health and broken families, and who had turned to crime and vice and drunkeness—as unfit. The lower class was characterized as brutish and roguish, while the upper class developed its refined, ultra-civilized cultural style. Britain, under the influence of Social Darwinism, may be the only nation in the world wherein its own lower class came to be categorized as subhuman and unfit to survive.

The extension of this negative definition beyond Britain's shores to Ireland was an easy one—all of the Irish then being characterized as beastial, degenerate, and therefore unfit as a "race." The British Social Darwinists then further extended this categorization to the Australian Aborigines, the East Indians, the American Indians, Africans, and other "lesser races." Eventually, this insidious, vulgarized doctrine would capture the imagination of the proto-fascists in Europe and come to fruition in the hideous eugenic and genocidal acts of Nazism.

The British upper class spoke over and over again of "good breeding." Not culturally instilled manners, but "good breeding," like that of a race horse as opposed to a plow horse, or a pure-bred dog as opposed to a mongrel. "Good breeding" became the term substituted for educational and socializational processes. In what other intellectual setting could Eliza Doolittle's transformations be viewed as titillating?[62]

With such an ideology, it became inconceivable to develop programs for the rehabilitation and upgrading of the poor to middle class status.

Social Darwinism, therefore, became a justifying ideology for the dramatic wealth differentials exhibited in Britain. Since wretched poverty was justified as part of the struggle for survival, and the "fit" were deemed biologically heroic, oligarchy seemed right and natural, and the deteriorating condition of the poor seemed proof of their inferior nature.

LIBERAL UTOPIANIZING

Conditions were not emerging as the state of nature theorists had imagined they would.

Against this context of a drift away from liberal ideals, a strain of utopian thinking began to emerge. Utilitarianism, as best presented by Jeremy Bentham,[63] was the central current of this utopianism. Bentham's utopian vision attempted to reinforce the original logic from which liberal society was supposed to have sprung. The utilitarians wanted to give competitive individualism a chance. They believed, and perhaps rightfully so, that unfettered individual economic and political competition had never really occurred, so that the ills of the emerging society could not actually be blamed on it.

Bentham and the utilitarians were certain that if only the conditions for free competition were fostered, the result would be an expanding wealth pool and a more equitable society. They were convinced that free competition would bring out the most in humanity—that individuals would maximize their profit-drive in the most rational way. This free competition, while obviously more favorable in end-result for the successful than the unsuccessful, would nonetheless produce the greatest benefits for the whole society. Since the competition would raise up the economic level of the entire society, it would, in the long run, produce the greatest benefits for all involved.

Utilitarian logic seems sound on this. In the long run, if the economic condition of the entire society is greatly raised through economic competition, then everyone's lifestyle and income should eventually improve. The basic problem with this logic is that in the actual industrial-capitalist world of economic development, there was a continuing tendency toward monopoly, while in the actual political sphere there was a tenacious clinging to oligarchy. And while in the long run in capitalist-industrial societies, the economic condition of everyone in society certainly did improve, it did not improve through laissez-faire processes alone.

Since the economic and political reality of capitalist-industrial legal society was different than the utopian logic supporting it, the change in the conditions of the middle classes and the poor occurred also in a reality different from the utopian logic. That is, the eventual growth of the middle class and rise in the income of the poor occurred, *not* through the process of free competition, but rather through: (1) the organization of the middle class in the "Chartist Movement" (which demanded the right to vote be extended to all male citizens), (2) through the expansion of the white collar professions attached to the giant monopolistic firms (and the technological base they engendered), and (3) through the organization of the poor into unions supported by socialist ideology.

This is a reality quite distant from the utilitarian's utopian vision of pure competitive individualism operating in a free market.

Still, Bentham's utilitarian utopianizing is seductive. For somehow, the dream goes, *if* the conditions for pure laissez faire could be fostered, the economic and political condition of everyone would be improved, and the best and most just distribution of wealth and power would emerge. No correctives would be necessary. All interferences would be counter-productive.

Rawls has argued brilliantly against the logic of the utilitarians.[64] First, their position is utopian in that the conditions for such a pure competition can never be fully established, because industrial capitalism itself tends toward the establishment of the giant industrial firm, and second, success in democratic politics (within mass society) depends on the formation of national organized "interest groups."[65]

But more importantly—and this is the heart of Rawls' critique of utilitarianism—*where the condition of free competition is approached historically, wealth differentials do not tend to lessen*. Rather, extremes of poverty and wealth come to typify the society, even though the general level of technological and industrial development rises. In the late 19th and early 20th centuries, when the major industrial expansion in the capitalist nations occurred, the middle classes and the poor did not fare well. The "market" did not automatically improve their condition, as it did the condition of the rich industrialists. Political and economic organizations, counter vailing[66] the power of the rich, were necessary in order to force the reallocation of resources from the rich to the middle classes and the poor.

If a theory does not correspond with reality, yet its logic is consistent within itself, then that theory must be categorized as utopian. Utopian visions are like fairy tales that cannot come true. We love the fantasy, but reality intrudes. The perfect world of competitive individualism can never be real, just as the perfect world of pure communism can never be real. Therefore, if romantic socialism must be avoided, so too utilitarianism must be rejected. Utilitarianism does not reinforce the liberal political and economic institutions that its proponents wish to sustain. Rather, such utopianizing strengthens the forces opposing liberalism.

The State of Nature and the Liberal-Utopian Vision

Liberal utopianizing actually began with the conception of the "state of nature" itself—especially the version promulgated by Locke. In liberal state of nature theory it is assumed that the guarantee of political rights and property rights and protection against governmental interference is enough to create a near-perfect social world. Free property development and full political protection from the power of the state were supposed to lead to the legal-democratic "mixed polity" and "proportionate equality," which Aristotle had held was the best practical form of polity.

Locke and his political followers were Aristotelians (and excoriated as such by the Hobbesians, who held a different view of the state).[67] However, the Lockians missed the second step of the Aristotelian program. The split of the victorious commercial classes into rich and middling, and the exclusion of the poor from the polity, were never analyzed in Aristotelian terms. Instead, state of nature liberalism split into two trends, the one defending oligarchy, the other utopianizing on the eventual idyllic outcome of the "social contract." We have described these trends already, and how far they stray from the Aristotelian program out of which they were originally derived. Vulgarized protestantism and Social Darwinism disallowed ameliorating the condition of the poor and, along with utilitarian utopianizing, made inconceivable the utilization of the wealth of the rich for the civic good.

Looking back upon this, Rawls saw that the state of nature theory was logically flawed,[68] that in its inception it was unfair, and that therefore in its results it would be equally unfair. We have described Rawls' revision of the philosophical state of nature. We mention it again here because Rawls' revision engenders a set of correctives fully consonant with the principles of Aristotle.

Rawls describes a *two step* process, the first of which establishes the political and economic freedoms that we cherish and must maintain at all costs, the second of which establishes a set of correctives that improves the economic fairness of the system. Rawls' position is that without the second step, although the system may remain constitutionally beautiful, it becomes economically unjust.

Conclusions on the Two-Step Theory of Legal-Democratic Stability

In conclusion on the liberal conception of polity, the key for us is that in the social reality of history, wherein the liberal political program is played out, it turns out that without enormous pressure for greater economic equality, society splits toward concentrations of wealth at the top and massive poverty at the bottom. This destabilizes the legal-democratic system and leaves it vulnerable to oligarchy and tyranny. A middle class majority does not grow automatically out of the dynamics of individualist competition or entrepreneurial activity. The middle class can be politically alienated and economically debilitated by the actual historical conditions engendered by capitalist-industrialism within a legal setting. The upward mobility of the poor is also not automatically assured within such a system. Finally, the actions of the rich industrialists and businessmen do not necessarily, in and of themselves, benefit the economic condition of the middle and lower classes. This is why liberalism alone is an inadequate theory of legal-democratic politics.

Liberal justifications for the economic and political flaw in the system serve to discredit liberalism rather than to reinforce it. Liberal utopianizing simply obscures the inadequacy of the program, and worse, generates its counterpart, socialist utopianizing. Neither brand of utopianizing serves to stabilize legal-democratic reality.

Therefore, the Aristotelian and Rawlsian correctives become necessary. Necessary, as part of the liberal program itself, established to reinforce that program and stabilize it (not to replace it or override it).

The Aristotelian and Rawlsian *second step* is not utopian; it is a social engineering[69] corrective directed toward the proper balancing of the class structure such that the liberal political institutions and processes may be stabilized and maintained.

CONTEMPORARY JUSTIFIERS AND UTOPIANS

In the modern world, there are still strong currents of thought linked to past trends, which in attempting to reinforce liberalism and the inherent goodness of its program, tend to either justify its ills or utopianize on how these ills could be removed through an extension of the liberal program itself.

In terms of justification, there is an undercurrent of Social Darwinism that is quite virulent in the United States, Britain, and Germany. Although this philosophy led to racism at its best and genocidal Nazism at its worst, it still persists. Bio-sociology, for instance, although very interesting in-itself and by no means illegitimate as an approach to social analysis, nonetheless—in its vulgarized form[70]—has led to some fairly blatant racism against blacks and against the "less intelligent." Arthur R. Jensen and Carlton Coon began writing about the inferiority of blacks in intellectuality as racially determined.[71] A sperm bank for artificial insemination was begun by a Social-Darwinist clique of Nobel Laureates who believed their genes were superior.[72] Films produced by bio-sociologists depict naked "savages" in Brazil engaging in aggression and sexuality—proving, of course, that they must be lower forms of beastial life?[73] Such films, while purporting to explain human social action through genetic causality, tend to reaffirm the Social Darwinist notion that some people are less "fit" and therefore do not deserve to survive.

In the United States a blatant rejection of the poor, and especially the black poor, accompanied the revival of Social Darwinism, while at the same time, the naked Amer-indians depicted in the bio-sociology film were marked for extermination by urban Brazilians seeking to develop the raw materials in their land. This latter situation reached such tragic proportions that a group of humanistic anthropologists[74] made a counter-series of films and television programs in which the headman of one of the groups of Indians marked for genocide tells the viewers, "You must understand, we are people—please tell others that we are people."

Let me emphasize that it is vulgarized bio-sociology that led to the Social Darwinist conclusions. There are also wonderful, sophisticated works in this field that have enhanced our understanding of both human beings and animals.[75] However, I did not think I would see the day when vulgarized biologism would return; but it did, and it is very much with us in our perception of the poor today.

The protestant rejection of the poor as lazy and unwilling to work is still around as well. Most Americans are amazed to discover that the working-poor exist, and that whenever job-openings, such as police or transit or sanitation worker, open up, thousands of poor people wait in line for these jobs. Americans still share the protestant belief that the poor are welfare cheats, immoral, lazy, and unwilling to work. Americans prefer the "workfare" program not because it is a better rehabilitative program, but because it will *force* the poor to work. "Blaming the victim"[76] is the modern-day version of the protestant "work gets you to heaven, sloth sends you to hell" ideology.

Given the protestant rejection of the poor and the undercurrent of Social Darwinism that still pervades our society, the incompleteness of liberalism becomes difficult to rectify. Yet, given such justifying ideologies, pressure for the "second step"—or the establishment of greater relative equality—becomes all the more necessary.

Left to itself, liberalism engenders law and democracy and civil liberties and protects us from the power of the state. But left to itself it also engenders poverty, crime, and violence, and a selfish, self-righteous disregard for the less advantaged and the less successful. If the numbers of these latter were small, liberalism could stand on its own. But since the numbers of the poor have been historically great, and their condition, even in this modern age, socially and physically wretched (please check the infant-mortality rate at Harlem Hospital or the rate of family violence and sexual abuse among the rural and urban poor in contemporary America), liberalism must be seen as an incomplete system in need of the Aristotelian-Rawlsian corrective.

MODERN-DAY LIBERAL–UTOPIANS: NOZICK AND FRIEDMAN

Taken together, the works of Nozick and Friedman spell out the most extensive attempt at liberal-utopianizing since the days of the utilitarians. Their works are as seductive as those of the utilitarians were in their day.

The utilitarians created a utopian ideal of liberalism, asserting that in its pure form—fully unfettered by state interference—competitive individualist action would create the most beneficial world possible. Just so Nozick and Friedman have reasserted this position within the context of modern society.

Nozick: The Ultraminimalist State and Utopia

Nozick, in *Anarchy, State, and Utopia*,[77] favors the "minimal state" advocated by liberal theory. His entire thesis is actually a defense of the minimalist state. So worried is he that the state will be extended in a welfare-state direction that he takes us on a mind-journey in the other direction, toward a state *more* minimal than the minimal state. He postulates an "ultraminimal" state—the only function of which is the maintenance of order. He goes further in his logic, still, past the ultraminimal state and to a situation of anarchy in which order is maintained by "protection associations," whose services one purchases like an insurance policy.

Nozick, however, carefully describes why the "protective associations" would be inadequate and why the ultraminimal state would be necessary to prevent protective associations from becoming "rogue" organizations. Then he analyzes the inadequacy of the ultraminimal state, the protective services of which would be extended only to those who could afford to pay for it. He then takes us back to the minimal state—a minimal state that provides order and protection for all citizens, regardless of wealth.

As we come back to the minimal state and away from anarchy, the journey seems long and we are grateful to be back at rest with the minimal state. Nozick then argues that no extension of the state, beyond the minimal—or "nightwatchman"—state is necessary or justifiable: "We argue that no state *more* powerful or extensive than the minimal state is legitimate or justifiable."[78]

Nozick then goes further yet with his analysis of the minimal state. The minimal state has no function beyond "protection"—all other functions are provided by the "market." Even payment for the "nightwatchman" state itself is to come from a market-oriented mechanism, that is, a Friedman voucher program.[79]

The minimal (night-watchman) state is equivalent to the ultraminimal state conjoined with . . . a Friedmanesque voucher plan financed from tax revenues. Under this plan all people, or some (for example, those in need), are given tax-financed vouchers that can be used for their purchase of a protective policy from the ultraminimal state.[80]

I have already stated that utopianism is different from theorizing in that the "model" created is too far from social reality to provide us with practical institutions and processes that we can slowly improve. The "utopian vision" draws us away from the realities of social life and toward a form of society that cannot be. That vision, because it is too far from reality, induces us to engage in mistaken social constructions that do not produce their intended effect.

The utopian vision of the romantic socialists should stand as a warning to all utopianizers that their dreams are too close to fantasy and too far removed from reality. Was it not Marx who said that "the state would wither away," and so too would all class divisions? Yet the realities of socialized control of the means of production have engendered a monolithic bureaucratic despotic state, and class divisions have ineluctably emerged with the modern technocratic division of labor.

However, is not postulating the "ultraminimalist" state like fantasizing the "withering away" of the state? Doesn't it push us toward the belief that in the practical world of modern reality, we can—and ought to—diminish the state to minimalist standards? Why is this utopianizing and why is it dangerous?

We don't have a minimalist state. And even if we minimized every vestige of social programs and social agencies from our modern state, it would still be a large-scale state with immense administrative functions and enormously powerful military and police sectors under the direction of the executive branch. The administrative segment cannot be eliminated: taxes need to be collected and social security dispensed; airlines need to be overseen on safety standards; money has to be printed and the money-supply regulated, and so forth. With no social programs at all, the size of the administrative portion of the modern state would remain enormous.

Not only can the military and police segments of the modern state not be eliminated, but under the impact of increasing world tensions and the organized nature of modern crime, they have been expanding. The military, police, and administrative portions of the government alone have expanded it to such proportions and with such power-potential as to send it beyond the realm of minimalist theory.[81]

If we pursue the utopianizing directions, then we should keep trying to diminish this "Leviathan"[82] until it approaches or becomes a minimal state. This is the core of liberal utopianizing. If, however, we discover that in reality we cannot approach the minimalist situation because we cannot minimize the functions of the state (necessitated by our mass society), then we should follow out the logic and precepts of *liberal theory* (as opposed to liberal-utopianism) and apply and extend liberal theory to our modern situation.

That is, since we don't have a minimal state, and since if we did it would be inadequate to our modern needs, then if we want to maintain our rights in the modern state, we must analyze it as it has evolved, and then extend the power-limiting and power-checking mechanisms we have against it.[83] We must extend the theory of Locke, Montesquieu, Jefferson, and the Federalists into the modern context. We must not dream of a utopian world wherein the state could be brought to minimalist proportions.

In terms of extending liberal theory, for instance, the addition of a national ombudsman[84] system could be established, as a kind of second supreme court system—but with prosecutorial and investigative functions designed to protect the rights of the individual citizens from the (real) government bureaucracies. As instituted in Germany, the ombudsman system could be established with three branches: to protect citizens (1) from the civil bureaucracy, (2) from the military bureaucracy, and (3) from the corporate bureaucracies.[85] Another possibility would be to create a special Congressional "watchdog" committee, whose task would be specifically to oversee the actions of administrative, military, and policing agencies whose connection to the executive branch empowers them beyond the design of legal-democratic constitutions (emergent as they were in the 18th and 19th centuries).[86]

Clearly, newly specified limitations of power will have to be placed over the use of computers (for the compilation of "dossiers" on citizens) and over the use of audio-video surveillance devices. The privacy of the citizen must be protected from the "Big Brother" potential of the modern state.[87] Perhaps, as Robert Dahl[88] has suggested, democratically elected "boards of directors" will have to be empowered against corporate managers and bureau managers, whose control of great bureaucratic corporations has become a threat to citizens' rights.

These are just a few suggestions of ways in which the liberal theory of power-limitations and power-checking should be extended into the context of the modern bureaucratic state and mass society.

WHY ANARCHISM IS NOT LIBERALISM AND PRESENTS A FALSE BASIS FOR THE MINIMAL STATE

Anarchism mistrusts, or has no conception of, democracy—representative or otherwise. No positive role for the state is accepted—no citizen's participation, representative debate, or jury trial emanates from anarchism.

Liberalism, although a theory grounded in limitation of the power and scope of the state, has always been wedded with democratic theory. Devoid of it, it becomes an arid anarchism in which the state appears as a reified monster—a Leviathan[89] or Behemoth[90]—rather than an institution of men and women limited by constitutional-legal constraints.

In anarchism the state can do no good. But in liberalism, wedded with democratic theory, within the power-limited state the government "of the people" (through its elected representatives) can do good "for the people." There is a positive role for government to play, welfare-statism aside. New laws covering new situations must be made by the legislature. Leadership must be provided by the executive in national and international affairs—all this sounds so elementary, yet, liberalism without democratic theory is an incomplete theory.

Nozick, in his defense of the minimal state from his anarchistic position, says this about our elected representatives: "Is there really someone who, searching for a group of wise and sensitive persons to regulate him for his own good, would choose that group who constitute the membership of both houses of Congress?"[91]

From the above view, one would have to become either a Platonist-elitist or an anarchist. Yet later in his treatise, Nozick comes out strongly for the minimal state, which he suggests is "not uninspiring." But the minimal state is genuinely inspiring because it at once limits the power of the state and protects the rights of individuals, while at the same time provides a democratic structure through which the protected individuals can assert their positive in-put into the policies and programs of the state.

The democratic state is not meant simply to do *nothing* that will impinge on the rights of citizens. It is also meant to do *something* that those citizens want. In this latter function it is different from anarchy. The magnificence of "Western democracy," as it has emerged in its mass form in the modern world, is that it combines the theory of Greek participatory democracy with the power-limitation theory of the Enlightenment. Liberalism alone degenerates into anarchism. Liberalism combined with the theory of representative democracy lifts us to our best practical potential under the real conditions of modern mass society.

The minimalist state that Nozick describes is not the state "of the people, by the people, and for the people" that Abraham Lincoln was afraid would "perish from this earth."[92] The minimal state of Nozick is not the state defended by Pericles in his "funeral oration"[93] or that which Thucydides feared would vanish with a Spartan victory[94] (or worse, a victory by Persia over war-torn Greece).[95]

During the week of the "Ides of March," 1988, in the United States, the C-Span cable channel carried the debate on Nicaragua between those representatives of the people who favored U.S. invasion and those who favored U.S. withdrawal. The debate was passionate and eloquent—perhaps it was not the Athenian assembly debating over the invasion of Syracuse,[96] but it was a well-argued democratic debate constrained by well-drawn legal rules. Why mention this? Because anarchists cannot conceive of *any* positive function for government, save, at the outer limit of their tolerance, the maintenance of order and defense. Democratic participation and representative government are simply not valued in the anarchistic vision. Yet liberalism, without the legal-democratic participatory processes that have always been taken for granted as a parallel set of political processes, becomes a dreary doctrine indeed, emphasizing only the ills that government may inflict on the individual[97] and the "nasty, brutish"[98] quality of human interaction.

We should treasure the liberal tradition because it protects us from the worst in ourselves and the inherent despotic potentiality of the state. However, we should avoid anarchism because it denies the positive citizen's role in the legal-democratic state and is blind to the positive legislative and administrative functions of the state.

Friedman: Free Market Utopianism

Friedman, in *Capitalism and Freedom*,[99] begins with Hayek's argument on the correlative relationship between capitalism and democracy:

By removing the organization of economic activity from the control of political authority, the market eliminates this source of coercive power. It enables economic strength to be a check to political power rather than a reinforcement.[100]

This position is a crucial one, and we have already discussed its urgent acceptance in our section on Hayek. However, Friedman goes much further than Hayek, extending the idea of market economics beyond the bounds of economic activity, to its outer limits: including all organized activities in society, such as education and medical care, old age insurance and parks, the postal service and even military service.[101]

For Friedman, the separation of the economic sphere from the political sphere not only protects us from despotism, but provides us with a free market mechanism for the provision of *all* our needs. Government in his model becomes almost an epiphenomenon—unnecessary save for the minimal provision of protection (which Friedman, unlike the liberal political theorists, barely dwells on).

The wider the range of activities covered by the market, the fewer are the issues on which explicitly political decisions are required and hence on which it is necessary to achieve agreement. In turn, the fewer the issues on which agreement is necessary, the greater is the likelihood of getting agreement while maintaining a free society.[102]

If we look carefully at Friedman's position on this we find that (1) it denigrates democracy by asserting that the democratic process cannot handle political conflict, and (2) it utopianizes the market by asserting that activities organized by the market will not generate political conflict! This latter is a far cry from reality and drifts dangerously into utopian fantasy, as I hope to show. For left to market mechanisms, political differences often widen as wealth differentials widen—exacerbating, not ameliorating, the political conflict inherent in the process involved.

Furthermore, both Hayek[103] and Popper[104] accept the need for safety net programs emanating from government, and have never suggested the free market as some sort of magical device for the resolution of all of society's ills. Maintaining the free market as the basis for democracy is one thing; projecting it as the panacea for all organized activities in society is another. For Friedman, it is almost as if politics can be replaced by market activities. Get government out of our lives and everything will run smoothly.

If it were up to Friedman, and it almost was during the Nixon–Carter–Reagan years, government would be withdrawn from all regulatory activity over the economy, and from all services to the public. Both of these sectors would be self-regulated and self-provided by the free market. Friedman states without reservation:

[G]overnment would have clearly limited functions and would refrain from a host of activities that are now undertaken by federal and state governments in the United States, and their counterparts in other Western countries. . . . [I]t may help to give a sense of proportion about the role that a liberal would assign government simply to list . . . some activities currently undertaken by government in the United States that cannot validly be justified:

1. Parity price support programs for agriculture
2. Tariffs . . .
3. Government control of output—farm, oil, or other
4. Rent control
5. Minimum wage rates or maximum prices
6. The regulation of industry, such as interstate commerce or banking
7. Control of T.V. and radio by the F.C.C.
8. The Social Security program
9. Licensure provisions on professions
10. Public housing and F.H.A. or V.A. mortgage programs
11. The military draft
12. National Parks
13. The Public Post Office
14. Federal or state toll roads
15. Public schools[105]

All of these and more Friedman would have us remove from government control and allow free market play.

This sounds interesting. Indeed, it is so seductive because in our everyday experience we have found government agencies to be generally less efficient and more officious than private companies. Therefore, it would seem that it certainly would make sense to privatize most services.

But, let us look more closely at what actually happens when the free market is allowed full reign.

The post office is a good example to begin with because it is such an inefficient unit that it may make sense to privatize it. There are already companies, like Federal Express, which do the job better. But please understand that the private competitive postal service might cost *more*, not less. Right now, private services do cost more than the post office. From Friedman's model, private services should cost less. However, there are realities such as advertising costs that would soar under competitive conditions, and the probability that management executives would gain much higher salaries and usurp a wide range of expensive corporate perks. The modernization of equipment—which would improve service—would also cost the consumer more.

Still, we could live with the added cost if the service were sufficiently improved.

The case of the railroads is different, however. When the free market governed the rails, passenger service was terminated on most important commuter links nationwide. Why? Because passenger service was not profitable compared with freight. AMTRAC was not created by phantom American socialists, but by abandoned commuters (through their democratically elected representatives). Further—and Friedman knew of this—Penn Central, for instance, was mismanaged, and while its corporate profits were declining, its managers were taking million-dollar bonuses. By the time the Penn Central Board of Directors discovered this situation, it was too late and the corporation collapsed.[106] Penn Central was as inefficient as the post office, although it was privately run. (We may also recall the many privately run nursing homes in this same vein).[107]

Still, I would agree that most private corporations are more efficient than most government bureaus. But would allowing the free market in its purest condition produce all good things? The case of the Friedman school-voucher program is illustrative of some of the unforeseen pitfalls in this approach.

The Voucher Program

Friedman's free market program reached its pinnacle with the voucher plan. Through this program, citizens would gain government funding for such services as education and health care, but the services would be provided by private organizations. Again, this is so seductive. The public schools are not very good in America, by and large, while some private schools are very good. Private hospitals, on the whole, tend to be better than public ones, as well. So we think to ourselves, yes, let's go the private route. Get government out of services and all will be well. A whole school of "public choice" policymakers has arisen in Friedman's wake.[108]

What is the reality in this proposal? Let us look at the school situation, for this was Friedman's most widely discussed proposal.

Friedman's school voucher program, which would have eliminated public schools and replaced them with private schools open to all and funded for all by government-supplied vouchers, is again instructive as to reality vs. utopian fantasy. In the utopian view, if all schools were private and all individuals could choose any school, a marvelous diversity of schools would emerge—better than the public schools, and supportive of democracy. However, Friedman himself admits that the situation began to turn out differently when the movement toward private schools and away from public schools actually started to occur in the late 1960s and early 1970s.

First Friedman states his market-utopian proposal:

Government could require a minimum level of schooling financed by giving parents vouchers redeemable for a specified maximum sum per child per year if spent on "approved" educational services. Parents would then be free to spend this sum and any additional sum they themselves provided on purchasing educational services from an "approved" institution of their own choice.[109]

This sounds quite interesting, given the generally low quality of our public schools. But notice already that with Friedman's proposal, the richer citizens could spend more on their children than the middling or poor. Friedman admits there may be problems involved with his private-school voucher program. For instance:

[The existence of] private schools would tend to exacerbate class distinctions. Given greater freedom about where to send their children, parents of a kind would flock together and so prevent a healthy intermingling of children from decidedly different backgrounds.[110]

Friedman plays down this latter trend, although this trend did, in actuality, exhibit itself. He also points to another "potential" problem:

It might be impossible to provide the common core of values deemed requisite for social stability. . . . The issue can be illustrated concretely in terms of schools run by different religious groups. Such schools, it can be argued, will instill sets of values that are inconsistent with one another and secular schools. . . . [I]n this way they convert education into a divisive rather than a unifying force.[111]

This, of course, is precisely what would occur if the voucher system were adopted. For in actuality a trend toward the expansion of religious schools and ideologically-narrow schools did begin to emerge. If this is the reality that would follow, then leaving education to the free market would not reduce the political conflicts of society, but would exacerbate them in terms of class and creed. Friedman admits that:

A stable and democratic society is impossible without a minimum degree of literacy and knowledge on the part of most citizens and without widespread acceptance of some common set of values.[112]

But he will not see that the public schools were created for precisely that reason. Jefferson understood political reality, while Friedman would have us work from a utopian fantasy that could destroy Jefferson's practical program.[113]

Another point needs to be made in terms of private vs. public schools. In the last five years (1983–1988) the prestigious Westinghouse scholarship awards have gone to students largely from public high schools. Schools such as Bronx Science, Stuyvesant, and Cardozo, in New York, rather than prestigious private schools, such as Dalton, Fieldstone, or the wealthy boarding schools (such as Andover or Choate), have produced America's scientists, scholars, and innovators. Why? Because the rich private schools have tended toward upper class snobbery, rather than toward the inculcation of intellectual excellence, while the lower-middle class private schools have tended toward the inculcation of religious parochialism.

If privatization is better—and remember, most of us are seduced by this idea—why are the private schools not producing our intellectual leaders? There is a warning in this example: Friedman's voucher program—so beloved by America's neoconservatives—is a utopian trap, leading us away from the kind of practical improvements our society really needs. If we want better schools, we should establish better schools; the market might not do it for us.

In this same vein, and again ignoring the reality of the market, Friedman suggested the elimination of the government-guaranteed social security system. He would have us replace it with a retirement system linked to the stock market. Pierre Dupont campaigned for the presidency with this as a major plank in his platform (1988). For Friedman, there was no risk in the market. However, since the market crash of "Black Monday," October 1987, can we really think of social security without its government guarantee?

Here again Friedman departs from theorists such as Hayek and Popper, who, while favoring the market economy, accepted the idea of a set of social "safety net" programs guaranteed by the government.[114] Pardon the metaphor, but Friedman would allow us the risk of falling from the high wire as the market economy swings in and out of balance.

Friedman's Myopic View of the Past Blurs His Vision of the Future

One should be very cautious about Friedman's view of the future if it is based on his view of the past. For instance, this is what Friedman says about the Great Depression:

The Great Depression in the United States, far from being a sign of the inherent instability of the private enterprise system, is a testament to how much harm can be done by mistakes in the past of a few men when they wield vast power over the monetary system.[115]

The fact is that the Great Depression, like most other periods of severe unemployment, was produced by *government mismanagement.*[116]

There are very few economists who would accuse Herbert Hoover and the Federal Reserve under him of controlling the economy to the point where their input engendered the Great Depression—but Friedman does. He glosses over the great "dust bowl" and the collapse of the farm economy in the same way. They just don't seem to have happened, but if they did, government was responsible.

Worse, this is what Friedman says about the economic transformation of Britain:

The reform of the economy in the direction of laissez faire . . . was accompanied by . . . an enormous increase in the well-being of the masses following this change in economic arrangements.[117]

Friedman skips the "Dickensesque" period. He goes from the early factory system and market directly to the early 20th century, as if the transition to a better lifestyle had been smooth and effortless and automatic. Friedman refers to this transition as, "the triumph of Benthamite liberalism in the nineteenth century."[118]

Friedman's description, if applied to Germany in its transition from monarchy to democracy, would then read something like this: The reform of the polity was accompanied by an enormous increase in the political freedom and legal protection of the populace. . . . This represented a triumph of Jeffersonian Democracy and Lockian Liberalism in 20th century Germany.

From Friedman's kind of analysis the horrors of the Nazi period would simply not be mentioned—or, if mentioned, blamed on something else. Could we accept such a view of the German transition to democracy? Can we accept such a view of the British transition to market economics?

If we cannot accept Friedman's view of the free-market past, we ought to be suspicious of his projected view of a free market future.

What are some of the jarring realities that have already marred the utopianism of Friedman's policies—as they were actually implemented by the Nixon, Carter, and Reagan administrations?

We have already discussed the disastrous results of the raised interest rates of Friedman's monetarist policy. The higher interest rates resulted in a bifurcation in the class structure, the rich getting richer, the poor poorer, and the middle class splitting apart.[119]

The encouragement of corporate competition—again, although in utopia leading to greater productivity and lower prices—actually led to widespread corporate collapses, paper mergers, buy-out mania, a *decline* in productivity and a continuing rise in prices.[120] Finally, the reduction of farm supports led to the near disappearance of the family farm, the emergence of monopoly farming, and a rise in the price of farm products.

FREE MARKETS ARE NOT ENOUGH

Without meaning to do so, Friedman lends support to the "two step" theory of legal-democracy that I have attempted to establish. He analyzes the situation in this way:

The major theme [of this book] is the role of competitive capitalism—the organization of the bulk of economic activity through private enterprise operating in a free market—as a system of economic freedom and a necessary condition for political freedom.[121]

History suggests only that capitalism is a necessary condition for political freedom.

Clearly it is not a sufficient condition. Fascist Italy and Fascist Spain, Germany at various times in the last seventy years, Japan before WWI and II, Tsarist Russia in the decades before WWI—are all societies that cannot conceivably be described as politically free. Yet, in each, private enterprise was the dominant form of economic organization.[122]

The fact that capitalism is a necessary, but not sufficient condition for the maintenance of democracy is precisely the reason that liberalism is an incomplete doctrine. Liberalism embodies step one only—the establishment of a market economy separated from state control. (As described, this would not be the market economy in its utopian, but in its actual institutional form.) Step two, however, is absolutely essential for the maintenance and stability of democracy. The middle class must be expanded and nurtured so that the democratic ''elective affinities'' that it carries can pervade the polity. The public school system must imbue all classes with a cultural proclivity for law and democracy. The free market cannot do everything. It cannot, in and of itself, produce an economic or political utopia.

7

The Economy: Modified Capitalism as the Model Economy for the Modern World

At the turn of the century, Max Weber described the structural dynamics of capitalist-industrialism.[1] This, in itself, would not have been any major achievement, as Marx had already described modern capitalist-industrialism in *Das Kapital*.[2] The critical difference, however, was that Weber predicted that capitalist-industrialism would be more rational and more efficient than a centralized, state-run, bureaucratized socialist economy.[3]

That is, the socialists harbored the dream that a socialized economy would be more rational than a capitalist one, because it would be *planned*, whereas capitalist production was left to the vagaries of the market—a market whose "invisible hand" had not, through the 19th century, led to an equitable distribution of goods, or even to an abundance of goods for the lower classes. Further, the socialists believed that a socialist economy would be more productive because the workers would work harder on their own behalf. Weber disputed this. Yet, as he wrote, there was no socialist economy existent, and therefore the socialists could still harbor their utopian dream.

Weber predicted, in remarkably precise terms, what would go wrong with the socialist economy.[4] He reasoned that the centralized planned economy projected by the socialists would crash against the rock of bureaucracy.[5] Rather than becoming more productive and more efficient than capitalism, the state-socialist economy would become a giant bureaucratic monstrosity, inefficient and autocratic in its functioning, and less productive for its lack of a profit motive. Nor would state-socialism produce for the necessities of the workers. If capitalism produced for the profits of the owners, rather than the needs of the workers, socialism would produce for the needs of the bureaucracy, and become even less attuned to the needs of the workers.[6] Socialism would not even be fair in its distribution procedures, because the bureaucratic hierarchy would claim a higher share of productivity than the workers.

In short, Weber was the first to predict, with a full analysis, what de Tocqueville had warned of: that state socialism would be less efficient and productive, and no more equitable, than capitalism. When the Bolshevik revolution occurred, Weber went so far as to say that it would eventuate in a new form of "patrimonialism."[7]

Given Weber's rejection of romantic socialism, and given the fact that his prediction has proven accurate, his analysis of the rationality of capitalism and its dynamic efficiency becomes even more efficacious now than when he first wrote it.

But, unlike Adam Smith, who had written so much earlier and never lived to see the actual capitalist factory system emerge full blown, Weber did not idealize the functioning of capitalism or its resultant social consequences. Accepting capitalism as at once the most efficient and productive form of industrial economy possible under practical conditions, and as the economic system that best undergirds the legal-democratic polity, he did not idealize capitalist-industrialism. In fact, he was quite sympathetic to the Social Democrats in their attempts to improve the condition of the workers. Though he was aware of his friend Robert Michels'[8] characterization of the Social Democrats as an authoritarian party, he was also aware of the need to improve the condition of the workers through unionization and the electoral process.

What are we trying to establish with out discussion of Weber's position? We are attempting to make a distinction between Weber's characterization of capitalism and the idealized analysis of Adam Smith. Smith, who wrote prior to the full emergence of the capitalist-industrial system, never saw the remarkable industrial firms, or the terrible toll the system took on its working poor.

Smith's work is monumental for its theory of economics, and as such, he is one of the great intellectual giants of history. In no way do I mean to denigrate his work. The point is that since Smith created his theoretical system before the reality was evident, it ought not to be used to continue to deny reality. In parallel terms, who would deny the genius of Newton or fail to teach with passion his magnificent theories of motion? Yet, who would teach Newton, today, without adding the correctives and extensions of Einstein, Bohr, and Heisenberg on relativity, quantum mechanics, and indeterminacy? The correctives and extensions do not make Newtonian theory less relevant; they make it more relevant. Just so with the theories of Smith (and the early economists).

Thus, as Weber describes it, the market *is* more efficient and creative than the bureaucratically planned, state-centralized economy. However, it is *the market of giant quasi-monopolistic corporate firms*,[9] not the market of competitive small firms.

Now, having established the modern capitalist-industrial system as more rational, efficient, and productive than bureaucratic socialism—a fact which has been reaffirmed by the post-WWII performance of the Soviet and Chinese economies as compared with their capitalist-industrial counterparts—we have to ask the key question: Is it laissez-faire capitalism in its primeval Smithian form that has become the model for the best practical economy under modern conditions? Or is it a modified form of capitalist-industrialism, as yet without a name, to which most contemporary nations are actually aspiring?

For example, let us look at the German economy (during Weber's lifetime and afterwards), the Japanese economy from the 1920s to the present, and the U.S. economy during WWII and the ensuing "Cold War."

What we find in each of these cases is a modified form of capitalism involving *government-corporate cooperation* and the domination of the market by giant firms.

Germany, a century late in its industrialization and desperate to catch up with Britain, produced an economic miracle of sorts, industrializing in less than half the time it took Britain. The German industrialization occurred with the *help* of the state, rather than without the state (or against a backdrop of state interference, as in France). By the time of WWI, the German industrialization had equaled or exceeded that of Britain. Following WWI, out of the ashes of the Great Depression, Germany's economy was to explode past the productive capacity of Britain,[10] which without the wartime support of the United States would have been overwhelmed by the industrial capacity of Germany during WWII (and not by the number of German troops).

Neither Bismarck's nor Hitler's Germany could be characterized as exhibiting laissez-faire market capitalism. Nor can modern Germany, whose economy is leading the world in consumer product development and industrial patents, be so characterized.

Japan industrialized even more quickly than Germany, and, after beginning by copying the United States, shifted toward the German model. The establishment of giant monopolistic firms was followed by the closest government-corporate partnership on record. The results were a productivity level that astonished the Western world and, of course, frightened the United States into a wartime economy resembling that of its new adversary.

The Japanese, of course, lost to the American war machine, but after WWII Japan further perfected the new modified form of capitalist-industrial production. Nowhere is government-corporate partnership better developed. And since such partnership is directed now toward consumer products, rather than military products, Japan has begun to lead the world in the production and marketing of such products.

Together the Germans and Japanese have begun to dominate the world markets in all but military goods, aircraft, and computers. The last category, computers, although invented and developed in the United States, is now being expanded and successfully marketed by European and Japanese firms. So successful has this modified model of capitalism become that such nations as France and Italy, moving in the German direction, are beginning, also, to compete successfully in the world market.

The contrast between the German and Japanese cases and that of the United States is most illuminating. After the Great Depression, Americans became confused and conflicted as to what was the best way to proceed in terms of economic production. Laissez faire certainly had its creative advantages. However it had left "a third of the nation ill-clothed and ill fed,"[11] it had left a "dust-bowl" in its wake, and after cresting like a tidal wave, it had sunk into a whirlpool of depression. Some modifications of the system had to be sought. The New Deal had not provided the answer, but before the situation could be thought out, WWII occurred.

It was the WWII economy of the United States that provided the answer for America's economic future—an answer which has never really been accepted.

The productivity of the American economy during WWII is legendary. It exceeded the wildest dreams of F.D.R., who could hardly believe that his war-crisis production goals were not only met, but dramatically exceeded. Yet that remarkable productivity was not a laissez-faire productivity, but rather a productivity born of government-corporate partnership and the organization of technology by the giant firms.

This modified form of capitalism would be retained in the United States after WWII because of the "Cold War." However the deeply ingrained cultural ideology supporting laissez-faire would create an ambivalence toward modified capitalism that would ruin the partnership and weaken the U.S. economy.

In the military sector, the government-corporate relationship continued, but without the kind of capitalist-efficient government-supportive partnership exhibited in Germany and Japan. In the United States after WWII, the government gave the corporations producing military goods carte blanche, and then looked away. Cost-efficiency and capitalist rationality were not demanded. Military production goals took precedence instead.

In the civic sector, government partnership was rejected by the corporations, and they moved farther away from such cooperation as the war receded into the past. In the civic sphere government became a regulator, but not a facilitator, of capitalist production.

The results in both the civic and military sectors of the U.S. economy were disappointing. The civic sector, while retaining entrepreneurial creativity and enjoying a period of postwar success (with the world economy bombed-out), fell behind the German and Japanese economies in both product development and industrial patents by the 1970s. The military sector drifted into the kind of inefficiency and excessive cost-overruns typical of state-run economies. Bifurcating away from the modified capitalist model, both sectors of the U.S. economy began to fail. Back to Max Weber.

Weber was not only the first in the modern world to show why capitalist-industrialism would be better than state-run socialist industrialism, but he was also the first to describe the *cooperative* relationship between the modern state and the corporate-capitalist economy. As Weber saw it, the modern rational-bureaucratic state, although not so competent as the capitalists themselves in managing the economy—hence the rejection of the state-controlled economy advocated by the socialists—played a decisive role in supporting and assisting the capitalists in the growth and stability of the industrial system.

It was precisely the success of the Prussian state, in its modern rational form, in assisting the industrial process that led Weber to predict the eventual expansion of the modern rational bureaucratic state, and to warn of the danger in this.[12] The danger was that of despotic authoritarian control, which could overwhelm legal-democracy and relegate it to a secondary level of institutional process— an analysis repeated by C. Wright Mills in his *Power Elite*.[13] As we have already described, this danger is made worse by socialism, which expands the administrative power of the state over the economy.

Therefore, retaining capitalism was critical for Weber, in that it would reduce the danger of authoritarian-bureaucratic state control. However, even with the retention of capitalism the role of the state would become increasingly important. According to Weber, the modern state is different from the "anciens regimes" observed by Locke and de Tocqueville. The modern state can martial expertise and wealth that, if placed under the direction of the entrepreneurs and managers of the capitalist-industrial system, can improve its performance, rather than inhibit it.

Thus Weber left us with a dual prediction, and a warning: (1) capitalism must be retained because of its efficiency and creativity; but (2) the modern state will play an increasingly important support role in the economic process—and, given this latter factor, we must take steps to safeguard our democratic processes from this necessary, but worrisome, modern state.

The warnings of de Tocqueville, Hayek, and Weber become all the more necessary given the reality in which modern capitalist economics has emerged. The need to protect democracy becomes ever more necessary as we move to a world of giant corporate firms and government-corporate cooperation. However, we must accept the reality of the modern, modified "mixed" economy if we want to properly protect our democratic system.[14] How can we protect our democratic rights if we are not absolutely clear about the economic and political context in which they are becoming enmeshed? Which economies are being studied and emulated—the German and Japanese modified capitalist economies, or the buckaneering, unrestrained capitalist economies of pre-Depression Britain and the United States?

The *two step* process in economics establishes these historical realities: the first step asserts the superiority of capitalism over socialism; the second step establishes the superiority of modified capitalism over laissez-faire capitalism.

MODIFIED CAPITALISM AS THE MOST PRODUCTIVE AND STABLE FORM OF MODERN ECONOMY

Capitalism evolved. It became the capitalist-industrial system of giant firms controlling much of a market share.[15] There is competition and there are market forces, but they operate within the context of national and transnational oligo-polies.[16]

Such a situation violates the classic principles set out by Smith, Ricardo, Say, and others, and leads, therefore, to problems unforeseen within their theoretical systems. Overproduction, for instance, became a reality of the market of giant monopolistic firms—whose technological productive capacity was never envi-sioned by Say or Ricardo (though certainly dreamed of by Smith). Overprod-uction ruins the neat demand/supply mechanism of the market and creates the necessity for massive and manipulative advertising programs. Veblen described the beginnings of this in his *Theory of the Leisure Class*[17] and *Theory of Business Enterprise*.[18] Yet, with all of the advertising, overproduction still leads to cycles of boom and bust.[19]

Keynes was aware of this boom and bust cycle, and set about to alter the theory to fit the new reality—and, of course, to help stabilize the actual capitalist-industrial system and save it from the horrors of depressions.

Keynes also noted, as we have described in detail, that unemployment was a regular feature of the capitalist reality. In principle it was not supposed to occur, but in reality it did occur. Hence another corrective became necessary if theory, attuned to reality, was to have a beneficial effect on the system—in this case the effect intended was to substantially reduce unemployment.

Finally, the capitalist rich, as rational economic beings, were supposed to invest their savings productively for the expansion and development of the cap-italist economic system, and by this, enhance the general civic good. However, the rich often removed their capital from the market or squandered it in coun-terproductive directions.

Keynes, and before him Veblen, saw that the capitalist-industrial system had evolved in precisely the direction that Smith[20] warned would destabilize it, and also that it had evolved to a technological proficiency beyond the imagination of the early theorists.

Given these dramatic changes in the system, Keynes, Veblen, and others (especially the Swedes in the 1930s[21]) developed a set of theories and strategies that would modify the capitalist-industrial system in such a way as to help stabilize it and eliminate its worst flaws, while at the same time retaining as much of its market-rationality and entrepreneurial creativity as possible.

Let us look at the modifications suggested.

THE KEYNESIAN CORRECTIVES

We have already analysed Keynes' correctives for the capitalist ills of insta-bility and unemployment. We have also mentioned that the Swedish economists arrived at the same set of solutions independently. It must also be mentioned that the Germans, under Bismarck (and later Hitler[22]), and the Japanese, arrived at a similar set of principles, but based much more on military development than the Keynesian or Swedish programs. Still, the parallels are remarkable.[23]

Since we have described the Keynesian modifications, we will simply list them here: Government-corporate partnership is the keystone of the program, with government-directed investment in productive areas of enterprise encouraged. The government, rather than becoming an inhibitor of entrepreneurial capitalism, as with the ancien (monarchical-bureaucratic) regimes of the 18th century, becomes a facilitator of entrepreneurial activity, guaranteeing contracts, capital investment, loans, and even purchases of manufactured goods (military and civilian).

The Japanese, apparently learning this technique from the Germans, perfected it. Japanese corporate-government productive and marketing strategies are legendary in the contemporary world.

The second Keynesian corrective has to do with unemployment. Here again classic capitalist theory was deficient and the evolving capitalist system changed the rules as well.

In terms of the theory, large-scale unemployment was simply not supposed to occur. When it did occur it was blamed on unions raising wages too high, or on workers unwilling to work. Does this not still sound familiar? Keynes, however, changed the theory. From his calculations, it was simply less profitable for producers to operate at a level of full employment. And from Marx's analysis, it depressed wages if producers kept an "army of unemployed workers" competing for the jobs of those who demanded higher wages.

Since unemployment continued and continues to occur, Keynes added to the theory, so that government investment would create more job opportunities, and absorbed the Marxian critique by theorizing that the government would *have* to become the employer of last resort for those not absorbed by the expanded opportunities.

Again, this was a modification of capitalism, intended to retain its strengths while minimizing its weaknesses.

Finally, as to unemployment: the "structural" unemployment created by the automation-computerization-robotization process (so recent that Keynes did not live to see it) needs little new theorizing. The Keynesian corrective works under the new conditions. Government still stimulates the economy through investments and guarantees, thus expanding the new technical, professional, managerial, and white collar career-line jobs. The government becomes the employer of last resort for those left out of this expanding job system. The only difference created by the newly evolved conditions is that education and educational support programs become a critical new aspect of job-training.

The Keynesian correctives on taxes and interest rates have already been described, but it needs to be emphasized that those nations that have more fully accepted the modified capitalist system have also been more willing to tax progressively and provide low interest loans. The German, Japanese, and Swedish governments tax their rich and their corporations at a higher rate than the United States. Yet their corporations have shown a more successful, more efficient performance level.

No idealization is intended here. For instance, the Germans are quite worried that their entrepreneurial level is quite poor compared to that of the United States, acknowledging that most of the creative business innovations and technological productive processes still emerge from the United States. And the Japanese firms suffer from the kind of rigid status hierarchies characterizing their militaristic cultural style.

Nonetheless, the increased taxation of the private and corporate rich, when turned to productive industrial investment and toward civic projects, does produce a more stable, expansive, and equitable system—a modified capitalist-industrial system close to that envisioned by Keynes.

VEBLEN'S INSIGHTS AND THE KEYNESIAN CORRECTIVES

Veblen, coming from a very different perspective than Keynes, presented a picture of the paradoxes of the capitalist-industrial system as it had emerged in his day. His *Theory of the Leisure Class*, is, of course, well known, but *The Theory of Business Enterprise* and *The Engineers and the Price System* also contain remarkable insights that can help us understand why a modified system of capitalism has become the most efficient and productive form of economy the world has ever known.

Veblen's ideas of "conspicuous consumption" and "conspicuous waste" have become part of our everyday discourse. They symbolized the decline of the puritan-ascetic culture from which capitalist-industrialism sprang.[24]

From *The Theory of Business Enterprise* we get his famous analysis of the technological overproduction of the giant firms and the need for mass advertising campaigns that this causes. This became the raison d'etre of economic activity, overriding the market mechanisms of supply and demand that were supposed to maintain business stability, set prices, and assure full employment. Boom and bust, expansion and depression came to characterize the system instead, with prices riding to higher levels than predicted by the market, and unemployment becoming endemic to the system.

As with Keynes, the realities that characterized the capitalist-industrial system struck Veblen as divergent from the theory that was supposed to undergird it.

In *The Engineers and the Price System*,[25] Veblen focused on a further development within the capitalist-industrial system—one that would demand a new level of modification. This level of modification has emerged, and is well understood in Japan, but it is still resisted in the United States. As such, it is creating havoc within our economic system.

The process that we refer to here, which Veblen brilliantly analyzed at the turn of the century, is the separation of capitalist financial dealings from the technological-industrial process. As Veblen described it, the early capitalist entrepreneurs—the "captains of industry"—combined the skills of capitalist *fi-*

nance with those of technological-industrial *inventing*. The captains of industry were inventors, producers, and financiers. They held all the skills.

However, as the technology became more complex, a separation occurred. Scientifically trained "engineers" came to be the industrial-technological innovators, while the captains of industry concentrated their effort on the business sector, becoming transformed into "captains of finance."[26]

The problem as identified by Veblen was that the needs of industrial (technological) production became different from, and divergent with, the needs of business and finance. Moneymaking—in its classic capitalist form—becomes separated from the dynamics of industrial production.[27]

Remember, capitalist business practices pre-existed the industrial revolution. Trade-capitalism existed for centuries, and it was from trade-capitalist dynamics that most of the theory of market economics emerged. It must also be understood that industrial production, with the advent of the Soviet Union (and then China), existed without capitalist business and financial institutions.

Thus, although fused in capitalist-industrialism, the two processes could exist separately, and they do engender different needs and different dynamic processes.

It was Veblen's observation that if the capitalist-system placed too much emphasis on financial dealings and too little on industrial-productive necessities, the system would not evolve properly.[28] In the short run this would not be noticed by the "captains of finance," who would still continue to expand their capital through the financial markets. However, in the long run, with industrial productivity neglected, the system would decline, and the profits of the captains of finance would decline with them.

Hence *Veblen's corrective* was to put the emphasis on the "engineers" in their effort to improve the production process, and to de-emphasize the financial machinations which, in his view, were diverting attention from the productive enterprise. Veblen in no way was suggesting the elimination of capitalist finance or the capitalist market. His idea of a "soviet of engineers" to oversee each industrial enterprise was based not on a socialist paradigm, but on a *technological-scientific paradigm* for industrial efficiency and expansion.

Whether Veblen's solution was sensible or not is not at issue here. What is important is Veblen's new insight: that scientific and engineering professionals, and technological-productive dynamics, were a new element in the reality of the capitalist-industrial system as it was evolving away from its trade-capitalist engendered theoretical principles.

In Germany and Japan where "engineering" dynamics are taken as seriously as market strategies and financial dealings, the economy is expanding in a stable manner, whereas in the United States, with the movement back toward laissez faire, the major effort of the last 15 years has been directed toward finance—in terms of stock profits, corporate-mergers, and takeovers (based on stock control). The industrial segment of the economy has declined (in all but the military and computer sectors, where government and corporate efforts at industrial-technological development have been high).

The events of the late 1980s in the United States should certainly reinforce Veblen's theory, and to any rational economic human, call out for the Veblen corrective, entailing a higher concern for the technological-scientific industrial productive processes and a shift of emphasis away from financial wheeling and dealing and paper profit-taking.

Let me make it clear that the capitalist financial segment is a crucial portion of the capitalist-industrial economy. Without it, a deadening, bureaucratic, non-entrepreneurial economic system with lowered efficiency and less productivity results. This latter, which the Soviets and Chinese are moving away from, is *not* where the Veblen corrective leads. The Veblen corrective leads toward the modified capitalist-industrial economy we have been describing. It is consonant with the Keynesian corrective, but focuses our attention more fully on the differential needs of the technological-industrial segment of the economy, which functions according to dynamics that are different from those of the financial system.

If brought into proper balance, the industrial and financial dynamics create the most vibrant form of economy. Either set of dynamics, if pursued alone, leads to a less productive economy—the capitalist, because it leads toward excessive paper transactions and financial profit-taking, and the industrial, because it leads to bureaucratic-managerial decision making, which is inhibiting to entrepreneurial creativity.

From Keynes and Veblen (and the Swedes), we get the additions to classic economic theory that explain why a modified form of capitalism is emerging as a more efficient and productive form of economy than laissez faire or bureaucratic socialism. These correctives bring economic theory into consonance with economic reality.

8

Ethics: Isaiah and Adam Smith

As with political and economic processes, liberalism has presented the world with an ethical jewel. Liberalism's ethical gift to the world is *self-actualizing individualism*—the ideology that encourages the individual to make the best of him or her self. Prior to liberalism, individuals usually found ideological justification for accepting their "fate" and wallowing in the mire of social degradation.

Liberalism holds out a torch and says "run with it," and whether you win or not, go for your "personal best." You may not be an olympian, but you will have raised yourself to heights that you hardly believed you were capable of.

When the United States, as a nation, held out the torch to the world, millions flocked to our shores to work hard and achieve their "personal best" within a context of free economic activity and political liberties.

Liberalism at its best places the individual—every individual—at center stage. Everyone is important; no one's life is meaningless or worthless—there are no "untouchables" or slaves or serfs or servants who are expendable; there are no aristocrats or lords who, like gods, think they are better than anyone else. This individualism, which we now take for granted in the modern world, came to us from liberalism.

This ethical gift of liberalism is *not* utopian. It is real. Under liberal democratic political and economic institutions, the individual is endowed with inalienable rights and encouraged to maximize his or her economic profits. This is the ethical jewel so precious to the world. What, then, is the flaw in the gem?

Taken to its logical extreme, liberal individualism projects that the world of individual achievement will result in a new perfect world of collective results. If every individual works toward his or her own rationally maximized individual development, the whole social world will be raised up through these individual efforts. This was Bentham's dream, but it was not a reality in Bentham's time, and it is not a reality in our time. Actualizing-individualism, if taken to its logical extreme, becomes utopian. Everyone can't win a race, and what becomes of those who can't run or run slowly?

As wonderful as the liberal ethical system is, it is incomplete, for, if it is not tempered by the ethics of social justice, it leads toward a nasty, selfish, self-righteous neglect of those individuals who fail.

INDIVIDUALISM AND THE CULTURE OF SELFISHNESS: MISERS AND NARCISSISTS

From the works of Locke, Smith, and Bentham, the ideology emerged that competitive individualism alone, within the context of market economics and government by law, would engender a near-perfect world. Nobody needed to help anyone else—that would be against the rules of the game. Everyone simply needed to help themselves.

Again, this was a revolutionary doctrine, that led to so much good, but taken to its utopian extreme, engenders so much misery.

The tale of Tiny Tim and Scrooge in the *Christmas Carol* of Charles Dickens[1] has become the folk legend of the flaw in liberal ethics. The name Scrooge is synonymous with the kind of selfishness and miserliness that characterizes liberal society (along with law and democracy). Why are there misers in liberal society? Let us look at the vulgarized doctrine of protestantism again.

Money was viewed as the "sign of grace," yet money could not be spent on the accumulation of luxury goods. The accumulation of luxury goods was forbidden by ascetic protestantism. Money could not even be given to the church, for this would corrupt the church, as the Catholic Church of Rome had been corrupted. And, of course, money could never be given to the poor, for they were damned.

Money, therefore, could not be used, except to make more money. One could never get enough money, because the more one accumulated, the surer the sign of heavenly grace. Hence, the miser syndrome.

The miser syndrome was good for capitalist development in its earlier years. Since moneymaking for the sake of moneymaking became an obsession, the capital buildup and industrial expansion resultant from this were remarkable.[2] However, the miserly attitude came to characterize the holders of wealth in these nations at the same time.

Now, before we discuss the "voices of Christmas" that Scrooge began to hear in his dreams—the voices that altered his miserly attitude—let us first discuss the alteration of the vulgarized protestant doctrine with the decline of puritan asceticism after World War II.

Christopher Lasch has documented this dramatic change in his book, *The Culture of Narcissism.*[3] Puritan asceticism declined under the impact of rational science,[4] and the rise of the mass consumption, mass advertising economy.[5]

The elimination of magic and ritual from modern religion,[6] along with the widespread absorption of the rational-scientific worldview by the population at large, has left religion as a more purely mystical quest. Religion remains, but in a rarefied form, as the search for meaning and order in an infinite and, though scientifically analyzed, essentially chaotic universe.

At the same time, the massive overproduction of the high-tech industrial economy has engendered an advertising blitz on the consumer public. This advertising blitz is now carried by the dramatically expanding mass media, whose hard-sell "message"[7] is often purveyed in sexual terms. The media's advertising message is, "Buy and be sexual."

Battered by the rationality of science and bludgeoned by the sexually oriented media attack, ascetic protestantism is dying fitfully.

However the vulgarized protestant doctrine, that the rich deserve their full reward and that the poor are damned, has not declined. Rather, it has re-emerged, divorced from its ascetic base. With asceticism removed, the accumulation of luxury goods becomes allowable. The accumulation of luxury goods and their conspicuous display[8]—designer labels and logos emblazoned for a better view—has become the new sign, the sign of entrance into the social "elect." The "lifestyle of the rich and famous" is that which is desired by all, and the poor are ignored. Narcissistic selfishness has replaced miserly selfishness.

Self-actualization has been taken to its ultimate extreme in post-puritan capitalist-industrial societies. And, as with liberalism in general, on the one hand it is wonderful, and on the other tragic. The wonderment lies with the real and remarkable achievements of the self-actualizing narcissist. That is, such a modern individual—male or female—may run marathons, or if this is not enough of an achievement, triathalons or super-marathons (50 to 100 miles); such an individual may work-out on Nautilus machines, developing a body rivaling the statues of the Greek gods. Workaholic self-actualization may result in career success and financial aggrandizement or the personal development of a special talent, artistic, literary or other.

The positive side of the self-actualizing syndrome should not be denigrated. But we must remember that Narcissus—in the myth—came to grief for falling in love with his own image, and the culture of narcissism—in reality—has brought our society a great deal of grief as well. Everyday, hoards of self-actualizing narcissists step over the bodies of homeless poor accumulating at the door of their luxury condominiums, and continue on to their all-consuming workaholic world or to their all-consuming recreational world of non-leisured leisure. Tiny Tim waits, but the yuppy-Scrooge will not allow Christmas to come.

HIGH PROTESTANTISM VS. THE VULGARIZED DOCTRINE

Protestantism, at its essence, engenders individualism, for each individual develops a personal relationship with god. This personal relationship with the deity takes the form of a personal dialogue with Christ. From this dialogue, "the exemplary life of Christ" emerges as a model for everyday action.

Is the Jesus of the New Testament a miser or a narcissist who ignores or rejects the downtrodden of the earth? Obviously not. The ethical doctrine of protestantism in its *pure* form is derived from the ethical actions of Jesus. Jesus took care of the lepers, whom no one would touch,[9] and gave his cloak to those left out in the cold.

It is important to make the distinction between pure protestantism and its vulgarized form. For it is from pure protestantism that the corrective to liberalism's ethical incompleteness can be derived. Scrooge, after all, in the end, hears the voices of his Christian conscience, exhorting him to override the self-righteous miserliness that had prevented him from acting with Christian charity.

The "exemplary life of Christ" exists as an ethical corrective to the withholding selfishness of the vulgarized doctrine. In this sense, Jesus speaks as the last in the line of the Old Testament prophets. Jesus said,

Blessed are the poor in spirit, for theirs is the kingdom of heaven. . . . Blessed are the meek, for they shall inherit the earth, Blessed are those who hunger and thirst for righteousness, for they shall be satisfied, Blessed are the merciful, for they shall obtain mercy. . . . Blessed are the peacemakers, for they shall be called sons of God. . . . Think not that I have come to abolish the law and the prophets; I have come not to abolish them but to fulfill them.[10]

THE JEWISH PROPHETS AND THE ETHIC OF SOCIAL JUSTICE

Western civilization gained rational science from ancient Greece, individualism from reformation protestantism, and the ethic of social justice from the Jewish prophets of the Biblical era. Contained within the works of Amos, Isaiah, Micah, and the other prophets is a powerful message of morality. In no uncertain terms the prophets warn the people that they must not turn away from the poor, the widowed, the orphaned; that they must not display their wealth at the expense of their brethren; and that they must not use their wealth to buy sexual favors and destroy their family life. They rose against unfair business practices and, finally, implored the leaders of the world's peoples to make peace and stop the horrors of war. Isaiah said:

Their land is filled with silver and gold, and there is no end to their treasures; . . . Their land is filled with idols; they bow down to the work of their own hands. . . . So man is humbled and men are brought low . . .[11]

What do you mean by crushing my people, by grinding the face of the poor? . . .[12]

Cease to do evil, learn to do good; seek justice, correct oppression: defend the fatherless, plead for the widow.[13]

And Amos said,

Therefore because you trample upon the poor and take from him exactions of wheat, you have built houses of hewn stone, but you shall not dwell in them . . . you who afflict the righteous, who take a bribe, and turn aside the needy in the gate . . . Hate evil, and love good; and establish justice in the gate . . .[14]

I hate, I despise your feasts . . . take away from me the noise of your songs . . . But let justice roll down like waters, and righteousness like an ever flowing stream.[15]

And Micah said,

He has showed you, O man, what is good; and what does the Lord require of you but to do justice, and to love kindness, and to walk humbly with your God.[16]

. . . and they shall beat their swords into plowshares, and their spears into pruning hooks; nation shall not lift up sword against nation, neither shall they learn war anymore; but they shall sit every man under his vine and under his fig tree, and none shall make them afraid.[17]

The ethic of social justice handed down from the prophets presents us with a necessary corrective to liberalism's competitive individualism. For if competitive individualism is left to its own dynamics, it leaves us with a residue of human degradation, greed, and selfishness.

We need competitive individualism, just as we need modern science—together they engender a creative and technologically expansive society. But without the ethic of social justice, the society produced by individualism and science remains ethically incomplete.

I am fully aware that religion, as an ethical system, is declining in the modern world. I have already described this. Therefore, why mention high protestantism and the Jewish prophets? Because there is a current of *ethical humanism* emerging in modern society along with the narcissism. This humanism, although divorced from religious mysticism and ritual, is nevertheless based in its ethical roots on the Judeo-Christian tradition derived from the prophets.

Humanistic cause groups, such as Amnesty International, implore the governments of the world to stop making war, to stop torturing prisoners, to free political detainees. Oxfam, and other groups focused on world hunger, raise money and buy food and feed the starving of the Earth. Coalitions for the homeless find shelter for those with no roofs over their heads. Church groups and secular groups tend to the needs of the needy in modern society. The outpouring of caring and love that went into the Ethiopian hunger-relief effort should make us aware of the reservoir of humanism that lies stagnant in our society and that ought to be tapped.

What is the point here? The fact is that the ethic of social justice is still vibrant in individualist, capitalist-industrial, legal-democratic societies. However, this humanistic current must be institutionally reinforced or it will be overwhelmed by the counter-current of narcissistic self-indulgence inherent in the vulgarized doctrine of the new non-ascetic individualism.

LIBERALISM AND HUMANISM

How can we institutionalize the ethic of social justice alongside competitive individualism without destroying the liberal structure of legal-democracy and market economics?

The whole of this book has been addressed to this question. The theories and programs presented in this volume relate precisely to the establishment of social justice within the context of law, democracy, and free enterprise.

Both liberal utopianism and socialist utopianism are romantic illusions. In the world of reality it is time that we stopped blaming the victim *and* stopped blaming the system. If we believe that liberalism is worth saving and that its contributions to the world of politics, economics, and ethics are unique, then *we must save liberalism from itself*, by adding the political, economic, and ethical correctives necessary for its viability.

These correctives must be added with the utmost care, for liberalism is a fragile gem. Therefore, with the "doctrine of least harm"[18] in the foreground of our vision, we should proceed cautiously, but responsibly, to correct the flaws of liberal society, without losing its essence.

Notes

INTRODUCTION

1. Alexis de Tocqueville, *The Old Regime and the French Revolution*. Translated by Henry Reeve. London: Murray, 1888.

2. For the Weber–Lukacs interchange, see Zoltan Tar, "The Weber–Lukacs Dialogue," in Glassman and Murvar (eds.), *Max Weber's Political Sociology*. Westport, CT: Greenwood Press, 1983.

3. Vatro Murvar, "The New Patrimonialism in Russia, " in Glassman and Murvar, Ibid.

4. Friedrich Von Hayek, *The Road to Serfdom*. Chicago: University of Chicago Press, 1969.

5. Karl Popper, *The Open Society and Its Enemies*. Princeton, NJ: Princeton University Press, 1951.

6. Robert Nozick, *Anarchy, State, and Utopia*. New York: Basic Books, 1971.

7. Charles Murray, *Losing Ground*. New York: Basic Books, 1984.

8. See my chapter on the neoconservatives.

9. Charles Dickens, *Oliver Twist*. Oxford, UK: Clarendon Press, 1966.

10. C. Wright Mills, *The Power Elite*. New York: Oxford University Press, 1959.

11. Robert Dahl, *After the Revolution*. New Haven, CT: Yale University Press, 1971. Ralph Nader and Mark Green, *Taming the Giant Corporation*. New York: Norton, 1982.

12. John Locke, *Treatise on Civil Government*. Chicago: Gateway Edition, 1962.

13. Jeremy Bentham, *The Work of Jeremy Bentham*. New York: Russel and Russel, 1962.

CHAPTER 1

All quotations in the text are from: Aristotle, *The Politics*. Translated by Ernest Barker. New York: Oxford University Press, 1961.

1. Ronald M. Glassman, *Democracy and Despotism in Primitive Societies*. New York: Associated Faculty Press, 1987. Lewis Henry Morgan, *Ancient Society*. New York: Holt & Co., 1878. E. Adamson Hoebel, *The Cheyenne*. New York: Holt & Co., 1960.

2. Colin Turnbull, *The Forest People*. New York: Simon and Schuster, 1962.

3. Abraham Lincoln, the Gettysburg Address.

4. Secular law emerged as contract law for trade transactions.

5. Glassman, *Democracy and Despotism in Primitive Societies*.

6. Ibid.

7. Hoebel, *The Cheyenne*.

8. Lewis Mumford, *The Myth of the Machine*. New York: Harcourt, Brace, and World, 1967–70.

9. Ronald M. Glassman, "Manufactured Charisma and Legitimacy," in Glassman and Swatos (eds.), *Charisma, History and Social Structure*. Westport, CT: Greenwood Press, 1986.

10. Henri Frankfort, *Kingship and the Gods*. Boston: Beacon, 1968. Karl Polanyi, *Trade and Market in Early Empires*. Glencoe, IL: Free Press, 1967.

11. Ronald M. Glassman, *The New Middle Class and Democracy*. Forthcoming.

12. Karl Polanyi, *Trade and Market in Early Empires*. Max Weber, *The Protestant Ethic and the Spirit of Capitalism*. New York: Charles Scribner and Sons, 1968.

13. Max Weber, *The City*. Glencoe, IL: Free Press, 1958.

14. Thucydides, *The Peloponnesian Wars*. Baltimore: Penguin Books, 1972.

15. Plato, *The Republic*. Baltimore: Penguin Classics, 1969.

16. Karl Popper, *The Open Society and Its Enemies*. Princeton, NJ: Princeton University Press, 1966.

17. Thucydides, *The Peloponnesian Wars*.

18. In Cambodia, Pol Pot became a murderous Communist dictator, as bad as Stalin had been.

19. Popper, *The Open Society and Its Enemies*.

20. Glassman, *The New Middle Class and Democracy*.

21. Ibid.

22. Polybius, Book VI, *The Histories*. Bloomington, IN: University of Indiana Press, 1962.

23. Durkheim, *The Rules for Sociological Method*. Glencoe, IL: Free Press, 1950. Idem., *Suicide*. Glencoe, IL: Free Press, 1951.

24. Governor Kean of New Jersey, State of the State Message, 1986.

25. Richard A. Cloward and Lloyd E. Ohlin, *Delinquency and Opportunity*. Glencoe, IL: Free Press, 1960. Albert Cohen, *Delinquent Boys*. Glencoe, IL: Free Press, 1955.

26. Human Serve is a voter registration organization working to register the poor.

27. Fundamentalist groups and the moral majority are working to register the white Southern poor.

28. Durkheim, *The Rules; Suicide*.

29. Ibid.

30. Ibid.

31. Weber, *The Protestant Ethic and the Spirit of Capitalism*.

32. Hanna Arendt, *The Human Condition*. Chicago, IL: University of Chicago Press, 1958.

33. James Burnham, *The Managerial Revolution*. New York: The John Day Co., 1941. A. A. Berle and Gardner Means, *The Modern Corporation and Private Property*.

New York: Harcourt, Brace, 1968. J. K. Galbraith, *The New Industrial State*. Boston: Houghton Mifflin, 1968.

34. John Maynard Keynes, *The General Theory*. New York: Harcourt, Brace, 1935.

35. Thorstein Veblen, *The Engineers and the Price System*. New York: Viking, 1954.

36. Keynes pressed for the progressive income tax; with the notable exception of Hayek, most economists accept this principle.

37. This is good Keynesian economics, not classic economics.

38. A. A. Berle and Gardner Means, *The Modern Corporation and Private Property*.

39. Maurice Zeitlin, "Who Controls the Corporation," in *American Society Inc.* Chicago: Markham Pub. Co., 1970.

40. G. William Domhoff, *Who Rules America Now*. Englewood Cliffs, NJ: Prentice-Hall, 1967.

41. David Bazelon, *The Paper Economy*. New York: Random House, 1963.

42. C. Wright Mills, *White Collar*. New York: Oxford University Press, 1958.

43. The Kodak Company has a very good ESOP plan, as do all Swedish companies.

44. ESOPs were "invented" in a book called *The Capitalist Manifesto*, by Louis O. Kelso and Mortimer Adler (New York: Random House, 1958).

45. Robert Dahl, *After the Revolution*. New Haven, CT: Yale University Press, 1970.

46. Berle and Means, *The Modern Corporation and Private Property*.

47. Ralph Nader, Mark Green, and Joel Seligman, *Taming the Giant Corporation*. New York: Norton, 1976.

48. Dahl, *After the Revolution*.

49. Keynes, *General Theory*.

50. Mark Green, *Where Should America Go*. New York: Grossman, 1984.

51. Max Weber, "Politics as a Vocation," in Gerth and Mills (eds.), *From Max Weber*. Glencoe, IL: Free Press, 1970.

52. Ronald M. Glassman and Mark Green, *A Democracy Agenda for the Year 2000*. New York: Democracy Project, 1988.

53. Ralph Nader and Mark Green, *Big Business Reader*. New York: Grossman, 1987.

54. Family breakups and urban isolation are also causes for the violence.

55. Christopher Lasch, *The Culture of Narcissism*. New York: Norton, 1968.

56. C. Wright Mills, *White Collar*.

57. Mills, *The Power Elite*. New York: Oxford University Press, 1959.

58. Glassman, *New Middle Class and Democracy*.

59. Weber, *The Protestant Ethic and the Spirit of Capitalism*.

60. Donald Rowat, *Ombudsman: Citizen's Defender*. London: Allen and Unwin, 1965.

61. Dahl, *After the Revolution*.

62. Glassman, *New Middle Class and Democracy*.

CHAPTER 2

All quotations in the text are from: John Rawls, *A Theory of Justice*. Cambridge, MA: Harvard University Press, 1971.

1. John Locke, *Treatise on Civil Government*. Chicago: Gateway Edition, Henry Regnery Company, 1964.

2. Ibid. Chapter on "property," pp. 21–40.

3. Ibid.

4. Ibid.

5. Chares Louis de Secandat Baron de Montesquieu, *The Spirit of the Laws*. Trans. by David Wallace Carrithers. Berkeley, CA: University of California Press, 1977.

6. Karl Marx and Fredrich Engels, *The Communist Manifesto*. Moscow: Foreign Language Press, 1951.

7. Karl Marx and Fredrich Engels, *The Paris Commune*. Edited by Ital Draper. Boston: Beacon Press, 1968. In this treatise, Draper (editor) undertakes a defense of Marx and Engels in the use of their phrase, "dictatorship of the proletariat." However, the historical reality of Leninism and Stalinism still stands as a warning against the defense. See Ira Cohen, "Marx and Weber on Democracy," in Robert J. Antonio and Ronald M. Glassman (eds.), *A Weber–Marx Dialogue* (Lawrence, Kansas: University of Kansas Press, 1986) for a critique of Marx on his understanding of democracy.

8. Locke, *Civil Government*, chapter on "property."

9. Jeremy Bentham, *Bentham's Economic Writings*. Edited by W. Stark, London: Blackwell, 1973.

10. Aristotle, *The Politics* (see chapter in this book).

11. Lord John Acton, the famous phrase, "power corrupts, absolute power corrupts absolutely." See also Acton, *A History of Freedom*. Boston: Beacon Press, 1948.

12. Charles Dickens' work presents a picture of extreme wealth differentials focusing on the poor; see Veblen, *The Theory of the Leisure Class* (New York: Mentor Books, 1951) for a view of the rich.

13. Daniel Bell, *The Coming of Post Industrial Society*. New York: Basic Books, 1968; also Norman Podhoretz's many articles in *Commentary* Magazine, against the use of quotas.

14. Senator Moynihan, when working for Nixon, coined the phrase, "benign neglect" as a policy for the poor.

15. Christopher Lasch, *The Culture of Narcissism*.

16. There is a television show entitled, "Lifestyles of the Rich and Famous"; "yuppyism" is also a lifestyle trend wherein designer labels are exhibited as badges of personal success.

17. See Ernest Kilker, "Weber on Socialism," in Ronald M. Glassman, William Swatos, and Paul Rosen, *Bureaucracy Against Democracy and Socialism*. Westport, CT: Greenwood Press, 1987.

18. Aristotle, chapter in this book.

19. Karl Marx and Fredrich Engels, *Communist Manifesto*.

20. Glassman, *The New Middle Class and Democracy* (Bks. I and II).

21. Locke, *Treatise on Civil Government*, chapter on property.

22. Thomas Hobbes, *Leviathan*. London: Penguin Classics, 1958. Hobbes, not a democrat, helped set the stage for legal-democracy by asserting the right of self-defense of the individual against the state.

23. See the statistics compiled by *The Center for Budget and Policy Priorities*, Washington, D.C., Robert Greenstein, Director.

24. Labeling the poor as "slothful" and "of the devil" comes out of the protestant "work ethic" tradition. This was reinforced by theorists such as Malthus, who labeled the poor as sexually uncontrolled, and then by the Social Darwinists (Huxley and Spencer), who labeled the poor as "unfit" to survive.

25. The Carnegie Foundations are well known in America, but less well known is

that Carlsberg in Denmark left all profits from the Carlsberg Brewery to the Danish people for use in educational and cultural programs.

26. Lasch, *The Culture of Narcissism.*

27. Keynes, *The General Theory* (see my chapter in this book).

28. Ibid.

29. Sheila Kammerman and Robert Kahn have published numerous papers on family allowance programs in Europe.

30. See The Canadian Universal Family Allowance Program. Details available from Ottawa, in the form of a pamphlet.

31. The "negative income tax" was a theory developed by Milton Friedman. For a critique of Friedman, see Galbraith, *Economics in Perspective* (Boston: Houghton Mifflin, 1987).

32. There was a pilot project in Seattle, Washington, that showed that the negative income tax reduced work incentive. This project was initiated by Daniel Moynihan while working for the Nixon Administration.

33. Ibid.

34. See my chapter on Aristotle.

35. Jefferson believed, with Aristotle, that everyone should have at least a modest but adequate amount of property.

36. Jerold Graubard, on ESOPs, in *Dissent* (Spring 1985); see also Kelso and Adler, *The Capitalist Manifesto* (New York: Random House, 1958).

37. David Bazelon, *The Paper Economy.* New York: Vintage, 1963.

38. Weber, *The Protestant Ethic and the Spirit of Capitalism*; "sensualists without heart, technicians without spirit," pp. 181–82. See also Lasch, *The Culture of Narcissism.*

CHAPTER 3

1. Carl Polanyi, "Aristotle Discovers the Economy," in *Trade and Market in the Early Empire.* Chicago: Gateway, 1957.

2. John Kenneth Galbraith, *Economics in Perspective.* Boston: Houghton Mifflin, 1987.

3. Karl Polanyi, *The Great Transformation.* Boston: Beacon Press, 1957.

4. Thorstein Veblen, *The Engineers and the Price System.* New York: Harcourt, Brace, and World, 1963.

5. Galbraith, *Economics in Perspective.*

6. Adam Smith, *The Wealth of Nations.* London: Heath and Co., 1948.

7. Galbraith, *Economics in Perspective*; Galbraith discusses Smith's "invisible hand" theory in the sections on classic economic theory.

8. Jeremy Bentham, *Economic Writings.* London: Blackwell, 1973.

9. Smith, *The Wealth of Nations* (see the chapter on "monopoly" and its *negative* effects).

10. John Stuart Mill, *Political Economy.* London: Penguin Classics, 1967; see chapter on "worker's cooperatives."

11. Karl Marx and Friedrich Engels, *Capital.* New York: International Publishers, 1948.

12. Karl Marx and Friedrich Engels, *The Communist Manifesto.* New York: International Publishers, 1948.

13. Marx and Engels, *The Communist Manifesto.*

14. Galbraith, *Economics in Perspective*.

15. Marx and Engels, *The Paris Commune*. Edited by Hal Draper. Boston: Beacon Press, 1968.

16. Thorstein Veblen, *The Theory of Business Enterprise*. New York: Mentor Books, 1958.

17. John Maynard Keynes, *The General Theory*. New York: Harbinger, 1965; p. 372. All subsequent references in the text are to this edition.

18. For a discussion of ''The Levellers,'' see Chapter 6 in this volume.

19. The principle of ''progressive taxation'' was derived from Marx and Engels in *The Communist Manifesto*.

20. Galbraith, *Economics in Perspective*.

21. Galbraith, in *Economics in Perspective*, discusses ''Says Law'' in his chapter on classic economics.

22. Ibid.

23. Galbraith, *Economics in Perspective*, p. 267.

24. Ibid., pp. 269–70.

25. Ibid., p. 267.

26. Ibid., p. 269.

27. Ibid., p. 273.

28. Ibid.

29. Robert Greenstein, *Center for Budget and Policy Priorities*, Washington, D.C.

30. Galbraith, *Economics in Perspective*, p. 274.

31. Ibid.

32. Ibid., p. 275.

33. Robert Eisner, *How Real Is the Budget Deficit?* New York: Free Press, 1986.

34. Ibid., p. 2.

35. Ibid., p. 3.

36. Ibid., pp. 23–25.

37. Ibid., p. 7.

38. Ibid., p. 7; pp. 114–128.

39. Ibid., p. 10.

40. Ibid., p. 3.

41. Ibid.

42. Ibid., p. 180.

43. Ibid., p. 5.

44. Ibid., Conclusions.

45. Thorstein Veblen, *The Theory of the Leisure Class*. New York: Mentor, 1953.

46. Ibid.

47. Galbraith, *Economics in Perspective*, chapter on ''monetarist policy.''

48. Keynes, *The General Theory*, pp. 380–81.

49. Veblen, *The Engineers and the Price System*.

50. Robert Reich has written extensively on ''re-industrialization.''

51. *Scientific American*, throughout the Reagan years, carried criticisms of the abandonment of scientific projects in space, and especially of the ''shuttle program.''

52. ''Star Wars'' was initiated.

53. Park West Village, owned by Harry Helmsley, was found to be operating at a profit in 1985.

54. Ortega y Gasset, *The Revolt of the Masses* (any edition).

55. Harvey Swados, *The Myth of the Happy Worker*. New York: Random House, 1963.

CHAPTER 4

1. Vatro Murvar, "Patrimonialism in Russia," in Glassman and Murvar (eds.), *Max Weber's Political Sociology*. Westport, CT: Greenwood Press, 1983.

2. Alexis de Tocqueville, *The Old Regime and the French Revolution*. Translated by Henry Reeve. London: Murray, 1888, p. 143.

3. de Tocqueville, pp. 143–44.

4. Ibid., p. 29.

5. Ibid.

6. Ibid., p. 34.

7. Ibid., p. 56.

8. Ibid., p. 59.

9. Glassman, Swatos, and Rosen, *Bureaucracy Against Democracy and Socialism*. Westport, CT: Greenwood Press, 1987, Introduction.

10. de Tocqueville, pp. 59–60.

11. Ibid., pp. 139–40.

12. Ibid., p. 140.

13. Ibid., pp. 140–41.

14. Karl Popper, *The Open Society and Its Enemies*. Princeton, NJ: Princeton University Press, 1950.

15. de Tocqueville, pp. 140–41.

16. de Tocqueville, in F. Von Hayek, *The Road to Serfdom* (Chicago: University of Chicago Press, 1975 edition; Phoenix Books Paperback), Introduction, p. xi.

17. Alexis de Tocqueville, *Democracy in America*. New York: Vintage Books, 1945.

18. Ibid.

19. Popper, *The Open Society*.

20. de Tocqueville, in Hayek, *The Road to Serfdom*, footnote 10, p. xvi, in Introduction.

21. Glassman, Swatos, and Rosen, *Bureaucracy Against Democracy and Socialism*.

22. Wolfgang Mommsen, *The Age of Bureaucracy*. New York: Harper and Row, 1974.

23. See Gunther Roth, "Marx' and Weber's Predictions," in Antonio and Glassman, *A Weber–Marx Dialogue*. Lawrence, Kansas: University of Kansas Press, 1986.

24. Zoltan Tar, "The Weber–Lukacs Dialogue," in Glassman and Murvar, *Max Weber's Political Sociology*.

25. Hans Gerth and C. Wright Mills, *From Max Weber*. New York: Oxford University Press, 1958; essays on Politics and Science, pp. 77–129.

26. Ronald M. Glassman and Arthur J. Vidich, *Conflict and Control*. Beverly Hills, CA: Sage Publications, 1979.

27. Lewis Mumford, *The Myth of the Machine*. New York: Harcourt, Brace, and World, 1966/67.

28. Max Weber, *Economy and Society*. Translated by Roth and Wittich. New York: Bedminster Press, 1978, p. 1402.

29. Ibid., pp. 1402–03

30. Ibid., p. 1453.

31. Max Weber, *The Interpretation of Social Reality*. New York: Scribners, 1971, p. 209.

32. Hans Gerth and C. Wright Mills, *From Max Weber*. New York: Oxford Press, 1958, p. 182.

33. Weber, *Economy and Society*, p. 1403.

34. Popper, *Open Society*.

35. Robert Michels, *Political Parties*. Glencoe, IL: Free Press, 1949.

36. Hayek, *The Road to Serfdom*.

37. Friedrich Von Hayek, *The Constitution of Liberty*. Chicago: University of Chicago Press, 1978.

38. Barbara Wooten, *Freedom Under Planning*. Chapel Hill, NC: University of North Carolina Press, 1945.

39. Hayek, *Serfdom* (new Foreword).

40. Ibid., p. xi.

41. Ibid., p. x.

42. Ibid., p. 31.

43. Ibid., Foreword.

44. Ibid.

45. Ibid.

46. Ibid., p. xix.

47. Both Weber and Keynes emphasize the importance of the separation of the economic sphere from the state; see Keynes in this volume; see Weber, *Economy and Society*, pp. 1402–04.

48. Hayek, *Serfdom*, pp. 102–04.

49. Ibid., p. 102.

50. Glassman, *New Middle Class and Democracy*, Bk. I, Pt. II.

51. Hayek, *Serfdom*, p. 120.

52. Ibid., p. 121.

53. Ibid.

54. Hayek, *Constitution*, pp. 258–89.

55. Arthur Schweitzer, "On Hitler's Charisma," in Ronald M. Glassman and William Swatos (eds.), *Charisma, History, and Social Structure*. Westport, CT: Greenwood Press, 1986.

56. Hayek, *Serfdom*, p. 209.

57. Ralph Nader and Mark Green, *The Big Business Reader*. New York: Norton, 1986.

58. Ira Glasser, *Doing Good*. New York: Pantheon Books, 1974.

59. Manhattan Borough President Andrew Stein's investigations into the nursing home scandal in New York gained him headlines for months in the 1970s.

60. Paul Rosen, "Bureaucracies in Hospitals," in Glassman, Swatos, and Rosen, *Bureaucracy Against Democracy and Socialism*.

61. Ira Glasser, *Doing Good*.

62. Donald Rowat, "The Ombudsman," in Glassman, Swatos, and Rosen, *Bureaucracy Against Democracy and Socialism*.

63. A. A. Berle and Gardner Means, *The Modern Corporation and Private Property*. New York: Harcourt, Brace, 1958.

64. Robert Dahl, *After the Revolution*. New Haven, CT: Yale University Press, 1972; Nader and Green, *Taming the Giant Corporation*. New York: Norton, 1984.

65. Glasser, *Doing Good*; Nader and Green, *Taming the Giant Corporation*.

66. Glasser, *Doing Good*.

67. Glassman, *New Middle Class and Democracy*.

68. Aldous Huxley, *Brave New World*. New York: Harper and Row, 1932.

69. George Orwell, *1984*. New York: New American Library, 1983.

70. John Wicklein, *Electronic Nightmare*, New York: Viking, 1981.

71. Nader and Green, *Taming the Giant Corporation*.

72. Donald Rowat, "The Ombudsman," in Glassman, Swatos, and Rosen, *Bureaucracy Against Democracy and Socialism*.

CHAPTER 5

1. Robert Nozick, *Anarchy, State, and Utopia*. New York: Basic Books, 1974.

2. Milton Friedman, *Capitalism and Freedom*. Chicago: University of Chicago Press, 1982.

3. Ibid.

4. Daniel Bell, *The Coming of Post Industrial Society*. New York: Basic Books, 1968.

5. Norman Podhoretz is the editor of *Commentary* Magazine, which became an organ for neoconservative discourse.

6. In foreign policy, the Arab–Israeli conflict and the Soviet anti-Jewish policies conservatized many Jewish intellectuals. Also the American blacks' embrace of the Moslem religion frightened Jewish intellectuals.

7. Nathan Glazer, *Affirmative Discrimination: Ethnic Inequality and Public Policy*. New York: Basic Books, 1975.

8. Daniel Patrick Moynihan, *The Moynihan Report on the Black Family*. United States Dept. of Information, Wash. D.C.; the Senate Information Office, Capitol Hill, 1965.

9. Daniel Patrick Moynihan, *Maximum Feasible Misunderstanding*. New York: Free Press, 1969.

10. The phrase "benign neglect" was coined by Moynihan, and became Nixon's policy toward the blacks.

11. Seymour Martin Lipset, paper on "Equality of Opportunity vs. Equality of End Result," available through The Hoover Institute, Stanford University, Palo Alto, California.

12. Daniel Bell, *The Coming of Post Industrial Society*.

13. Ibid.

14. Charles Murray, *Losing Ground*. New York: Basic Books, 1984.

15. Ibid., p. 18.

16. Ibid., p. 18.

17. Ibid., p. 16.

18. Ibid., p. 23.

19. Ibid., p. 23.

20. Ibid., pp. 24–5.

21. Ibid., p. 23.

22. Ibid., p. 33.

23. Ibid., p. 93.

24. Ibid., p. 43.

25. Bell, *Post Industrial Society*.

26. Ibid., p. 416.

27. Ibid., p. 426.

28. Especially in *Commentary* Magazine, but also in *The New Republic, Time, News-week, U.S. News and World Report*.

29. Bell, p. 439.

30. Ibid., p. 450.

31. Murray, p. 233.

32. Ibid., p. 36.

33. Ibid.

34. Ibid., pp. 36–7.

35. Ibid., p. 70.

36. From the Columbia University School of Social Work there were: Richard Cloward, Harry Spect, Frank Riesman, and others.

37. From N.Y.U., Sherman Barr and others.

38. Murray, p. 70.

39. Some of the street workers actually risked their lives working with the gangs. The process of pacification was, however, relatively successful.

40. Murray, p. 70.

41. In Mobilization for Youth, a Kennedy program on the Lower East Side of Manhattan, many of the girls trained well and were successful, although they did get pregnant.

42. Murray, p. 70.

43. Daniel Patrick Moynihan and Nathan Glazer, *Beyond the Melting Pot*. Cambridge, Mass: M.I.T. Press, 1963. Richard Cloward and Lloyd Ohlin, *Delinquency and Opportunity*. Robert Merton, "Social Structure and Anomie," in *Social Theory and Social Structure*. New York: Columbia University Press, 1952.

44. Murray, p. 113.

45. Ibid., p. 117.

46. Ibid., p. 188.

47. Ibid.

48. Ibid., p. 49.

49. Ibid., p. 63.

50. Ibid., p. 64.

51. Ibid., pp. 146, 149.

52. Ibid., p. 150.

53. Alexander Sutherland Neil, *Summerhill*. New York: Schocken Books, 1973.

54. For "The New Math," see some works by Max Bieberman.

55. Metropolitan Opera school program, Young People's Concerts of the New York Philharmonic, theater productions, etc.

56. Murray, pp. 105–06.

57. Joe Clark, Paterson High School principal; *Time* Magazine cover story, Jan. 27, 1988.

58. A New York millionaire, Maurice Lang, gives college scholarships to minority students attending his old grade school. The program has been so successful that Governor Cuomo may expand it. Corporate millionaires in Paterson, N.J., may do the same at Joe Clark's high school.

59. Governor Mario Cuomo, "Liberty Scholarships."

60. Charles Murray, in a Ken Auletta interview on CBS news.

61. Paterson High School expelled many troublesome students.

62. Manhattan school districts 3 and 4 have gifted programs that are non-authoritarian. They have been successful.

63. Murray, p. 219.

64. Ibid., p. 190.

65. William Ryan, *Blaming the Victim*. New York: Vintage, 1976.

66. The idea of "social engineering," as opposed to utopianizing, was put forth by Max Weber in his essays on science and politics, in Gerth and Mills, *From Max Weber* (New York: Oxford Press, 1958).

67. Murray, pp. 202–03.

68. Ibid., p. 202.

69. Ibid., p. 233.

70. Ibid., p. 223.

71. Ibid., p. 190.

72. Ibid., p. 231.

73. Low- and middle-income housing funds were passed during the Kennedy–Johnson era, but sequestered under Nixon.

74. "Benign neglect" was the Nixon policy.

75. Statistics on this can be obtained from: Robert Greenstein, Center for Budget and Policy Priorities, Washington, D.C.

76. The "feminization" of poverty is now a well-known phenomenon.

77. In Venice, California, a lovely beach area, the homeless are camped in front of luxury condominiums.

78. The *New York Times* carried a picture of the homeless in Venice, California, Tues., March 5, 1988.

79. The "Upward Bound" program was housed at Yale and Connecticut College.

80. Hayek called this time period one in which we have a "breathing space" to evaluate the good and bad of socialism. See the chapter on Hayek in the text.

81. Milton Friedman, *Capitalism and Freedom*.

82. The Howard Beach incident in New York occurred during 1987; "Jimmy the Greek" made racial remarks on CBS in 1988.

83. Milton Friedman, Martin Feldstein, and other Nixon economic advisors.

84. Thorstein Veblen, *The Engineers and the Price System*. New York: Harcourt, Brace, and World, 1954.

85. Ralph Nader and Mark Green, *The Big Business Reader*. New York: Norton, 1984.

86. The Beechnut babyfood case—babies were given sugar water instead of juice; chemical dumping cases in New Jersey.

87. G. William Domhoff, *Who Rules America Now*. Englewood Cliffs, NJ: Prentice-Hall, 1967. Domhoff emphasizes the elite private schools and the relation to control by the rich.

88. Bell, *Post Industrial Society*.

89. Friedman, *Capitalism and Democracy*.

90. John Kenneth Galbraith, *Economics in Perspective*. Boston: Houghton Mifflin, 1987.

91. Friedman, *Capitalism and Freedom*.

92. Galbraith, *Economics in Perspective*.

93. Robert Reich has been critical of the mergers and breakups.

94. Ibid. Robert Reich appeared on "Nightline," ABC T.V., Thursday, January 21, 1988.

95. The Uniroyal executives took million dollar bonuses as the company was failing.

96. Leon Keyserling and John Kenneth Galbraith have spoken out for wage–price guidelines.

97. Robert Eisner, *How Real Is The Federal Deficit?* New York: Free Press, 1986.

98. John Maynard Keynes—see the chapter in this text.

99. The U.S. government is investigating Ivan Boesky, the trading company of E.F. Hutton, and other brokers.

100. The N.Y. Times *Magazine* spent an unprecedented two weeks on Lehman Brothers Brokers; see also Oliver Stone's movie, *Wall Street*.

101. Nader and Green, *The Big Business Reader*.

102. Milton Friedman championed the "voucher" system for private schools.

103. Bell, *Post Industrial Society*.

104. Domhoff, *Who Rules America Now*.

105. William Ryan, *Blaming the Victim*.

106. Bell, *Post Industrial Society*, p. 426.

CHAPTER 6

1. Ronald M. Glassman, *The Political History of Latin America*. New York: Funk and Wagnalls, 1960; see also, Glassman and Swatos, *Charisma, History, and Social Structure*. Westport, CT: Greenwood Press, 1986, Epilogue.

2. Ibid.

3. Ibid.

4. Stephen Shalom, *The Philippines Today*. Beverly Hills, CA: Westview Press, 1978.

5. Ibid.

6. David Apter, *Ghana in Transition*. Princeton: Princeton University Press, 1972; John Kautsky, *Political Change in Developing Nations*. New York: John Wiley, 1963.

7. Andrew Young, United Nations ambassador under President Carter.

8. Gunter Grass, comments on Calcutta in a forthcoming novel—to be published in 1988 (in English).

9. Max Weber, *The Religion of India*. Glencoe, IL: Free Press, 1953.

10. Ibid.

11. Beatrice Pitney Lamb, *India: A World in Transition*. New York: Praeger, 1975.

12. Hanna Arendt, *The Origins of Totalitarianism*. New York: Oxford University Press, 1951.

13. Henry Turner, *German Big Business and the Rise of Hitler*. New York: Oxford University Press, 1985. John Weiss, *The Rise of Fascism*. Princeton, NJ: Princeton University Press, 1983. F. L. Carsten, *The Rise of Fascism*. Berkeley, CA: University of California Press, 1969.

14. John Maynard Keynes, *The Social Consequences of the Peace*. Boston: D.C. Heath, 1947.

15. Aristotle, comments on "law." See the chapter on Aristotle in this volume.

16. Glassman, *The New Middle Class and Democracy*, chapter on education.

17. From John Locke (*Treatise on Civil Government*) to E. Digby Baltsel (*The Protestant Establishment*, New York: Oxford University Press, 1962), there have been justifiers of legal-oligarchy.

18. From Bentham to Friedman there have been liberal utopianizers.

19. There is a whole literature of debate on this: see Tawney, *Religion and the Rise of Capitalism* (New York: Mentor, 1954), Weber, *The Protestant Ethic and the Spirit of Capitalism*; see also Philip Taylor, *The Origins of the English Civil War* (Boston: D.C. Heath, 1960).

20. R. H. Tawney, *The Agrarian Problem in the Sixteenth Century*. New York: Harper Torch Books, 1967.

21. Eduard Bernstein, *Cromwell and Communism: Socialism and Democracy in the Great English Revolution*. Translated by H. J. Stenning. New York: A.M. Kelley, 1963.

22. Hans Rosenberg, *Bureaucracy, Aristocracy, Autocracy*. Boston: Beacon Press, 1958. See also Glassman, *The Political History of Latin America*.

23. Glassman, *The Political History of Latin America* (see the section on Spain for an analysis of Italy, as well as Spain).

24. Glassman and Vidich, *Conflict and Control: The Challenge to Legitimacy of the Twentieth Century*; see the Glassman essays, "Conflicts Between Legal and Bureaucratic Authority" and "Rational and Irrational Legitimacy."

25. For theories of power limitation, see the works of: Locke, Montesquieu, Jefferson, *The Federalist Papers*, Lord Acton's *History of Freedom*.

26. Glassman, *The New Middle Class and Democracy*, Bk. I, Pt. II, on the origins of law from "contract" law.

27. For an analysis of the *standestaat*, or "estate-state," see Weber, *Economy and Society*; Hans Rosenberg, *Bureaucracy, Aristocracy, Autocracy*.

28. Hobbes, *Leviathan*; Hobbes presents a debate over a unified or separated executive.

29. Tawney, *Agrarian Problem in the Sixteenth Century*.

30. Popper, *The Open Society and Its Enemies*.

31. Tawney, *Agrarian Problem in the Sixteenth Century*.

32. Karl Polanyi, *The Great Transformation*. Boston: Beacon, 1944.

33. Tawney, *Agrarian Problem in the Sixteenth Century*.

34. Ibid.; see also Philip Taylor, *The Origins of the English Civil War*.

35. Weber, *The Protestant Ethic*.

36. For the Weber–Tawney debate, see Weber, *The Protestant Ethic*, and Tawney, *Religion and the Rise of Capitalism* (New York: Mentor, 1954).

37. *Columbia University Source Books*. New York: Columbia University Press, 1950, pp. 67–8.

38. Christopher Hill, *God's Englishman*. New York: Dial Press, 1970, pp. 71–115.

39. See Phalleus, in Aristotle, *The Politics*. Translated by Ernest Berker. New York: Oxford University Press, 1961.

40. Karl Marx, *The German Ideology*; see also Marx and Engels, *The Paris Commune*, Hal Draper, ed.

41. Glassman and Swatos, *Charisma, History, and Social Structure* (Epilogue).

42. Lilburne, his Writings of the Levellers, in Christopher Hill, *God's Englishman*.

43. Trevor-Roper, thesis on the lesser gentry and the English Revolution, in Taylor, *The Origins of the English Civil War*.

44. Christopher Hill, *God's Englishman*.

45. Lord Acton, *A History of Freedom*. Acton had some revealing commentary on the United States—he believed that the English Revolution was *completed* in the United States.

46. Seymour Martin Lipset, *The First New Nation*. New York: Doubleday, 1958.

47. Gerald Straker, *The Revolution of 1688*. Boston: D.C. Heath, 1963.

48. Robert K. Merton, "Social Structure and Anomie," in *Social Theory and Social Structure*. New York: Columbia University Press, 1952.

49. Dorothy Thompson, *The Chartists*. New York: Pantheon Books, 1984, p. 335.

50. Weber, *The Protestant Ethic*; K. Polanyi, *The Great Transformation*.

51. Marx and Engels, *The Communist Manifesto*.

52. Veblen, *The Engineers and the Price System*.

53. Karl Marx, *Das Kapital*. Moscow: Foreign Language Press, 1949.

54. Charles Dickens, *A Christmas Carol*. Boston: Page Books, 1913; *Oliver Twist*. Oxford: Clarendon, 1966.

55. C Wright Mills, *White Collar*. New York: Oxford University Press, 1958.

56. John Stuart Mill, *Political Economy*. London: Penguin Classics, 1962.

57. John Stuart Mill, *On Representative Government*. New York and London: Penguin Classics, 1958.

58. Weber, *The Protestant Ethic*.

59. Ibid.

60. Paraphrase of a quote from William Jennings Bryan at the "Scope's Monkey Trial."

61. Charles Darwin, *The Origin of the Species*. Oxford: Clarendon, 1954.

62. George Bernard Shaw, *Pygmalian*.

63. Jeremy Bentham, *Works of Jeremy Bentham*. New York: Russel & Russel, 1962.

64. Rawls, *A Theory of Justice*. Cambridge, MA: Harvard University Press, 1961 (chapter on the "Utilitarians").

65. Robert Dahl, *Who Governs*. New Haven: Yale University Press, 1959. "Interest group" pluralist theory is spelled out by Dahl.

66. John Kenneth Galbraith, *The Affluent Society*. Boston: Houghton Mifflin, 1969.

67. Thomas Hobbes, *Leviathan*; Hobbes criticizes Aristotle as the "worst" theorist for suggesting a mixed, rather than unified, polity.

68. Rawls, *A Theory of Justice*.

69. Popper, *The Open Society*; Weber, "The Ethic of Responsibility" in "Science as a Vocation," and "Politics as a Vocation," in *From Max Weber*, edited by Gerth and Mills, (New York: Oxford Press, 1958).

70. For vulgarized bio-sociology see Robert Ardrey, *African Genesis*, (New York: Athenium Press, 1961); for excellent bio-sociology, see Jane Goodall, *In the Shadow of Man* (Boston: Houghton Mifflin, 1971).

71. Jensen wrote articles on black I.Q. scores, insisting blacks were genetically inferior; so too did Carlton Coon, a well known anthropologist. See Arthur Robert Jensen, *Educability and Group Differences*, New York: Harper and Row, 1973.

72. The sperm bank for Nobel Laureates is in San Diego. For information write to "Nightline," Ted Koppel, WABC News, Columbus Ave. at 67th Street, New York, N.Y. (March 30, 1988, program).

73. Film on Socio-Biology, Dept. of Sociology, William Paterson College.

74. Film on the plight of the Brazilian Indians on PBS.

75. Jane Goodall and other students of Leaky have produced marvelous bio-sociology studies.

76. Julius Wilson, *The Truly Disadvantaged*. Chicago: University of Chicago Press, 1987.

77. Robert Nozick, *Anarchy, State, and Utopia*. New York: Basic Books, 1971.

78. Ibid. Conclusions.

79. Milton Friedman, *Capitalism and Democracy*. Chicago: University of Chicago Press, 1971.

80. Nozick, pp. 26–27.

81. Glassman, *The New Middle Class and Democracy*.

82. Hobbes, *Leviathan*.

83. Glassman, *The New Middle Class and Democracy*.

84. Donald Rowat, *The Ombudsman: Citizen's Defender*.

85. Ibid.

86. Glassman, *The New Middle Class and Democracy*; see also, the Oliver North "Iran-Scam" case; special prosecutors have intervened against the presidency four times in the last 18 years (1970–1988).

87. John Wicklein, *Electronic Nightmare*. New York: Viking, 1981.

88. Robert Dahl, *After the Revolution*.

89. Hobbes, *Leviathan*.

90. Hobbes, *Behemoth*.

91. Nozick, *Anarchy, State, and Utopia* (see quote in section on Nozick in text).

92. Abraham Lincoln, the Gettysburg Address.

93. Pericles, "Funeral Oration," in Thucydides, *The Peloponnesian Wars*.

94. Ibid.

95. Herodotus, *The Persian Wars*.

96. Thucydides, *The Peloponnesian Wars*.

97. Proudhon quotation in Nozick, *Anarchy, State, and Utopia*, p. 11.

98. Hobbes, *Leviathan*.

99. Friedman, *Capitalism and Freedom*.

100. Ibid., p. 15.

101. Ibid., p. 34–36.

102. Ibid., p. 24.

103. Hayek, *The Road to Serfdom* and *Constitution of Liberty* (he agrees that safety net programs are necessary).

104. Popper, *Open Society*, also agrees that safety net programs are necessary.

105. Friedman, pp. 34–36.

106. See the Penn Central scandal and the many articles it generated, 1967.

107. Andrew Stein, in the 1970s, as Manhattan borough president, made his career by exposing the nursing home horrors. See also Ira Glasser, *Doing Good*.

108. James Gwartney and Richard E. Wagner, "The Public Choice Revolution," in *The Intercollegiate Review* (Spring 1988).

109. Friedman, p. 90.

110. Ibid., p. 92.

111. Ibid., p. 90.

112. Ibid.

113. Jefferson, in Carl Cohen, *Communism, Fascism, and Democracy*. Chicago: University of Chicago Press, 1981, p. 486.

114. Hayek and Popper on safety net programs—see above citations.

115. Friedman, p. 50.

116. Ibid., p. 38.

117. Ibid., p. 10.

118. Ibid.

119. J. K. Galbraith, *Economics in Perspective*. Boston: Houghton Mifflin, 1987.

120. Ibid.; see also Robert Reich—many books and articles on the topic.

121. Friedman, p. 4.

122. Ibid., p. 10.

CHAPTER 7

1. Max Weber, *Economy and Society*. Translation by Roth and Wittich. New York: Bedminster Press, 1978. Idem. *General Economic History*. New York: Greenberg, 1927, Trans. Frank H. Knight.

2. Karl Marx, *Das Kapital*. Moscow: Foreign Language Press, 1949.

3. Weber, *Economy and Society*; see also Glassman and Murvar (eds.), *Max Weber's Political Sociology* (Westport, CT: Greenwood Press, 1983).

4. Weber, *Economy and Society*; Glassman and Murvar, *Max Weber's Political Sociology*.

5. Glassman, Swatos, and Rosen, *Bureaucracy Against Democracy and Socialism*. Westport, CT: Greenwood Press, 1987. See essays by Wolfgang Schluchter and Ernest Kilker.

6. Max Weber, *Economy and Society*.

7. Vatro Murvar, "Patrimonialism in Russia," in Glassman and Murvar. *Max Weber's Political Sociology*.

8. Robert Michels, on the "iron law of oligarchy," in *Political Parties*; New York: Free Press, 1962. See also letters between Weber and Michels.

9. John Kenneth Galbraith, *The New Industrial State*. Boston: Houghton Mifflin, 1972.

10. John Kenneth Galbraith, *Economics in Perspective*. Boston: Houghton Mifflin, 1987.

11. Franklin Delano Roosevelt, the radio speech in which he referred to "a third of a nation as ill clothed . . . ," etc.

12. Glassman, Swatos, and Rosen, *Bureaucracy Against Democracy and Socialism*.

13. C. Wright Mills, *The Power Elite*. New York: Oxford University Press, 1961.

14. Glassman, *The New Middle Class and Democracy*.

15. Galbraith, *Economics in Perspective*.

16. Ibid.

17. Veblen, *Theory of the Leisure Class*. New York: Mentor Books, 1951.

18. Veblen, *Theory of Business Enterprise*. New York: Mentor Books, 1958.

19. Ibid.

20. Adam Smith, *The Wealth of Nations*. Oxford, U.K.: Clarendon Press, 1976, chapter on monopoly.

21. Galbraith, *Economics in Perspective*.

22. Ibid.

23. Ibid.

24. Max Weber, *The Protestant Ethic*.

25. Veblen, *The Engineers and the Price System*. New York: Viking, 1954.
26. Ibid.

CHAPTER 8

1. Charles Dickens, *A Christmas Carol*.
2. Max Weber, *The Protestant Ethic and the Spirit of Capitalism*.
3. Christopher Lasch, *The Culture of Narcissism*.
4. Max Weber, *The Protestant Ethic*.
5. Thorstein Veblen, *The Theory of the Leisure Class*, and *The Theory of Business Enterprise*.
6. Max Weber, "The Sociology of Religion," in *Economy and Society*, Translated by Roth and Wittich. New York: Bedminster Press, 1978.
7. Marshall McLuhan, *Understanding Media*. New York: McGraw Hill, 1965; *The Medium Is the Message*. New York: Bantam Books, 1967.
8. Thorstein Veblen, *The Theory of the Leisure Class*.
9. Matthew, the *New Testament*, pp. 1179–80, *The Oxford Annotated Bible*, edited by Herbert G. May and Bruce M. Metzger. New York: Oxford University Press, 1962.
10. Jesus, "The Sermon on the Mount," in Matthew, the *New Testament*, pp. 1175–76, *The Oxford Annotated Bible*.
11. Isaiah, *Old Testament*, p. 825, *The Oxford Annotated Bible*.
12. Ibid., p. 827.
13. Ibid., p. 824.
14. Amos, p. 1112, Ibid.
15. Ibid., p. 1113.
16. Micah, p. 1129, Ibid.
17. Ibid., p. 1126.
18. Ira Glasser, *Doing Good*. New York: Pantheon Books, 1979.

Bibliography

Acton, Lord John. *A History of Freedom*. Boston: Beacon Press, 1948.

Aristotle. *The Politics*. Translated by Ernest Barker. New York: Oxford University Press, 1961.

Bell, Daniel. *The Coming of Post Industrial Society*. New York: Basic Books, 1968.

Berle, A. A., and Gardiner Means. *The Modern Corporation and Private Property*. New York: Harcourt, Brace, 1968.

Bernstein, Eduard. *Cromwell and Communism: Socialism and Democracy in the Great English Revolution*. Translated by H. J. Stenning. New York: A. M. Kelley, 1963.

Cloward, Richard, and Lloyd Ohlin. *Delinquency and Opportunity*. Glencoe, Ill.: Free Press, 1960.

Dahl, Robert. *After the Revolution*. New Haven: Yale University Press, 1971.

de Tocqueville, Alexis. *Democracy in America*. New York: Vintage Books, 1945.

———. *The Old Regime and the French Revolution*. Translated by Henry Reeve. London: Murray, 1888.

Eisner, Robert. *How Real is the Budget Deficit?* New York: Free Press, 1986.

Friedman, Milton. *Capitalism and Freedom*. Chicago: University of Chicago Press, 1982.

Galbraith, John Kenneth. *Economics in Perspective*. Boston: Houghton Mifflin, 1987.

———. *The New Industrial State*. Boston: Houghton Mifflin, 1972.

Glasser, Ira. *Doing Good*. New York: Pantheon, 1974.

Glassman, Ronald. *Democracy and Despotism in Primitive Societies*. New York: Associated Faculty Press, 1987.

———. *The New Middle Class and Democracy*. Forthcoming.

———. *The Political History of Latin America*. New York: Funk and Wagnalls, 1969.

Glassman, Ronald, and Robert Antonio (eds.). *A Weber-Marx Dialogue*. Lawrence: University of Kansas Press, 1985.

Glassman, Ronald, and Vatro Murvar (eds.). *Max Weber's Political Sociology*. Westport, CT: Greenwood Press, 1981.

Glassman, Ronald, William Swatos, and Paul Rosen. *Bureaucracy Against Democracy and Socialism*. Westport, CT: Greenwood Press, 1987.

Hayek, Friedrich Von. *The Constitution of Liberty*. Chicago: University of Chicago Press, 1978.

———. *The Road to Serfdom*. Chicago: University of Chicago Press, 1969.

Keynes, John Maynard. *The General Theory*. New York: Harcourt, Brace, and World, 1935.

Lasch, Christopher. *The Culture of Narcissism*. New York: Norton, 1968.

Locke, John. *On Civil Government*. Chicago: Gateway Edition, 1962.

Marx, Karl, and Friedrich Engels. *The Communist Manifesto*. Moscow: Foreign Language Press, 1951.

———. *The Paris Commune*. Edited by Hal Draper. Boston: Beacon Press, 1968.

Mill, John Stuart. *Political Economy*. London: Penguin Classics, 1962.

Mills, C. Wright. *The Power Elite*. New York: Oxford University Press, 1959.

———. *White Collar*. New York: Oxford University Press, 1958.

Mommsen, Wolfgang. *The Age of Bureaucracy*. New York: Harper and Row, 1974.

Mumford, Lewis. *The Myth of the Machine*. New York: Harcourt, Brace, and World, 1966/67.

Murray, Charles. *Losing Ground*. New York: Basic Books, 1984.

Nader, Ralph, Mark Green, and Joel Seligman. *Taming the Giant Corporation*. New York: Norton, 1982.

Nozick, Robert. *Anarchy, State, and Utopia*. New York: Basic Books, 1971.

Polanyi, Karl. *The Great Transformation*. Boston: Beacon Press, 1957.

———. *Trade and Market in Early Empires*. Glencoe, Ill.: Free Press, 1967.

Popper, Karl. *The Open Society and Its Enemies*. Princeton, N.J.: Princeton University Press, 1951.

Rawls, John. *A Theory of Justice*. Cambridge, Mass.: Harvard University Press, 1961.

Smith, Adam. *The Wealth of Nations*. Oxford, U.K.: Clarendon Press, 1976.

Tawney, R. H. *Religion and the Rise of Capitalism*. New York: Mentor, 1954.

———. *The Agrarian Problem in the Sixteenth Century*. New York: Harper Torch Books, 1967.

Taylor, Philip. *The Origins of the English Civil War*. Boston: D.C. Heath, 1960.

Thucydides. *The Peloponnesian Wars*. Translated by Crawley. New York: Modern Library, 1951.

Veblen, Thorstein. *The Engineers and the Price System*. New York: Viking, 1954.

———. *The Theory of Business Enterprise*. New York: Mentor Books, 1958.

Weber, Max. *Economy and Society*. Translated by Gunter Roth and Klaus Wittich. New York: Bedminster Press, 1978.

———. *The Protestant Ethic and the Spirit of Capitalism*. New York: Charles Scribner & Sons, 1968.

Index

About the Author

RONALD M. GLASSMAN has written numerous volumes, including *The Political History of Latin America, Democracy and Despotism in Primitive Societies, The New Middle Class and Democracy*, and with Mark Green, *A Democracy Agenda for the Year 2000*. He has also edited various volumes, such as: *Conflict and Control* (with Arthur J. Vidich), *Max Weber's Political Sociology* (with Vatro Murvar), *A Weber–Marx Dialogue* (with Robert J. Antonio), *Charisma, History, and Social Structure* (with William Swatos, Jr.), and *Bureaucracy Against Democracy and Socialism* (with William Swatos, Jr. and Paul Rosen).

The author has been active in the sociology profession and was the founder and first chair of the Comparative Historical Sociology section of the American Sociological Association. To further the goal of creating a truly comparative-historical sociology, Professor Glassman is currently involved in an NEH Scholars Seminar on modern China at Columbia University, and has previously been associated with a similar seminar analyzing fascism, at Yale.

Political action is also his forte. Ronald Glassman is currently executive director of New York City Americans for Democratic Action and has been actively involved in many political campaigns. He was also the chair of the University Professors Committee Against the War in Vietnam, and believes that the trauma of the Vietnam War—for both the United States and Southeast Asia—needs renewed discussion and debate today.

As a professor, the author believes deeply in the value of good teaching, and is proud of the two citations for teaching excellence that he has received. The first was at Connecticut College, where he was cited in *The Underground Guide to the College of Your Choice* as one of the two most interesting professors at the college. The other was at the State University of New Jersey, William Paterson College (Wayne, N.J.) where he is currently tenured as a professor of sociology.